PRAISE FOR
SUSAN BURTON AND
BECOMING MS. BURTON

"Susan Burton is a national treasure . . . her life story is testimony to the human capacity for resilience and recovery . . . [*Becoming Ms. Burton* is] a stunning memoir."

—Nicholas Kristof, in *The New York Times*

"Valuable . . . [like Michelle] Alexander's *The New Jim Crow,* Nell Bernstein's *Burning Down the House,* and Bryan Stevenson's *Just Mercy.* But rarely has such a powerful, personal perspective been made available to us. . . . Our understanding of the criminal justice system is immeasurably strengthened by Susan Burton's fierce, compassionate, and expressive voice."

—*Los Angeles Review of Books*

"A dramatic, honest, moving narrative of how hard life can get and how one can still overcome seemingly insurmountable adversity to do good in the world."

—*Kirkus Reviews*

"Burton has helped thousands of formerly incarcerated and homeless individuals and now, by telling her story, she continues to advocate for a more humane justice system guided by compassion and dignity."

—*Booklist* (starred)

"More than just a memoir, this account provides an intimate glimpse into the problems that plague the U.S. prison system."

—*Library Journal*

"The book documents Burton's tireless efforts to effect change first helping individual women, released from prison with few resources, to make a new start, and then snowballing advocacy efforts at the state and national level to reshape how the United States treats those with criminal records."

—*Publishers Weekly*

"Susan Burton's life and work are a testament to the power of second chances and the impact one person can have on the lives of others. Her book is a stirring and moving tour-de-force—a beautiful inspiration for all of us to continue to fight for justice."

—John Legend, actor, singer, and songwriter

"Miraculously inspirational. . . . *Becoming Ms. Burton* is most of all a book about trauma, fair justice, inequality, healing, resiliency and selfless humanity. It is a life changer."

—Vivian Nixon, executive director of College and Community Fellowship and co-founder of the Education from the Inside Out Coalition

"Susan Burton is someone who inspires while she educates. Her powerful and compelling memoir is an unforgettable journey and also an extraordinary light for all who are looking for answers on how we must recover, restore, and redeem those who have been incarcerated. This is a must-read."

—Bryan Stevenson, executive director of the Equal Justice Initiative and author of *Just Mercy*

"*Becoming Ms. Burton* eloquently shows why the voices of formerly incarcerated women *must* be at the center of efforts to reconstruct the criminal legal system. This is critical reading for champions of justice everywhere."

—Monique W. Morris, author of *Pushout*

BECOMING
MS. BURTON

FROM PRISON TO RECOVERY
TO LEADING THE FIGHT FOR
INCARCERATED WOMEN

SUSAN BURTON and CARI LYNN

THE NEW PRESS

25 YEARS

NEW YORK
LONDON

Requests for permission to reproduce selections from this book should be mailed to:
Permissions Department, The New Press, 120 Wall Street, 31st floor, New York, NY
10005.

Published in the United States by The New Press, New York, 2017
Distributed by Perseus Distribution

ISBN 978-1-62097-212-0 (hc)
ISBN 978-1-62097-213-7 (e-book)
CIP data is available

The New Press publishes books that promote and enrich public discussion and
understanding of the issues vital to our democracy and to a more equitable world. These
books are made possible by the enthusiasm of our readers; the support of a committed
group of donors, large and small; the collaboration of our many partners in the
independent media and the not-for-profit sector; booksellers, who often hand-sell New
Press books; librarians; and above all by our authors.

www.thenewpress.com

Book design and composition by Bookbright Media
This book was set in Minion Pro and Bembo

Printed in the United States of America

10 9 8 7 6 5 4 3 2

Most women in U.S. prisons were, first, victims.

It's estimated that 85 percent of locked-up women were, at some or many points in their lives, physically or sexually abused, or both. Disproportionately, these women are black and poor.

I was born and raised in those statistics. My life is now devoted to stopping this cycle.

This book is dedicated to my son, K.K.

And to my daughter, Toni, and granddaughter, Ellesse.

And to all the women who may lie on their prison bed dreaming of a new way of life.

A NOTE TO THE READER

This book is drawn from my own life and experiences. It is also a book of memory and opinion—and memory and opinion, as we all know, may have their own stories to tell. The names and identifying details of some individuals have been changed out of respect for their privacy; the first occurrence of a changed name is indicated in the notes for each chapter that appear at the end of the book. —SB

CONTENTS

PART II: MS. BURTON

FOREWORD

MICHELLE ALEXANDER

There once lived a woman with deep brown skin and black hair who freed people from bondage and ushered them to safety. She welcomed them to safe homes and offered food, shelter, and help reuniting with family and loved ones. She met them wherever they could be found and organized countless others to provide support and aid in various forms so they would not be recaptured and sent back to captivity. This courageous soul knew well the fear and desperation of each one who came to her, seeing in their eyes all the pain she felt years ago when she had been abused and shackled and finally began her own journey to freedom.

Deep in the night she cried out to God begging for strength, and when she woke she began her work all over again, opening doors, planning escape routes, and holding hands with mothers as they wept for children they hoped to see again. A relentless advocate for justice, this woman was a proud abolitionist and freedom fighter. She told the unadorned truth to whomever would listen and spent countless hours training and organizing others, determined to grow the movement. She served not only as a profound inspiration to those who knew her, but as a literal gateway to freedom for hundreds whose lives were changed forever by her heroism.

Some people know this woman by the name Harriet Tubman. I know her as Susan.

I met Susan Burton in 2010, but I had learned her name years before. I was doing research about the challenges of re-entry for people incarcerated due to our nation's cruel and biased drug war. At the time, I was in the process of writing *The New Jim Crow: Mass Incarceration in the Age of Colorblindness*—a book that aimed to expose the ways the War on Drugs had not only decimated impoverished communities of color but had also helped to birth a new system of racial and social control eerily reminiscent of an era we supposedly left behind.

The United States has become the world leader in imprisonment, having quintupled our prison population in a few short decades through a drug war and "get tough" movement aimed at the poorest and darkest among us. I was writing a chapter that explains how tens of millions of people branded criminals and felons have been stripped of the very rights supposedly won in the civil rights movement, including the right to vote, the right to serve on juries, and the right to be free of legal discrimination in employment, housing, access to education, and public benefits. I had mountains of policy analyses and data, but was disturbed by the fact that few voices of those who had actually been impacted by these modern-day Jim Crow policies could be found in the research.

I scanned dozens of articles online, then paused when I stumbled upon an interview with a woman named Susan Burton. The integrity and authenticity of her voice were undeniable. She told the reporter plainly and directly what it felt like, as a recovering drug addict released from prison and struggling to survive, to be forced to "check the box" on the ubiquitous employment, housing, and food stamp applications that asked the dreaded question, "have you ever been convicted of a felony?" She knew full well that, once that box was checked, her application would be thrown straight in the trash. How would she survive without food, shelter, or a job? She described with clarity and conviction what it meant to be a second-class citizen in the so-called land of the free, and she insisted that she was determined to do everything she could to ensure that the laws, rules, policies, and practices that authorize legal discrimination against people with convictions are eventually abandoned, and that we begin to provide drug treatment rather than prison cells to people struggling with addiction and drug abuse. I learned Susan had created several safe homes for formerly incarcerated women and that she was part of a small but growing movement for the restoration of basic civil and human rights for people who have spent time behind bars. The interview moved me, and I thought, *I have to meet this woman.*

Shortly after *The New Jim Crow* was published, I had my chance. A mutual friend introduced us via email and Susan invited me to come to Los Angeles and visit the nonprofit organization she founded, A New Way of Life. She thanked me profusely for my book and said that she, along with the formerly incarcerated women currently residing at the safe homes, wanted to organize a book event for me at a local community center. I told her that I would be thrilled to come and hoped to learn more about her work and lend support as best I could.

I was not prepared for what followed. Upon my arrival, Susan gave me a tour of the safe homes for formerly incarcerated women that operate as part of A New Way of Life. I'm not certain what I expected, but probably something similar to various halfway houses I've seen over the years. Instead, I discovered something else entirely. These were not facilities or shelters or way stations or simply housing for people released from prison who need support services. These were homes. Loving homes. Susan took me from house to house and showed me where the women slept and worked. The residents and staff greeted Susan with a measure of formality—"Good afternoon, Ms. Burton!"—yet the warmth and love were palpable. In some of the bedrooms, paint was peeling off the walls, and mattresses for children were on the floor along with a few scattered stuffed animals. Clearly, every penny raised was immediately invested in providing more beds, houses, and services. The accommodations were sparse, to say the least. But they were also immaculate, and every woman I met expressed enormous gratitude for Susan and the lifeline she provided. Susan offered not just a place to sleep and to get desperately needed assistance, but also emotional support as the women struggled to meet the seemingly endless and impossible requirements of parole and probation officers, as well as the demands of the most feared agency of them all: child protective services.

In California, as in most states, women released from prison must meet a dizzying list of requirements if they hope to regain custody of their children, including showing they have secured employment and housing. Meeting these requirements is no small feat, particularly when hundreds of categories of jobs are off-limits to people with felony records, discrimination is still legal against them, public housing agencies routinely deny access to people based on criminal records, and—until recently—even food stamps weren't available to people with drug convictions. Susan and her staff work tirelessly to help women at A New Way of Life meet these conditions, but they also go to court with them, hold hands with them, and pray with them, as judges decide whether custody will be terminated forever.

I remember calling Susan one day, long after my first visit, and catching her when she was at the courthouse with a young woman who had just lost custody—permanently—of her daughter. Susan's voice was cracking and breaking over the phone, failing to hold back tears, as she erupted: "I've been down here all week at the courthouse, watching and waiting as these families are torn apart. I see these women doing everything they can, and still their babies are taken away. How can we do this to people? Does anyone really understand what's going on here? We're willing to spend countless dollars putting people who need help in cages, and then when they get out we say you can't have a job, and you can't have housing, and because you don't have either we're going to take your kids too. Sometimes I think I can't go on, that I just can't bear to watch this or do this anymore."

But she does. Day in and day out, Susan is always there, welcoming women returning home from prison, providing them with as much support and guidance as possible, and walking with them into the courthouse. Over and over again. Like Harriet Tubman, who famously helped to build the underground railroad for runaway slaves who yearned to be free and reunite with their loved ones, Susan has committed her life to helping those held captive today make a genuine break for freedom, attempt to rebuild their lives and families, and hopefully begin to heal from the trauma of it all.

I don't think I understood the full extent of the trauma experienced by people who churn through America's prisons until I began taking the time to listen to their stories. Research suggests that people rarely change their minds or form a new worldview based on facts or data alone; it is through stories (and the values systems embedded within them) that we come to reinterpret the world and develop empathy and compassion for others. Susan Burton's life story—filled with trauma, struggle, and true heroism—is precisely the kind of story that has the potential to change the way we view our world. It is impossible to read her story and not feel challenged to reconsider basic assumptions about our criminal injustice system, as well as the conscious and subconscious beliefs we hold about the living, breathing human beings we, as a nation, have condemned and discarded. In today's political environment we are constantly encouraged—through the media, politicians, and government bureaucracies—to view certain groups of people defined by race and class as undeserving of care and concern, especially the drug addicts, criminals, and so-called illegals who are trapped in prisons, detention centers, and ghettos across the United States.

During my first visit to A New Way of Life, Susan sat me down on a couch in an empty safe home—the residents were out for the moment—and quietly began to tell her story. She explained that her odyssey with the criminal justice system began when her five-year-old son was accidentally killed by a police officer employed by the Los Angeles Police Department. The officer was driving down her street in her South Central neighborhood and ran over her boy while he was crossing the street. The LAPD initially offered no compensation, no counseling, no trauma support—not even an apology. Susan fell into a deep, seemingly bottomless well of grief and depression.

I have no doubt things would've turned out differently if Susan had been wealthy and white. Even if she was middle class and had access to a good health insurance plan, she could've afforded years of therapy and been prescribed the best legal drugs available to help her cope with her trauma. But things were different for Susan. Lacking money and a support system, she turned to illegal drugs and became addicted to crack cocaine. Living in an impoverished black community under siege during the height of the War on Drugs, it was only a matter of time before Susan was arrested and offered her first plea deal. It would not be her last. Susan cycled in and out of prison for fifteen years, trapped in a virtual undercaste—a parallel social universe that exists for those labeled criminals and felons in the era of mass incarceration. Every time she was released, she faced a web of discriminatory rules and laws that made survival next to impossible, and she continued to self-medicate with illegal drugs.

By no small miracle, Susan was eventually granted admission to a private drug treatment facility and given a job. When she became clean, she decided to devote her life to ensuring that no other woman would ever have to suffer what she had been through. She began meeting the prison bus as it released women onto the streets carrying nothing but a cardboard box with their belongings and a few dollars in their pockets. She said to these women, who were strangers to her, "Come home with me, sleep on my couch or on my floor. I'll make sure you have a roof over your head and food to eat. You don't have to turn to the streets tonight."

Susan explained to me that, in the beginning, she simply wanted to give women who were struggling to make it on the outside food, shelter, safety, and some support as they pieced their lives back together again. But now, Susan said, she sees her mission and purpose as much broader. She aims to help build a movement, a human rights movement that will provide a path to a new way of life for all of us. She co-founded All of Us or None, an organization dedicated to the restoration of basic civil and human rights for formerly incarcerated people, and has begun training the women who are part of

A New Way of Life to be leaders, spokespeople, and organizers. She views the women who live and work with her not merely as people to be "helped," but as women who are joining in a shared struggle to remake their individual lives, while transforming their communities and the nation as a whole.

Since that talk on her couch several years ago, Susan and I have had many conversations about the future of movement-building and advocacy to end mass incarceration. She has become a friend and a confidante, as well as my personal sh-ero. Every time I speak with her I am reminded of why it is so critically important for people who have been directly impacted by injustice to emerge as partners and leaders of the movements for justice we aim to build. As a lawyer and an academic, I am often surrounded by people who think they know the answers, as well as how to define the problem, and have endless opinions about what to do next. They've done their research and studied the data and read the reports and they know how to navigate the halls of power. Yet often what they lack is relevant life experience—the deep, profound ways of knowing and seeing that come from living through severe racial and social injustice and making a way out of no way. What I have found is that I have much more to learn from Susan Burton than she does from me, despite all of the research and writing I have done on these issues over the years.

The book you hold in your hands right now is not simply a story about a formerly incarcerated woman dedicated to working for justice and freedom in the era of mass incarceration. It is a story of a black woman who, as she often tells me, is "nothing special" and yet has somehow managed to transform her own life as well as hundreds of lives around her. She has emerged as a leading figure in the movement to end mass incarceration, always leading by example and never leading alone. This book tells a story of one woman known to staff and residents as Ms. Burton, but it is also tells a much broader, universal story about the utter fragility and breathtaking resilience of the human spirit—even in the face of severe sexual, physical, and emotional abuse. In the end, this is a story about how an entire system of oppressive rules, laws, policies, and practices has failed to permanently crush one woman's spirit and the spirits of the many women who have walked through the doors of A New Way of Life, though surely that system has tried. To borrow the poetry of Maya Angelou, "And still like dust they rise."

When Susan first began working on this book, she told me how emotionally difficult it was for her to revisit her childhood and speak openly and honestly about the years she spent addicted to drugs, living on the streets and in cages. There were days she wanted to abandon the project, feeling she couldn't muster the emotional strength to speak publicly about the rape and emotional abuse she experienced as a child and young woman. I didn't realize, until I read the manuscript, how much courage it took for her to share this story. I thought I knew her story, but as I turned the pages I realized I didn't know the half of it. I am so proud of Susan for sharing her journey in this way. I know there are thousands of women who will receive this book as nothing short of a transformative gift, an open door to a new way of life.

There's an African proverb that says, until the lions have their own historians, the history of the hunt will always glorify the hunter. I could not be more grateful that Susan Burton has found her own historian, Cari Lynn. If the arc of the moral universe truly bends toward justice, one day this beautiful, bold, courageous lioness named Susan Burton—and the thousands of other courageous women and men who are making a way out of no way for themselves and others—will receive their glory, and the freedom fighters who came before them will look down from the heavens and smile.

PROLOGUE

I hadn't seen Ingrid in several years when I picked her up in downtown Los Angeles. In her prison-issue clothes, she looked worn and weary, not at all like when she first showed up to my house in 2007, twenty-four years old and holding the hand of her five-year-old daughter, Simone.

As Ingrid got in my van, her once-sparkly eyes filled with tears. "I should have called you, Ms. Burton," she said.

"You did call me," I said. "That's why I'm here."

She shook her head. "Before I was arrested. I wasn't doing so well. Simone kept telling me to call you, that you would help me. But . . . I felt I'd let you down. I wasn't working because I had two babies one after the other. I gave up my housing to move in with my new baby's father. But it was a bad relationship. I was bruised up." Her voice quivered. "I didn't want you to see me like that."

As I listened, I recognized that fierce combination of pride and shame, how such opposite emotions could consume a person, forcing you into thinking you can manage, you can do it all, all by yourself. I drove Ingrid back to my house in Watts, a working-class black community of Los Angeles, immortalized in 1965 by racial tension and police brutality that sparked bloody riots. In a way, Watts was emblematic of so many of its residents. Efforts at revitalization were continuously overshadowed by staid perceptions of violence, gangs, and crime. Even in the face of a dramatic and steady decrease in violent crime, Watts still struggled for redemption. To me, this was a community of perseverance.

Nearly ten years ago, in my two-story, pink stucco bungalow, Ingrid and Simone had thrived, and I'd grown attached to those two. Little Simone, with her mother's sweet smile, knock-kneed to the point you'd think one leg was gonna trip over the other. Ingrid, with smooth charcoal skin and full lips, her effervescence belying the many lives she'd lived in not so many years. I'd taken Ingrid with me to meetings with policymakers and political activists, discovering what family and teachers should have been nurturing in her all along: she had a sharp mind and an ease with public speaking. I'd watch Ingrid stand before crowds and tell her story.

"I can count the times I saw my mother sober," she'd begin. "My childhood memories are filled with violence. I can't remember any happy times, just black. Until one day, my dad came and got me, and I lived with him for a month. He bought me toys and set up an area for me to play. He made me breakfast every morning and took me places, to see family, to get ice cream. I never saw him angry. But he couldn't keep me because he had a felony record. That was the best month on my life." She went on to describe years of group homes and boot camp, and eventually escaping to the streets of South Central L.A., selling drugs to get by, giving birth at nineteen to Simone, being incarcerated shortly after.

Ingrid's story pierced me so deeply because she reminded me of my younger self, a strong-willed woman swirling in trauma and tragedy, with so much to offer if only given the chance. She'd tell me, "Every time we go speak, it makes me want to be involved more and more. I can see the bigger picture, and I want to be part of that."

Now, Ingrid was thirty-four years old. Her life had changed in a single day, outside a Dollar General store. Having scrounged up the money to buy Pampers and baby formula, she took her screaming toddler with her and made a bottle in the checkout line, but left her sleeping baby in the car, the windows open for air. Not more than

ten minutes later, when she returned to her car, the police were
there. She was arrested for child endangerment, though the baby
was unharmed. The police impounded the diapers and baby formula
in the car, despite Ingrid's pleas that the children were hungry and
needed changing. Because of her history, she was guilty before ever
standing trial. She was sentenced to three years in prison and lost
custody of all three of her daughters.

I was silent while she blamed everything on herself, how she'd
been frazzled and sleep-deprived and, looking back, perhaps had
postpartum depression. Okay, I thought, but had Ingrid been a person of means, had she been in a different neighborhood, had she
not been black, would she have been sentenced to years in prison?
Or would she have been given help, sent to parenting classes and
therapy—resources that existed for certain people but not others?

Did I even need to ask the question?

Ingrid's story could have—should have—been different. Same with
my own story, and the stories of most of the one thousand women
and their children who've come through the doors of A New Way of
Life, seeking safety, productivity, meaning, and fulfillment.

So I keep asking questions. Why are black Americans incarcerated
at nearly six times the rate of whites? Why are prison sentences for
African Americans disproportionately higher? Once released, why
do people face a lifetime of discriminatory policies and practices that
smother any chance of a better life?

Nearly twenty years ago, before I began looking at the big
picture—before I fully recognized there *was* a big picture—I set out
to offer the type of refuge and support I wished I'd had: a house of
women helping women. I came at it with only a GED earned in prison, without mentors, without funding. All I had was life experience.
All I knew was there had to be a better way.

Now, every year in South L.A., around a hundred newly released
women and their children call A New Way of Life home. In a state
where more than half of all people with a felony conviction will
return to prison, our program has a mere 4 percent recidivism rate.

We assist women in completing their education and finding jobs; we help women regain custody of their children; we provide twelve-step programs, counseling, and peer support groups. All for less than a third of the cost of incarceration. Our annual cost per woman at A New Way of Life is $16,000—compared to the annual cost of up to $60,000 to incarcerate a woman.

But something bigger than I could ever have imagined happened. As we women began telling our stories and talking about what was going on around us, I found my voice. I could no longer shake my head and helplessly ask the same questions over and over again. It was time to change the answers. To do that meant tackling the many institutional barriers—the laws, policies, and attitudes—that created mass incarceration and that continue to punish people long after they've served time.

The Thirteenth Amendment to the U.S. Constitution abolished slavery other than in prisons—but it was a lie that you regained your freedom once you left the prison gates. Upon release and for the rest of your life, you faced a massive wall of No. The American Bar Association documented 45,000 legal sanctions and restrictions imposed upon people with criminal records, a near-impenetrable barrier denying access to employment, student loans, housing, public assistance, custody of your children, the right to vote—in many places, the formerly incarcerated are even blocked from visiting a loved one in prison.

The minute I picked up a supposedly free Ingrid, these collateral consequences stared her square in the face. The highest priority was to get her kids back. But before she could even attempt to regain custody of her daughters, we had to get her set up in permanent housing. But she had to have money to cover rent, so first we had to find her employment. Of course only a limited number of jobs existed for someone with a conviction. Are you starting to get the picture? By design, Ingrid's hopes and dreams were all but snuffed out, and her children's lives thrown into permanent disarray, that day she made a faulty decision outside the Dollar General store.

———

This isn't a problem that's going to go away all on its own. The United States has the largest prison population in the world, and most of those prisoners will one day be released. I realized that formerly incarcerated people had no voice, and no one seemed willing to speak for us. As I built A New Way of Life, it sometimes felt as though a new underground railroad was taking shape. We, the people of the community, weren't going to let each other fall. We would rescue each other, and deliver people to a lasting freedom. We would do all we could so that women like Ingrid could get their lives back, and make better lives for their children.

Through the network I'd cultivated over the past two decades, we began chipping away at what was once nearly impossible. We found Ingrid a job doing intake at a women's homeless shelter. Working closely with the Department of Children and Family Services, and with proof of her residence at A New Way of Life, Ingrid was approved to have her children on weekends while she pursued the longer process of regaining full custody. She was putting money into a savings account, and working with housing agencies to find a permanent residence.

"Ms. Burton," she said, the sparkle having returned to her eyes, "I'm moving my life along."

PART I

SUE

1
NOW WHAT?

The United States, with 2.2 million people behind bars, imprisons more people than any other country in the world.

Since 1980, the rate of incarceration for women has risen more than 700 percent. The majority of these women are imprisoned for nonviolent offenses.

The women take their first step of freedom at the Greyhound bus station in downtown Los Angeles, around the corner from Skid Row, where America's largest concentration of homeless people live on the sidewalk, the lucky ones in makeshift tents. It's nothing like the freedom you'd dreamed about in your cell. This freedom smells of urine and stale beer. Lingering to check out the new releases are pimps and drug dealers and down-on-their-luck others who may not be intentional predators but who are desperate to find someone to hang on to. Or someone to drag down with them. They all know you are easy prey.

You can almost touch the desperation, the doom in the air. You can feel it on you. On your prison-issue clothes. Everyone recognizes the ill-fitting clothes stitched by inmates: the muumuus with the garish pink and orange and yellow flower pattern; the baseball shirt;

the state jeans, so stiff they can nearly stand up on their own—no designer label on the back pocket of these jeans. In order to walk out of prison you had to buy yourself some clothes with the $200 you were given upon release. That money went quickly after you also had to buy your bus ticket, a prison guard watching while you went to the Greyhound window and waiting until you got on that bus and it drove away.

Away, to freedom that was hardly freedom at all but a plan practically set in stone for people like me who came into this world in the county hospital, then grew up in the projects. Or maybe it wasn't a plan at all; maybe it was the complete absence of any plan.

When you step off at the bus station, you have at most $100 left in your pocket, maybe less if you were only granted half your allowed amount, the rest to be doled out to you months later by your parole officer. There's no reason why some people have their gate money withheld. Just like there's no reason to anything in prison. No reason why, on a whim, a guard raids your locker, tearing through your only belongings, dumping your soap powder, and mixing your baby powder into your instant coffee, spoiling both. No reason why some women inmates are assigned to spend their days in a parenting class even if they don't have children, while others must push a mop around for eight cents an hour, and others have to report to fire camp, going through weeks of rigorous physical training to be awarded an orange uniform and delivered to the front lines of a California wildfire for $1 an hour.

There's also no logical reason why federal prisons offer halfway houses to those newly released, but state prisons provide nothing. Four thousand newly released women arrive in Los Angeles County every year to nothing. No re-entry programs, no counseling, no services, no assistance. You have no house key, no credit card, no checkbook, no driver's license, no Social Security card, no identification of any sort because anything you were carrying when you were arrested has been destroyed by the state. You're just one woman in the crowd of mostly black and brown faces, one number in the recidivism stats that are decidedly not in your favor. Like vultures, the pimps circle, eyeing you, assessing you. The drug dealers circle. You know them from the old neighborhood, and they call you by name, offering their brand of a welcome home party. You have little incentive to say no. Ego tells you you're gonna make it by any means necessary. Ego tells you you're a grown woman. But you're scared. How do you calm yourself? How do you connect with something healthy and hopeful when you're surrounded by Skid Row? When you haven't been allowed to make a decision in five, ten, twenty years? When all you want to do is wash prison off you, but you can't, because it's in you. It's seeped into your psyche and into your soul.

One time I stepped off that bus and my father was there to pick me up. But by going with him I stepped right back into a bad dynamic, reconnecting with all the anger and abuse that had sent me out of control in the first place. My whole family, all five of my brothers, have had run-ins with the prison system.

Another time, my husband was there, and I stepped from the prison gates right back into an unhealthy relationship. What else was I going to do? Where else was I going to go? Nothing I possessed was going to get me any closer to a new way of life. I couldn't even imagine what a new way of life might be. A discarded lottery ticket offered better odds.

All I wanted was to ease the fear, ease the self-loathing, ease the hopelessness. It seemed the only thing in the world I was certain of was how to escape by taking drugs, by self-medicating. Three days: that's the average time for someone to relapse after getting out of prison. I knew nothing about statistics, but I knew that, in a drug high, I could escape into silence.

The last time I stepped off that bus, I didn't know it would be the last time. Every time I left prison I left saying to myself, *I'm not gonna get caught up again.* Saying to myself, *I'm gonna make a better life. I won't be back*. The prison guard who put me on the bus waved and said, "We got your bed waiting for you. See you soon."

Six times I'd been imprisoned and each time I held hope that it would be the last time, but deep down I knew I wasn't prepared for life "outside." I'd been arrested over and over again for possession of a controlled substance. You'd think someone in the system might have gotten the bright idea that I needed drug treatment, that I needed therapy. But I was never offered help, and I didn't know to ask for it because I didn't know what to ask for. People with my color skin, and who grew up where I did, didn't know concepts like *rehab*. I was always remanded to prison.

Even going back some fifteen-plus years, back to before I was first incarcerated, when assistance should have been mine for the taking and when it could have made all the difference. Back to that day when my five-year-old son came in the house to give me a beautiful chrysanthemum he'd picked. "For you, Mama," he said, then went back outside to play. Marque, my little boy. We called him K.K. He was tall and slim, his skin caramel, his energy boundless. It was a day like any other. I'd picked K.K. up from kindergarten and we'd walked home and it was now around two in the afternoon. I looked down at the chrysanthemum he'd so proudly given me. The cushion of pink petals was crawling with ants. And then, brakes wailed and tires shrieked. The flower filled with ants dropped to the kitchen linoleum.

K.K. had run across the crosswalk and was hit. It could have been anyone at the wheel, but it happened to be a policeman driving an unmarked van. He didn't see my son. Nor did he stick around. Neighbors and bystanders rushed over. But it was too late.

The loss of my baby filled me with a rage so powerful I no longer recognized myself. I knew K.K.'s death had been an accident, but when there's an accident, it should be acknowledged. It was, however, no accident that I never did receive an acknowledgment—not from that policeman, or from the department, or from the city. Nothing would have brought my son back, of course, but just that small gesture, just someone bothering to say, "Ms. Burton, I'm sorry," would have meant something.

When time's numbing effect began to take hold, my rage was replaced by a depression so deep I felt hollow. How my body kept going was a mystery to me. If I could have stopped myself from breathing, I probably would have. My older child, Antoinette, whom we called Toni, was fifteen when K.K. was killed. She not only lost her brother but also the mother she'd known. My days had no meaning and my nights were sleepless.

I was afraid to sleep. I would see his face, hear him calling to me. I tried everything I could get my hands on to alleviate my pain. It was the early 1980s, the beginning of the crack epidemic, and on the streets of South Los Angeles, there was a lot someone like me could get her hands on.

2

LAND OF OPPORTUNITY

In Los Angeles from 1940 to 1945, the white population
rose less than 20 percent, while the black population
increased nearly 110 percent. Yet only 5 percent of the
city's residential areas allowed blacks.

My five brothers and I were born and raised in California,
though my family on both sides came from Texas. My parents
rarely spoke of our roots, and I never knew any grandparents, all of
whom passed before I was born. It was only when my mother was
getting on in years, her mind starting to short-circuit, that she'd blurt
out flashes of memory.

"My papa, he was so light in color, he could pass," she said one day.
"He'd sneak into KKK meetings a few towns over so he could come
back and warn people of their plans."

I knew my mother was the second-youngest of nine kids. Her
mother had died giving birth to twin girls, taking one of the babies
with her. "No sooner was she gone," Mama scoffed, "than my papa
had some woman in her place."

Out of the blue one day she said, "My papa, he liked me. I was
Papa's pick." She didn't say this with the sweetness of being Daddy's
little girl. The way she said it made my flesh creep.

On the first family vacation of my life, when I was about to turn six years old, we drove to visit Mama's family near Dallas. The image is still vivid of my father behind the wheel of his brand-new 1957 blue-and-white Pontiac station wagon. Mama was proud to be seen in that new car. Somewhere in Texas we stopped at a restaurant. As we entered, heads turned, then voices scolded us. Mama got angry and said, "I am *not* going to any back door for food." I remember how quiet the restaurant became, booths of white faces, pausing mid-bite, eyes unblinking. We returned to our car, Mama ranting that they didn't deserve our money.

This was my first time outside California, and this scene stayed with me, making me understand why my parents felt compelled to leave their entire families behind in the South. What I also remembered about that trip was that Mama's brother owned a liquor store and let us take bottles of soda for free.

Even though my parents grew up in nearby towns south of Dallas, they first met in Washington, D.C. Daddy fought in World War II and returned from the front to the nation's capital. He never spoke of his war years; I only saw a photograph of him in uniform, so that's how I knew. Daddy was handsome, his body tall and straight, his skin dark and flawless; and he had the biggest, brightest smile of perfect white teeth. His personality matched that smile: he was charismatic and quick to laugh, a boisterous jokester, a jiver. Mama had found herself a catch in Herman Burton.

She was a catch too. Flora Burnell Hughes, known to everyone as Nell. Mama was beautiful, and she was smart. How determined she must have been to get herself all the way to Howard University. She pursued a degree in Home Economics, one of the only majors available to women then. Everyone who knew my mother raved how beautiful she was: her creamy coffee skin, smooth and unblemished; her coal-black hair, twirling down her back. There was also the proud way she carried herself. She never cursed. She loved how Daddy had traveled the world, and how he'd take her by the waist and do the jitterbug.

These were the few sunny details I knew of my parents' lives before us kids. What I'd later learn was that my mother had been married once before, though I know nothing about that man, other than a passing comment that he'd gotten rough, too rough.

Like so many southern blacks, my parents migrated west, to the city W.E.B. DuBois touted as the most beautiful, intellectual, spirited land of opportunity for the Negro, where the air was scented with roses and orange blossoms. My father found a good job in a sheet metal factory, and he probably could have afforded to buy a house. But instead, my parents landed in Aliso Village, a housing project in East Los Angeles. Though it wasn't called Jim Crow in this part of the country, there were covenants and other unspoken—albeit organized and systematic—methods of keeping home ownership white.

There were no orange trees or rose bushes in Aliso Village. Mama was always harping about it. "I want to get out of these projects" was her frequent refrain and the way I learned that other people didn't live in projects; they lived somewhere better. Mama had a bit of a keeping-up-with-the-Joneses complex, a *bourgie* attitude, we called it, though she was kept in check by the fact that, with six kids, she couldn't afford to be frivolous. Still, she liked to think of herself as better than the other women in Aliso Village, even though she'd be out back just like the rest, pushing socks and underwear across the scrub-board, hanging them on the big line, going to the neighbor's to iron together.

Built during World War II on the razed site of some of the country's worst slums, Aliso Village, a massive thirty-five-acre complex with some three dozen buildings, was one of the country's first racially integrated projects and hailed as a model of the latest in urban planning. The homes' full, modern amenities were widely advertised: electric refrigerator, gas range, water heater, radiator, window shades, built-in laundry tub, and clotheslines. Situated between the L.A. River and the rail yard, the design included large, green, open spaces, making Aliso Village feel entirely separate from nearby downtown. No one dared think history would repeat itself, that just a few neglectful decades later, both the isolation and the open spaces would prove fatal design flaws, leading the *Los Angeles Times* to call Aliso Village the most violent neighborhood in L.A.

But growing up there in the early 1950s, all was still idealized and hopeful. My mother had six babies within eleven years. I had two older brothers, Michael and Billy, and three younger brothers, Melvin, Marvin, and Isaac.

My world consisted of the cluster of two-story apartments on our cul-de-sac, the families mostly black, with a handful of Mexican families. Next door was Miss Gerthree and her two daughters, who were older and younger than me; the eldest, Dorothy Sue, would kiss her boyfriends on the porch when her mother wasn't around, which was often, since Miss Gerthree worked three jobs. Then there were the Robinsons; tall, skinny Mr. Robinson, who worked at Lockheed, was so strict he'd order his sons to scrub the floor with a toothbrush. Ms. Robinson was strict too, with everyone's kids, and when I was little she once smacked me hard for twirling up my dress. There weren't any girls my age, only boys. Lots of boys. My brothers were always up to antics with the five sons of our neighbor Mr. Short, who drove a city bus, and together they created a big pack. Once, they heaved our refrigerator until it tipped over, cracking all the eggs and spilling the glass milk bottles and a big pitcher of orange juice. When my father came home, each boy blamed it on another. But that refrigerator was stout and heavy, the old kind with steel latches sealing the doors—there was no way they weren't all guilty.

Thankfully, there was Big Mama, the elder of the place. She'd sit on her porch, always wearing an apron, always dipping snuff and spitting in a can, and telling all the kids what was what. "Boy, quit throwing them rocks." "Boy, you get over here and sit down." "Y'all, don't be talking to them hobos." There were a lot of hobos passing through; they'd hop from boxcars and sleep in the tunnels by the river. We'd see them with a stick over their shoulder, their belongings tied to it in a sack. But they rarely bothered us, and back in those days, we didn't think to be frightened or put off by them.

My good memories of Aliso Village: behind our building, a dirt road with monkey bars and swings; across the street, a big lawn where the boys ran around, and I'd have tea parties with little metal cups and saucers Daddy bought me for Christmas. We were the first family I knew to get a TV, a great big box with a small black-and-white screen that stood proudly in the living room. I'd sit on the concrete floor and watch, not knowing that those bare concrete floors were one of the things that made the projects different from other people's houses. I liked the concrete; it was good for playing jacks.

Every Friday night, Daddy would take us and the neighborhood kids to the drive-in. We'd pile into his station wagon, the smaller kids hiding on the floor under blankets so we wouldn't be charged extra. Once there, the older boys climbed onto the roof of the car so we all got a view.

On Saturday nights, Mama and the neighbors had card parties. Walking out our front door, you practically fell right into Miss Gerthree's place, and that's where everyone gathered, the adults playing Tonk or Bid Whist—black folks' version of Bridge—while we kids played hide-and-seek and dodgeball on the big lawn. On hot summer nights, we'd build tents with branches and brooms pitched into the grass and sheets draped over, held down by bricks. Each family cooked a dish, and we had a smorgasbord of soul food and Mexican food. The kids fell asleep in the tents, while the parents stayed up talking and laughing and drinking until the wee hours.

And then there were other memories.

When I was around four years old, or maybe just three, my father's sister Elizabeth popped up from Texas and moved around the corner from Aliso Village into an efficiency apartment above a market that sold pickles for a nickel and candy two pieces for a penny. Aunt Elizabeth must've been over three hundred pounds, and the only boyfriend she could find lived at a place called Camarillo, about an hour away. On Saturday mornings, when her boyfriend, Curly, got temporary leave, my mother would drive Elizabeth all the way out there to pick him up, and I'd have to go with. I couldn't stand her crazy boyfriend. When my auntie babysat me, as she often did, Curly would make up reasons to send her out of the house. After Elizabeth left, Curly would take out his penis. He'd say to me, "Make it cry."

I'd say, "It don't smell good."

He'd say, "I've got a bag of candy for you."

I'd scrunch up my face, shake my head.

Then he'd order me, "Open your mouth."

I'd return home with a bag of candy, everyone thinking how nice Curly was to me. To remove its taint I'd dole out the candy to the neighborhood kids at my tea parties. Once I saw them happily eating the Tootsie Rolls and Smarties and Abba-Zabas, I could too. Eating away the nasty thoughts, the vile feelings, the things I knew were wrong but didn't know why and couldn't put into words even if I'd wanted to. It wouldn't be until decades later, when I was forty-three years old, that I finally spoke of this, describing to a prison instructor how I was only beginning to realize the impact of this early abuse.

One time, Aunt Elizabeth doubled back home when she was supposed to be out for a while, and she caught Curly standing in front of me with his pants down. She yanked me. "You dirty little girl," she scolded. "You better not say anything to your mother or father about what a dirty little girl you are."

That Sunday, just as most every Sunday, Mama and Elizabeth chatted and listened to the car radio up front, while I shared the backseat with Curly, drawing up as small as I could on the long drive to return him. My body would finally let go when he got out of the car at the Camarillo State Mental Hospital, the greasy scent of him lingering.

But my relief was always short-lived. Come Saturday, I'd feel a sickening dread as we got back in the car and drove that hour, turning off the freeway and heading down a long, straight road, what seemed the longest mile ever, lined with evenly spaced palm trees shooting tall into the cloudless sky. I'd count the palm trees: one down, two down, three down. At twenty-two down, danger arrived.

3

DADDY'S GIRL

Unemployment rates for blacks in America are consistently twice as high as for whites.

African Americans with a college education or beyond experience nearly the same rate of unemployment as whites with only a high school diploma.

M y father, at heart, was a family man. When I remember him, the first image that comes to mind is of Daddy cooking. He could turn an ordinary pot of red beans into a gourmet meal. Wielding a chopping knife with ease, stirring the simmering pots, he'd man our kitchen, taking swigs from a bottle of red wine he kept in the freezer.

He moved through life with a zest, a passion. He laughed easily and robustly. He was also an adventurer. Most people we knew didn't travel beyond the neighborhood, but Daddy took us to the Pike in Long Beach, where we'd ride the Cyclone Racer, an old wooden roller coaster that spanned beyond the shore, so when the cars twisted and plunged all you'd see beneath you was ocean. We spent many Saturdays in Lincoln Park, running around in the fields and playground while Daddy grilled. There was a lake, and we'd go out in a little boat, dangling handmade fishing poles baited with worms we dug up.

On the Fourth of July, Daddy went all out, and we'd head to Lincoln Park in the morning with blankets and coolers and a barrel barbecue pit, staking a spot under the biggest tree. Daddy grilled chicken and ribs and weenies and corn on the cob, with beans and potato salad he'd made the night before. Later, we ate watermelon by the slice while fireworks exploded over our heads. He celebrated every holiday with flair, but made the biggest hoopla of Christmas. The day after Thanksgiving we picked out the biggest tree on the lot. We didn't have keepsake ornaments or anything like that, but we strung lightbulbs and angel hair until the tree was in Technicolor. Christmas meant red wagons, Lionel trains, an Easy Bake Oven for me, and I'd bake Daddy little chocolate cakes to take to work.

But when I was around seven years old, everything changed. In the first wave of deindustrialization, the sheet metal factory closed down. This wasn't just a temporary blow, wasn't just a few months of tightening the belt while my father found another job. When the doors of that factory closed, my father's worth, his pride, got closed up in there too. Without his career, without that paycheck to provide for his family, he didn't know how to pick himself up day after day. All his life he had to move against a forceful undercurrent—growing up in Texas, he knew to look down when passing a white woman on the street; and when strange fruit hung from the trees, he tried not to look up. He fought for our country, but the army treated him like a second-class citizen. A charcoal-black man, he dared to have dreams for himself and his family. But at what point does that undercurrent overtake you? At what point does the struggle to, yet again, try to find a place for yourself in an unwelcoming world become too much? With the closing of that factory began the dismantling of our family.

I was still young, but I remember the swift change. A hopelessness gripped my dad. His flickering eyes turned sad. He used to say, "Come on, Susie Q, let's go," and we'd go to one of his friend's houses and they'd throw dice while I eagerly waited for someone to toss me a nickel. But Daddy didn't do that anymore. Friday nights, we kids would be ready to pile in his car for the drive-in, but there were no more movies. Instead, Daddy went out alone and returned hours later, slurring and walking sideways.

On it went: my father drank, and my mother worked. All day she cleaned white people's houses—a sad use of her Home Economics major—while he tried to numb the layers of disappointment, of hardship after hardship. She would come home bone tired; he would come home eyes red. They both came home angry.

Their fights grew louder and rougher. At night the walls vibrated with their shouting. Many mornings, Mama had a swollen eye or busted lip. One night the police showed up. I remember it was just after Christmas because my brothers had toy guns in holsters and sheriff badges pinned to their shirts, and a policeman told them to shoot the bad guys.

Often, Daddy lashed out at my brothers, too, especially Billy. We all knew Billy had a different father, Mr. Walker, who sometimes came around the house. I'm not sure how the events had gone down but, before I was born, my parents split and my mother moved in with Mr. Walker—until my daddy showed up, demanding his wife return home. Mr. Walker tried to make a relationship with Billy, but my father resented him coming around and reminding everyone of Mama's dalliance, even though my father himself had a loose definition of devotion.

Daddy would punish my brothers by ordering them to strip and endure a switch or razor strap. They were whipped until they fell to their knees, or until my father tired. Didn't matter if skin would break, if blood would come. This was how my parents had been disciplined. This was how their forefathers had had their souls beat out of them. But Daddy never so much as raised his voice, let alone a hand, to me—and neither did anyone else when he was around. When he wasn't there, though, I was at the mercy of everything, including my mother's wrath. Directed solely at me, her temper could be vicious.

We kids were the collateral damage of my parents' histories, of the worst and weakest parts of themselves, and of the plain fact that neither was around during the day and we were left to raise ourselves.

Meanwhile, Aliso Village was changing. Black and Mexican gangs began to face off by the big clothesline. Our neighbor Miss Gerthree took her daughters and moved away after one too many times of looking out the back window in broad daylight and seeing knife fights. Her eldest, Dorothy Sue, said she was worried about me, that I was such a friendly little girl, wandering around Aliso Village, saying hi to everyone. She said she hoped someone would keep an eye on me like she had.

Most days I was sent to Aunt Elizabeth's. Eventually, her crazy boyfriend vanished—I don't know if he'd been discharged from the hospital and dropped her, or if she finally got fed up with him. Even without Curly around I was on guard with my auntie. When she couldn't keep me for the day, Big Mama would, and the way I felt when I was with Big Mama was in stark contrast. I was too young to articulate it, but when I was in Big Mama's care, I felt free to be myself. I felt safe.

Other times I was left at home with my brothers. Probably because Daddy beat on them but spoiled me, they had no soft spot for their only sister. They often barricaded me in the closet or locked me out of house, laughing as I banged my fists and pleaded for hours.

All of us kids thought I was my father's only daughter. Until, one day, Celeste showed up for a visit. Her skin damn near white, she lived in New York with her mother and was thirteen years old—born before my parents had married. For the time Celeste was with us, everything was picture perfect. My brothers left me alone, and Daddy left them alone, and Mama didn't whoop me or scream at Daddy but moved gently, like it was she who was the visitor in the house. I didn't want Celeste to leave. With her there, our house felt like *Leave It to Beaver*. With her there, I felt safe. When Celeste told me she had to go back home, I begged to go with her. Ironically, years later she admitted she had envied *me*, because I had Daddy. But that one time she visited, she didn't really *see* Daddy, didn't know how the drink was wasting him, and how he was turning into a shadow of the man and father he'd once been.

I was shattered when Celeste left. And the chaos in the house started right back up. It's interesting, I suppose, to trace the trajectories of half sisters growing up across the country. When we met, Celesta and I were both studious and made good grades, but our paths diverged. She went on to college, eventually getting a job that brought her back to Los Angeles, working for Mayor Tom Bradley. By this point, I was in the midst of a reckless and dark time. I had become the bad seed. Although we were finally living in the same city, long-lost sisters, Celesta understandably distanced herself from me.

Not long after Celesta's visit my mother got wind of the fact that my father had another daughter in Long Beach, about twenty miles away. I was around six years old when Mama took me to meet my half sister LaRonda, who was two years younger. I was happy to have another sister, but, hardly surprising, my mom never paid another visit to Long Beach, and LaRonda and I were too young to keep in touch ourselves.

Decades later, in the early 1990s, I was reading the prison movement sheet, a daily bulletin that reported things like work detail openings and new inmates, when I saw the name LaRonda Burton. Out in the yard, I found her, my half sister, also serving time for possession of drugs.

4

HIT THE ROAD

*Over 42 percent of African American children under the
age of six live in poverty.*

When I was ten years old my mother bought a 45 of Ray
Charles's "Hit the Road Jack" and played the song over and
over. It filled our house, it filled my head, hearing her sing—*No more,
no more, no more, no more*—it filled that year. That song became my
mother's anthem as she mustered the courage to kick out my father.

I can still see clearly those final images of my father in our house:
he's drinking Seagram's gin. On the record player is "The Thrill Is
Gone," and his eyes are closed as he croons how lonely he will be.

I begged Mama to take Daddy back. He was the one who protected
me, who looked at me tenderly, who bought me things. But Mama
didn't take him back, and I grew deeply resentful.

Daddy got a job working as a chef for Amtrak and moved to the
other side of the world: Syracuse, New York. It would be nearly two
years before I saw him again. Every week when the *Sentinel* came
out, I'd mail him a copy so he could keep up on the black community in Los Angeles. At Christmas, he sent a big box of gifts, most
for me. Occasionally, he wrote or called. He told me how he earned
the nickname Soup Maker after his train was stocked with canned
soup and he threw a fit. He remained the only chef on Amtrak who

cooked everything from scratch. He always ended our calls saying he missed me.

Right away, Mama had a new boyfriend, Mr. Albertus Fisher. The story went that Mama had been walking down the street when Mr. Fisher, a widower with no children of his own, saw her and instantly fell in love. But I'd heard his name before—in fights between my parents, Daddy claiming my youngest brother Isaac belonged with Mr. Fisher; Mama swearing that wasn't true. No sooner was my father out than Mr. Fisher moved us from Aliso Village to a house on Olive Street in South L.A. My mother had finally made it out of the projects.

Our house had a garage in back, and behind that a gravel pile, where we'd have rock fights. My brothers and I found boxes of balloons in the garage, and we held them under the faucet and had water balloon fights. One day my mother saw one of my brothers holding a balloon. She looked at it funny, the long water balloon with a nipple on the end. She said, "Boy, where'd you get that?" We took her to the garage and showed her the boxes. She mumbled, "Those ain't balloons," and gathered up all the boxes.

If there's one thing I have to say for Mama, she and Mr. Fisher were very discreet. That's how Mama carried herself. Even though she and my father were separated, she was still a married woman and did not want to be seen going around with another man. Mr. Fisher never stayed with us. He never even came into the house and kicked back on the couch. The most I saw of him was when he'd pick up Mama in his gold Cadillac. A few hours later, the Cadillac would return to drop her off.

Unlike my father, Mr. Fisher was a man of few words. Daddy was spry and stood with command; Mr. Fisher seldom emerged from his car. Every few weeks Mr. Fisher would come by and my brothers would pile into the Cadillac and he'd drive them downtown to the barber college for haircuts. Though he drove that flashy car, Mr. Fisher wasn't flashy in other ways; his clothes were plain, he didn't wear jewelry. The only gift I recall he bought for us was a Monopoly game.

We knew he was in real estate, and we knew he had money. One day I was ear hustling when Mama said to a girlfriend, "We're at that motel so much, he might as well buy it." Mr. Fisher lived Monopoly; he was savvy and shrewd. We were just rolling the dice and playing the game. Mama still cleaned houses. She took the bus in the early morning to fancy parts of town, like Brentwood and Beverly Hills. One house she worked at belonged to film actor Robert Ryan. She spoke of him a lot because he was kind to her, unlike some of her other employers. She sometimes came home with bags of the Ryan kids' old clothes, though nothing looked old or raggedy. I could tell their clothes were different than ours by the feel of that nice fabric on my skin. Once, Mr. Ryan invited our family to his home for a party. When Mama told us, there was hesitation in her voice and, as she eyed us up and down, as though sizing up what we'd look like standing in that house, I saw a twitch of shame. She wagged her finger, "At Mr. Ryan's house, don't say, *Gimme*. Don't even say, *Can I have*." I was excited to go to a famous actor's house. But she must have decided against taking us, because we never went.

At 61st Street Elementary, I placed top in my class spelling contest, qualifying me to compete in the schoolwide spelling bee. I could tell Mama was proud. She and my brothers put on nice clothes, and I looked out from the stage and saw them. It's a pivotal memory: my family showing up for me, rooting for me. I stood in the spotlight, watching them applaud. But just as quickly and easily as a slipped-up letter, that moment was there, then gone. I can't remember the word I misspelled—or, for that matter, the words I spelled correctly. We went home, I changed out of my good clothes, and any remaining glow vanished, lost to the chaos around me.

My brothers had the run of the house. We were getting cereal one morning, Mama long gone on the bus, and I opened the silverware drawer but there were no spoons. Michael, the oldest, said, "You looking for spoons?" He thrust some at me—spoons that, unbeknownst to me, had been resting on the gas burner of the stove. When I reached for them, the burn went deep, so deep on my arm the white meat showed. I fell to the floor, kicking like a chicken. My brothers gathered around, deep-belly laughing.

They'd never have dared pull this kind of prank if Daddy had been around. I had to wait the whole day, my arm oozing, for Mama to come home. She told off Michael good, and bandaged me, but I didn't go to any doctor. The scar would be with me for life.

I'd think of that day some forty years later, at Michael's funeral. Alternating the image of Michael laughing while I writhed on the linoleum with another childhood night, around Christmastime, when Daddy came by the house with bikes for us, but he and Mama got into it. Daddy locked the front porch door, locking Mama in with him and the rest of us out, and Michael bravely tried to bust down the door to help Mama. I thought, too, about how, when Michael was a teenager, he fell asleep at the wheel and, though a narcolepsy diagnosis wouldn't come until years later, he was prosecuted and sent to live at a juvenile detention camp in the mountains. The police who'd taken Michael away came by that Christmas and brought me a Chatty Cathy doll. But I didn't want the doll, I wanted my brother back. Even though my brother had burned me, something made me connect the fact that Michael had been treated meanly by my father, and when you treat people mean they become mean.

In his thirties and forties, Michael turned to drugs and was eventually incarcerated for possession. While in prison, he got word that his wife, his childhood sweetheart, had stopped going to her kidney dialysis. She said it was all too much, she was too tired. Michael knew that without dialysis she'd die, but behind bars he was helpless to influence her or to provide her some comfort. At her funeral, my heart broke over Michael's absence. By the time he was released, it wasn't only his wife who was gone; he was too. He told me he had nothing left to live for. When a cut on his foot became infected, he wouldn't seek help. Gangrene ate up his foot and then his life. I tried to intervene, talking with doctors and hoping to convince Michael to amputate his foot in order to save himself. He refused. His life and its hardships and disappointments had left him so defeated he was no longer rational. What was the point of caring about yourself when life was so hard? How do you keep going when there's little hope of relief? I found a rest home for Michael and visited him every other day, up until the end.

When I was still in elementary school Mr. Fisher moved us from the nice house on Olive Street to a house on 41st and Figueroa, which butted up against the 110 freeway. I wondered if Mama and Mr. Fisher were on the outs or if he was angry at her. I also wondered why Mama let us move into that house. The ceiling was crumbling, and rats scurried along the floor and in and out of holes chewed between the kitchen cabinets. I'd never been to Mr. Fisher's house, but I knew he lived in Leimert Park, an upper-class area, and one of the first planned communities.

I'd heard Mama say Leimert Park was so nice the telephone wires were buried underground so no poles messed up the view. Our house had a view of the southbound ramp. But even in this rundown neighborhood with the freeway out your front door, none of the houses were as raggedy as ours.

My mother wasn't having it good. With her wages from cleaning unable to support six growing kids, she applied for welfare. I can only imagine the shame she must've felt, but she never said a thing. I grew accustomed to yearning for the first and fifteenth of the month, when the gray envelope from the government showed up. Then we could get groceries, though the food stamps never covered enough to fully feed us all.

Routinely, a white woman came to our house to look in the closets and search under the beds for any sign of my father. But this went beyond making sure my mother was, indeed, supporting us on her own. Years earlier, Daddy had been arrested for possession of marijuana, and with that felony record following him, he wasn't allowed to live with us so long as Mama was, as we called it, on the County. That government money we so desperately needed distanced me further from Daddy, and, in my young mind, created yet another barrier to my parents ever getting back together. I longed for that gray envelope, but I felt guilty, because I longed for Daddy more. I longed for the way things used to be.

One night, a rat crawled into my bed. It was as big as my foot, and I screamed and kicked it onto the floor, its thick tail thrashing as though it was a mile long. The rats were becoming more and more bold, like we were the visitors and they were residents in this house. Every morning Mama made me sit on the floor between her knees to do my hair: a ponytail on top, two on the side, and one or two ponytails in the back. She'd sing, "*Your hair is nappy, nappy to the gristle. Every time I comb your hair you jump up and whistle.*" I was jumping up because her yanking hurt, but also because I didn't want to be sitting on the floor, afraid those rats might bite me.

Mama said living in this house was only temporary, but month after month passed. For three years we lived in that hovel—which would be torn down the minute we moved out. Mama had eight or nine siblings, all in Texas, and I wondered why she never asked them for help. As I grew older, I understood more about her pride, realizing her family would've told her to come back to Texas or to go back to her husband, chastising her for having left both in the first place. So Mama soldiered on, in the only way she knew how. For those years, I lived in a constant state of fear. I was scared of my brothers and scared of my mother and scared of that house.

I tried to think up ways not to come home. My friend Kathy lived on the other side of the freeway, and it was her father raising her and her sister and they had a mean dog, but I spent a lot of time there. Another friend was Sharlene—we called her Shamp—and her house was my favorite. Her brother, Floyd, played music like Johnny "Guitar" Watson, and her mother cooked some really good beans. Their house was clean, orderly, calm, no rats.

School was also my safe place. In the afternoons, I'd stick around the schoolyard and play tetherball. I was excellent at tetherball. I learned that, just like my daddy, I had an anger brewing inside me, and I could shoot that anger to my fists and whack that tetherball so hard it wrapped itself all the way around the pole. Nobody could get that ball as high as I could. I'd stay until the playground closed—or until Mama showed up. Mama wanted me to come home and clean up the house, and if she got back and the house wasn't tidy, she'd come to the schoolyard holding an extension cord. Mama liked that six feet of cord. She'd make a noose, the rest wrapped around her hand for a tight grip, and she'd whoop me with that cord all the way home. She hit my thighs until U-shaped welts appeared. Sometimes, my skin opened.

Mama had two sides: the tornado of rage she unleashed on me, and the side she presented to everyone else. There wasn't a neighbor who wouldn't describe my mother as the sweetest person in the world, always generous, very soft-spoken. They wouldn't have believed she carried that extension cord like a threat all around the house.

Maybe my mother resented me for getting so much of my father's attention and love; maybe she resented the fact that she'd made it far from Texas in search of a better life, but this wasn't anything near what she'd had in mind. She was just trying to hold on—hold on to a life that shouldn't have been so hard. And maybe that's what made it possible for her, at one moment, to whip me, and another moment to open the back door to a tattered white man asking for food for his family and give him one of the three potatoes she had for her own six kids.

5

THE SACRIFICE

More than 60 percent of incarcerated women report having been sexually assaulted before the age of eighteen.

In the fourth grade, I became a teacher's helper for my youngest brother, Isaac's, kindergarten class. Every week, the kids brought quarters for milk, and I was supposed to take the quarters and put them in an envelope. I took the quarters, all right. I took the quarters because my brothers and I didn't always have our own milk money. Our sack lunches were often nothing but sugar sandwiches—a piece of white bread sprinkled with sugar.

With those quarters, I bought food from the market for my brothers and me. And I bought treats. Now I could join my friends who always had pickle money. We chose the biggest pickles from the barrel, then poked a peppermint stick through the pickle and ate it all together.

One day, the principal's finger was in my face. "Don't be saying you didn't take it, because a quarter fell out of your sock." I watched as the principal went through a ritual of picking a wooden paddle from a choice of different sizes. In my dress, I leaned over a chair, and he whacked my behind. But my shame was worse than the paddling. Surprisingly, I was allowed to remain a teacher's helper. A rare second chance, and I knew it. I never again took another quarter.

As if things couldn't get worse in our house, Aunt Elizabeth moved in. Now I had to share my twin bed with the massive weight and breathing and sweatiness of her. I squashed myself up against the wall, not wanting my skin to touch her skin, though it was inevitable. I'd wake to nightmares of her ex-boyfriend.

I'd also wake in the night because Elizabeth frequently wet the bed. In the morning she always blamed it on me. All I could do was silently stand there, burning with humiliation, swallowing back my fury. I was trained not to talk back, though this was about more than just respecting your elders. This went back to an archetypal core: you didn't speak up to the master, no matter what, no matter if the master was right or wrong or crazy as a loon, you didn't say a damn thing. That's how it was for my ancestors, and that's how they taught their children, and that's how my parents taught me.

If only I had understood the threat I posed to Aunt Elizabeth—that if Daddy ever found out his sister's role in what had happened to me with Curly, there's no telling what he'd have done. Looking back, she had to have realized this, and her solution was to intimidate, to lord over me. I never did tell Daddy. As far as I'm aware, he passed without ever knowing.

The only time I didn't seethe at Elizabeth was when we visited the hamburger stand where she worked, and she gave us free burgers. Still, I'd much rather have paid the quarter for a burger than have to see her face.

One night in the room we shared, Elizabeth was teasing me, bragging how much money she had and flashing her couple hundred dollars. She said, "Sue, put all your money down and watch my money run your money up under the bed." By the time she woke the next morning, I had squeezed my little hand in between that mattress and gotten all the money. No way was her money gonna run mine.

With her cash I went downtown to Lee's and bought myself some shoes and bought my friend Kathy some shoes, but I had to hide mine at Kathy's house. As soon as Elizabeth realized her money was gone, she told my mother I stole it. By some stroke of goodness toward me—or maybe exasperation with Elizabeth—Mama didn't believe her. The next day, Elizabeth moved out.

In those rare moments when my mother bothered to really notice me, she saw her daughter growing rough and wild. So she took me to Sears and enrolled me in charm class. At the time, it didn't occur to me how much this meant for Mama to spend her hard-earned money this way. I didn't like charm class, but I endured it, and it was someplace to go that wasn't home. I learned to walk straight and sit with my knees together and use a handkerchief. But then I'd return to the toughness of my brothers and that house, and it was like being thrown over-board and worrying about daintily swimming ashore. Gracefulness and manners were useless—detrimental, dangerous even—when you were fending for yourself. I needed more than charm school.

Next, Mama signed me up for Woodcraft Rangers, the poor girl's Brownies: no uniforms to purchase, no dues, no badges to stitch onto a sash. I never saw Brownies on my side of town; instead, Woodcraft Rangers was a charitable effort to build character and keep kids out of trouble. But I unknowingly walked right up to trouble and knocked on its door.

I was in the fifth grade and wanted to be the Woodcraft Ranger who sold the most boxes of cookies. Alone, I went door to door. A house across from school had a guest house around back, and I went around and knocked on that door, too. An older white man answered, and to my surprise he bought ten boxes of cookies. His name was Mr. Burke, and I gleefully recorded his order.

A couple weeks later, when I went to deliver the boxes of cookies, Mr. Burke invited me in. His house was tidy, and I sat at the kitchen table, my fingers idling on the vinyl tablecloth. He paid what he owed me, but told me I could keep the cookies. *Keep the cookies?* Though I hadn't won top cookie sales, I sure as heck beat out everyone for the most cookies brought back home! Then Mr. Burke asked where I lived.

I left with the money and the cookies, and soon Mr. Burke showed up at my mother's house. He and Mama talked for a while, and then he turned to me and said he'd like to invite me to his house again. Mama told me I should go. The next morning I stopped by Mr. Burke's on the way to school, and he gave me a dime just for coming by to say hello.

Mama began earning money doing Mr. Burke's laundry, and I continued to stop by Mr. Burke's to say hello and get a dime. One day, he invited me inside for a soda. Now I really had it good: a soda and a dime, all just for saying hello to an old man.

After a while, the dime turned into a quarter. And then a dollar.

Before long, things started happening in Mr. Burke's house, and I was no longer just saying hello. But when these things started happening, my family started eating very well. Mr. Burke owned restaurants, and we went from eating beans two weeks of the month to having bread and eggs and bacon, even steak. I noticed a difference, too, in my mother. Ever since her Mr. Fisher had disappeared I'd watched life wear on her, wringing out the fight in her. Though cleaning houses still made her achey and exhausted, she no longer sighed like it was a trapped scream, like all that was going through her mind was, *On my own, there's no way out and no way up.*

I don't remember how much money Mr. Burke offered to lure me into his bedroom. He told me not to be scared, that he wasn't going to hurt me. I clenched the bedspread, my body going stiff as a board. The next time it happened, it was as though my spirit jumped out of my body and hovered someplace else, someplace where nothing was seen, nothing was heard, nothing was known. And that's how it happened every time after that.

I kept returning to his house. I came back for $10, then $20, then $50. I taught myself how, the instant I walked through the door, to take my mind far away, to a place of silence and stillness. I got so good, all I had to tell myself was *Time to do the out-of-body thing.* Sadly, some decades later, this would make me good at prison, too.

I was ten years old, then eleven, then twelve, and I became accustomed to Mr. Burke's money. I'd take the bus downtown by myself and buy clothes for me and my brothers, and even for Mama. I'd dole out my purchases like I had some power in my family. I also began to argue with my mother and fight back with my brothers. I hit my brothers like I was pounding that tetherball, so hard they'd drop to their knees. All the while, Mama continued doing Mr. Burke's laundry. "Susan," she'd say, matter-of-factly, upon returning with her laundry wages. "Mr. Burke asked after you."

Around this time, I began to have a noticeable stutter and was sent to the speech therapist at school. The therapist, a white woman, called in my mother, and I overhead her telling Mama I was going to grow up to be a criminal. Mama didn't say anything in the meeting, but she took it back to the neighborhood, where she ranted, "How could that woman say such a thing about my child?"

Maybe within my stutter the therapist saw how life was shaping me, teaching me to build a razor wire around myself and showing me that nobody was going to take care of me but me.

Every week I had to go sit with that therapist, silently knowing what she thought of me. My younger brother Melvin, closest in age to me, stuttered too. He also had to sit with that therapist. Eventually, Melvin and I stopped stuttering, as though we simply outgrew it. But Melvin and I both grew into that therapist's prediction.

By the time I was in seventh grade, Mr. Burke was giving me $100 bills. He came by my mother's house one day that autumn and handed Mama cash. "Go to Bullock's," he said, "and get Sue something pretty to wear to junior high school."

Bullock's was a high-end department store, not the kind of place we shopped. But Mama took me to Bullock's and we picked out a beautiful dress for the first day of school: a jumper of royal blue felt with kelly green piping and two rows of gold buttons connected with little gold chains.

One day, I knocked on Mr. Burke's door, but a stranger answered. I was supposed to get money that visit and had already picked out a portable record player you could even take in the car that cost $140. The person at the door told me that Mr. Burke had a heart attack and died. I trudged home, disappointed because I'd really wanted that record player. Mr. Burke's loss evoked nothing in me, but I mourned the loss of his money.

I wore the jumper from Bullock's to school every week, maybe every other week, because it was my best and most favorite dress, and I didn't want to wear it out. In the hall one day, the principal stopped me, saying my dress looked short of code. I was thirteen years old and in the midst of a growth spurt—and because the jumper was felt, there was no hem to let down to stretch another year out of it. Without Mr. Burke's money, my family was back to scrounging; we barely had enough for food, let alone new clothes.

The principal made me kneel on a bench. The edge of my jumper was supposed to graze the bench. Instead, it hovered about an inch too high. I was suspended from school for two weeks on account of the inch.

I was more upset than Mama about my suspension. I wanted to be in school. She got on the bus to go to work like she always did, and I was left home, alone. Not wanting to be in that scary house, I made my way to the street. There, I discovered the kids drumming up trouble. There, I received an intensive education of another sort. In those two weeks of my suspension, I learned to smoke. I learned to hang out. I learned how to get with boys—and that I could pick the boys I wanted. I learned to buck authority, and I learned to be defiant.

By the time I returned to school, I'd fallen considerably behind, especially in math. The class had moved on to fractions, and I was lost. Having always been a good student, I didn't know how to ask for help. Or maybe I'd learned well from Mama to be too proud to ask. My teacher *had* to see I was struggling, had to notice the marked difference, but never offered me assistance. With each passing week, my confusion and stress mounted. And then it occurred to me: there was a way I could solve this. I could decide to stop caring about school. I could, instead, go hang out.

An unthinkable proposition just a couple of months earlier, when school had been my haven, but I now saw things differently. School had failed me. Just as everything up until that point had failed me. So when everything betrays you, what are you left with? If only I'd known that my contemplation, that the mental exercise of divvying up the mud pie of my days and calculating that school deserved the thinnest sliver . . . if only I'd known that *was* doing fractions.

I played "Dancing in the Streets" on the record player. I played "Party Lights." I could see those party lights before my eyes, and I was raring to go. Mama would lock me in my bedroom, but I'd crawl out the window. I was going to have it my way. One night I was trying to get out of the house and Mama was trying to hold me back from the front door. The door had a long glass panel with a decorative design inside, and in our wrangling I busted right through the glass panel. Only it wasn't glass, it was Plexiglas and the design inside was only cardboard. It took me a second to realize I wasn't all cut up, not even a scratch. Then I escaped into the night. When I returned home a day, maybe two, later, Mama said she was calling the police on me. I didn't believe her and was shocked when two policemen showed up at the door.

Calling me "incorrigible," they took me to Southwest Police Station. From there, I was delivered to Juvenile Hall, a heavy gate sliding shut behind the police car. I'd heard about kids, boys mostly, who'd landed in juvie. They weren't spelling-bee champs and teacher's helpers like me. Only, I wasn't like me anymore.

At Juvenile Hall, big pitchers of cold milk were placed on the communal tables at breakfast and pitchers of Kool-Aid at lunchtime, and we could drink all we wanted. There was bread with butter at every meal, and the meals changed day by day. It was clean; no rats. I was treated respectfully. But I was lonely, and I was ashamed. When my court date came, I went in front of the judge. He asked how old I was.

"Thirteen," I replied.

He looked at me with a nod of compassion. "I'm not going to send you to the Ventura School for Girls," he said.

I'd heard of Ventura—it was called a school, but was more like prison for kids. "You're too young," the judge said. "The exposure there isn't going to help you." With a smack of his gavel, the judge granted me leniency, assigning me a probation officer and releasing me back to my mother.

6

THINGS YOU DON'T TALK ABOUT

More than 75 percent of incarcerated women had at least one child as a teenager.

My probation officer was Ms. Strathy, a white woman, always with a Salem extended from her fingers, though she only smoked the tip because she said most of the nicotine was at the other end and this was her compromise with her husband, who wanted her to quit. I liked Ms. Strathy. She would ask how I was, and I felt I could talk to her. But not about what had gone on with Mr. Burke. I couldn't tell her that. Besides, he was dead, so I didn't see the point.

Ms. Strathy said I needed continuation school. In my neighborhood, we knew about these: the Betsy Ross school was for girls who were pregnant, and the Ramona school was for bad girls. But it was at the Ramona school where I began to reengage. The all-girls school was a mix of black, white, and Mexican. The teachers were mixed too, but unlike my old school, they seemed interested in the students. The classes were small, and I felt attended to. I felt safe. My art teacher gave me a thick book with a title I couldn't pronounce, but it was about a starving man imprisoned for stealing a loaf of bread and a young girl he later rescues named Cosette. I couldn't put the book down, and it made me fall in love with reading.

That August of 1965, my mother said some of her siblings from

Texas were coming to visit. I overhead her on the phone trying to make excuses why they shouldn't come to the house. I knew she was ashamed of how we lived. But they insisted, so Mama ran around trying to patch things up, moving a chair in front of a hole in the wall, rearranging a rug over bare spots in the floor. But there was no way to fully camouflage that kind of deterioration, like the rat holes—not little-bitty mice holes, but big holes—chewed, through all the kitchen cabinets and all over the place.

As her family approached our exit from the freeway, they saw deep black clouds billowing from the ground: South Los Angeles was on fire. Her brother kept driving past our exit and straight back to Texas. The Watts riots saved my mother from the visit.

White folks often called Watts "Mud Town" because of its lack of paved roads. During World War II, when the availability of defense factory jobs prompted thousands of black southerners to head to Los Angeles in search of a better life, Watts was one of the only areas blacks were permitted to live. Merely two square miles, Watts soon became the most densely populated neighborhood in the country. But when the war ended, thousands of "essential workers" were laid off, devastating Watts with mass unemployment. City government turned a blind eye, and wealthy, white Los Angeles easily avoided this no-man's-land in South Central.

Before the riots put Watts on the national map, all most Angelenos knew of Watts was the Watts Towers, an art structure of multiple spires made of discarded glass, broken pottery, tiles, and seashells. The artist, Simon Rodia, an Italian immigrant, spent thirty-four years creating the towers. But upon completion of his life's work in 1955, he deeded his property to a neighbor and up and left Watts.

By 1965, Watts was boiling over with decades of employment and housing discrimination, segregation, extreme poverty, and police abuse. On a scorching August night, when a white policeman arrested a young black man on suspicion of drunk driving—and then arrested his mother and brother, who showed up to the scene—a crowd of onlookers protested the officer's harsh treatment. More officers arrived with billy clubs, and that night the pressure cooker of Watts exploded.

My nose stung with the smell of smoke and char. Ashes floated in the air like snowflakes. The disc jockey on the radio, Magnificent Montague, used to say, "Burn, baby, burn!" Now he said, "Cool it, cool it." I didn't have a sense of the bigger picture, that this was an uprising. Didn't understand how these six days of fists and bricks and flames and bullets obliterated the country's illusion that civil rights was only a southern problem. Just the week before, President Johnson had signed into law the Voting Rights Act, but what impact did that have on me, on my family? In Los Angeles, we'd had the right to vote, and my parents did so proudly. But what was their vote doing for all of us in South L.A.? Every adult in my world was so tired and beaten down they couldn't think about life in a way that was beyond how to get by day by day. My mother could draw the curtain and pull the lever, but it didn't change the fact that she was a single mom raising six kids on a cleaning woman's wages, or that we lived in a house that should have been condemned, the government routinely visiting in search of evidence of my father, all the while turning a blind eye to the empty refrigerator, the collapsing ceiling, the scratching of rats in the walls.

As the riots fumed, the row of shops near my house on Vernon and Broadway were looted. Come daytime, I walked myself to the corner, surveying the mess of glass and bricks that had been a liquor store, a tuxedo shop, a wig shop. I stepped through the broken storefront window and took a straight red wig.

When Mama saw me in that wig, she yanked it off. "This has no business being on your head." Then she demanded to hear where I got it, though she knew full well. Mama was a by-the-book person; stealing was unacceptable—even if the place was scorched, a pile of rubble; even if the police knew it was no use stopping looters; even if someone else would've walked in a minute later and taken that wig, so it might as well have been mine.

The riots pounded on, the National Guard took over, and the city enforced a curfew at dusk. It was miserably hot in our house, and my brothers and I ventured onto our front porch, trying to catch a cool, night breeze. We had the Four Tops on the record player, the volume turned up and the front door open so we could hear. Before our eyes, a military tank rolled down 41st Street. Out jumped soldiers in combat gear, rifles pointed at us. "Get inside!" they ordered. We scrambled into that stifling, crumbling house so fast.

The riots raged for six days, leaving thirty-four people dead and over a thousand wounded, with four thousand arrests and tens of millions of dollars in property damage. The aftermath was merely a continuation of the devastation. If the community had been depleted before, now it was a big pile of ash and boarded-up buildings. Businesses would never bother to return. The streets remained in a state of disrepair. Schools were sorely lacking. Medical care was sparse. Watts had never been paid much mind, but now there was disinvestment in the place.

For my family, though, everything changed: not long after the riots, Mr. Fisher mysteriously reappeared. He moved us out of that rattrap and into a beautiful four-bedroom, two-bathroom house on Normandie Avenue and 42nd, a well-kept block across from the St. Cecilia Catholic church and school. I don't know what kind of rekindling took place between Mama and Mr. Fisher, but she stopped going to work cleaning houses. The shadows lifted from her eyes, and she moved about like she was younger, lighter.

I, too, felt something lifting. I had taken an inventory of my young life, reflecting on the bad things I'd done and what it had gotten me: it hadn't gotten me anything. I was still attending the Ramona school, and I liked my teachers and had made goods friends. I knew these people enjoyed seeing my face each day; I knew they cared about me. It was what I'd later come to know and value as a community. I quit boys, I quit weed, I quit hanging out. Instead, I was being the best person I could be.

Daddy called with the great news that his Amtrak route had changed—he was now the chef on the Los Angeles–to–Chicago train.

First thing he did upon returning to L.A. was drop off gifts at our house. To see his face—he was as handsome and debonair as in my memory. He rented a hotel room on 54th and Central, and my brothers and I visited him there every week or so. If no one was around to drive us, we'd walk, an hour each way, which required crossing the 110—we knew all the pedestrian bridges up and down that stretch of freeway. We crowded into that small hotel room, the five of them on the floor and the bed, while I sat in the window. Sometimes, Daddy would surprise me by coming by my school to walk me home. Looking back, he must have surmised more than I thought, because as we walked, he'd say things like, "Nobody putting his hand on my baby girl."

That Christmas Eve in 1965, I was fourteen years old. Mama let me open one gift from under the tree. It was a purple, long-sleeved tunic with big ruffles and a matching pair of purple pants, which I changed into immediately. I looked sharp in my new Christmas suit.

My friend Cupcake, who lived nearby, came over and together we walked several blocks to a party at another friend's house on 35th and Vermont. We danced for hours, records spinning; the Temptations were hotter than fish grease, the Supremes, Martha and the Vandellas, and, of course, James Brown. We ate Christmas cookies and drank Coca-Cola. At around 10:30, Cupcake and I said our goodbyes and started walking home. But we only made it a couple of blocks when a group of boys stood in our way.

"Hey, girl," someone leered. "Where ya going?"

We tried to turn around, but suddenly six or seven boys surrounded us. They hustled us into a backyard, and the next thing I knew we were pushed through a back door that led directly into a basement. I could hear voices, especially a woman's voice, coming from upstairs. I screamed as loud as I could. The boys pushed us down. I screamed again. But the woman upstairs kept talking and her footsteps kept easily moving around the floor. When it was over, Cupcake and I pulled up our pants and left.

As we ran home, Cupcake swore me to secrecy. Her mother was sickly, and Cupcake feared that if she found out what had happened she'd have a heart attack. I promised not to tell. When I got home I went straight to my room. I took off my Christmas suit. A little bow on the chest of the tunic was ripped. I stomped on the clothes, then buried them in the trash. And then I buried myself, too. I stepped out of my body and went to that other place that existed only in my imagination. I never spoke of that night, and no one around me noticed a thing.

Until some months later. My English teacher, Ms. Morgan, pulled me aside. I loved her class; she was warm and friendly and taught in a way that reached me. She said, "Susan, I think you're pregnant."

I didn't know what she was talking about. She said, "I'm going to drive you home." We got in her car.

Mama invited Ms. Morgan in, and we sat in the living room. Mama now had herself a lovely living room, carpeted, with a fireplace and big, comfortable couches. Mama looked expectantly, waiting for news that I'd either aced a test or uncharacteristically failed one. Ms. Morgan said, "I noticed Susan's nose looks different, broader. Sometimes that happens when you're pregnant."

My head spun. I watched the confusion on Mama's face melt into shame. And that made my shame turn into anger. But I stifled it as I told them what had happened on Christmas Eve. I didn't cry. I'd long ago learned tears were useless.

Here we were, at last in a nice house, I wasn't taking any beatings from my brothers, Mama's rage toward me had subsided, I periodically saw Daddy, I was making As in school. And this: upheaval. Mama thanked Ms. Morgan and showed her out. The rest of the night she and I were very quiet. The next day Mama took me to Ms. Strathy, my probation officer, and I repeated what had happened. I explained that Cupcake didn't want her mother to know. But Ms. Strathy explained that we were underage, so her mother had to be told. Then we all went in Ms. Strathy's car to the police station to file a report. The police drove me to 35th and Vermont, and I retraced the path Cupcake and I had walked, pointing out the house with the back door that led to a basement.

I watched the policemen recording what I said. I thought about all those other times I should have stood up for myself, but couldn't because I was there but not there, because I'd left my body, because I'd taught myself that the way to not go crazy was by disassociating, though I wouldn't learn that word until a lifetime later. For a fleeting moment, in that police car, I glimpsed how my voice had spurred action, and how that action filled a little bit of the hollowness in me. But it was too late. Ms. Morgan had been right. I was fourteen years old, and I was, indeed, pregnant.

Abortion wasn't legal, and though I'd heard the word, probably knew people who'd undergone abortions in back rooms, curtains drawn, I was too far along. The moment I started to show in places other than my nose, Mama told me to pack a bag. She drove us to the far eastern reaches of the city, pulling up to a pink stucco building on a tree-lined street, Booth Memorial Maternity Home.

Having had six children, Mama certainly knew how to care for her pregnant daughter. But it wasn't about care; it was about shame. In her mind, the circumstances of me being pregnant didn't matter. These were things respectable people didn't speak about. For the remaining five months I was to be hidden away. When I gave birth, the baby would be put up for adoption, and I'd return home and pretend none of it had ever happened.

The circumstances didn't seem to matter to anyone at Booth Memorial, either. I never received counseling, never spoke with anyone about the rape. The nurses at Booth had a mantra: *Don't worry, you'll forget all this.* But I knew I wouldn't.

Part of the Salvation Army, Booth Memorial was solely for expectant, unwed teenagers. I recall about thirty girls living there. Most were cute blondes and brunettes from places like Beverly Hills. They'd had accidents with their boyfriends, and now all their friends and neighbors thought they were traveling in Europe or caring for a sick aunt in someplace like Des Moines. Their situation was to be kept secret because girls like them who found themselves unmarried and pregnant were considered "fallen" or "wayward." In my neighborhood, we were trash and whores.

At Booth, we had school courses and chores and took long walks, an odd-looking group of dozens of pregnant teenagers lumbering around the neighborhood. The girls with spending money visited Thrifty's each afternoon for ice cream, though as the weeks passed they were reprimanded for gaining too much weight. We were taught to crochet and knit and given patterns for baby sweaters and booties. It seemed odd to be creating things for babies we wouldn't keep, babies we'd never know, babies whose existence in relation to us would be snuffed out, a dark, indecent thing that never happened, though of course it did.

My mother came to visit. One day she brought a sack of red cherries. We went for a drive and I was eating the cherries and spitting out the pits. Mama said, "Eat all the cherries you can, 'cause you sure don't have one anymore."

My head snapped to look at her. Her smug expression told me the words had been purposeful, meant to sting. I wanted to scream, *Don't you know I can* never *remember having one! You sit there like you don't know, but you do. You know!*

But I didn't say a thing. I abided by the unwritten code of silence. A silence that spit out the cherries but left the stones piling up inside me. My mother's shame was pervasive. But her shame had not been the opposite of pride; her shame had been the barrier to any means of rising above, to any method of healing and learning and vowing never to make the same mistakes again. Now, her shame had become mine. It would be another three decades before I'd finally confront my mother, and even after all that time it took vast courage to speak honestly to her.

I never told Daddy I was pregnant, though no doubt my mother did. Throughout the time I was at Booth, he and I had no contact. I missed him terribly, but couldn't bring myself to call or write; apparently, neither could he.

One day, I received a call that I was expected in court to testify. Just before I'd left for Booth, I had been walking near 42nd and Vermont, when I stopped cold at the sight of a young man at a hamburger stand. His face sent a shudder through me. And then, another guy joined him, and his face, too, jolted me. I found a pay phone and with shaking hands dialed Ms. Strathy. "I recognize two of them," I sputtered. "From that night."

She told me to stay put, a policeman was on the way. When the police car arrived, I got in the backseat, and the officer slowly drove by the hamburger stand and had me point out the two boys, sitting at a picnic table, laughing, devouring burgers and fries. Later, Ms. Strathy called to tell me the boys had been arrested, along with one of their mothers—the woman who'd been upstairs in the house while I screamed below.

Cupcake and I were called to testify. It was the same court where the judge had shown me compassion by deciding not to send me away to the Ventura School for Girls because I was too young for such a rough, dangerous environment. So much for trying to protect me. I met up with Cupcake in the courtroom. By the randomness of life I was pregnant, and she was not. I don't remember the trial, don't remember the boys or the mother. I only remember being given a lot of directions: go there, sit here, say this. I remember my hands resting on my swollen belly, wondering why this was my life. And then I was returned to Booth Memorial.

I grew sullen and sluggish. I felt hurt, rejected, and profoundly alone. I felt out of control of myself, of my body, of my life. I didn't know how I'd have this baby and then be expected to return to my mother's house like nothing had happened.

Nearly nine months along, I went for a walk by myself. I couldn't stop walking. I walked mile after mile, until I found myself on a bridge overlooking the freeway. I watched the cars below speeding by. I was overcome with the urge to jump, to hurl my pregnant body over the railing. If I ended it all, it would be best, for me, for my mother, for everyone. I stood there for what felt like a long while. Maybe I didn't have enough courage to jump. Or maybe I had enough courage not to. The sun was setting. I turned around and walked the miles back to Booth, not sure if I'd made the right decision.

When I returned, I was greeted with great relief. The nurses had been in a panic over my disappearance; the other girls said they missed me. I hadn't realized anyone noticed me, but here they were, glad I was back.

I was turning fifteen in a couple of days, and that night my mother called to ask what I wanted for my birthday. I said, "I just want to bring my baby home. That's all."

The day before I turned fifteen, I gave birth. The other girls didn't ever see the babies they birthed, but I was handed a bundle wrapped in a pink blanket. My daughter. I looked at her tiny face and couldn't bear the thought of parting. Couldn't bear not keeping my baby after all this. I was led to a phone, and I called Mama. I pleaded with her to let me bring my baby home. There was silence on the other end of the line, and then she said quietly, "Okay."

When the white girls cried and begged not to give up their babies, the nurses tried in earnest to talk them out of it. "There's a wonderful, loving family waiting for this baby. They'll give it a wonderful home. You can go back home and resume your life and have fun with your boyfriend and your friends. You have college and marriage and your whole life ahead of you, and you can be at peace knowing you did the right thing, the very best thing, for this child." But when I said I wanted to keep my baby, the nurses readily complied, adjusting the status change in my file. Apparently, in 1966, wonderful parents and wonderful homes weren't waiting for little black babies. Nor did I have a wonderful rest of my life full of opportunities to return to.

I thought about naming my daughter Cosette, after the book I loved. But then I latched on to Antoinette—Toni for short—and that's the name that stuck. I cradled her, this precious, innocent child. Love swelled within me. But so did panic. I would keep my baby, but then what?

———

My birthday gift was to bring Antoinette home, but I brought her back to a crazy house. The baby shifted the family dynamic tremendously. My mother, my brothers, they all got a second chance with my child. The baby was a blank slate, the girl my family could do better with, and I watched as the baby changed them into people I didn't recognize: they were kind, gentle, and protective with her. For my baby's sake, this was the best I could hope for. As for me, if I wasn't cooking their meals or washing the dishes, I had no use. I was, at best, the Cinderella of the house. And now they treated me like I was tainted, like a Cinderella who'd been around the block.

I had vowed that never would I work as a maid, like my mother, but that seemed the direction I was headed. Defiantly, I made a plan to better myself. I would learn to type and become a secretary. For a black girl in the mid-1960s, this was a respectable dream. Since I'd progressed beyond the Ramona school, I had to enroll in public high school. I signed up for a typing class, the one thing about which I was excited. On the first day I took a seat at the front of the class, behind a heavy, manual typewriter. The teacher had us go around room and tell what we did over summer break. I felt my mother's shame flaring up in me. But I didn't want to live under that shadow the way she did. When it came my turn, I said the truth. "I had a baby."

Heads turned.

The teacher said, "You had a baby?" as though he hadn't heard correctly.

I nodded, wanting to disappear into that typewriter.

The teacher said, "Then why are you here?"

There was sniggering, and I could feel eyes burning into me. This class was supposed to teach me a way out, a way up. Instead, I felt ousted, from the class and from hope. It's only looking back years later that I can see how this teacher's words, flippant and sexist, should have rolled off me, banished by each key I pounded on that typewriter. Instead, his words pummeled me, and I crumbled.

I'd been equipped with so little. I possessed no resources and no reserves. This felt like yet another betrayal, another failure, the only door I could see for miles slammed in my face. If only I'd known that, too often, black girls like me were considered dropouts but were really "push-outs"—pushed out of opportunities that school should have provided. If only I had someone to turn to, someone to tell me, "What happened to you was not your fault." But there was no one. My family—generation upon generation—had lived their lives helplessly swept along. We were victims of the limitations society hoisted on us, which we then internalized as our own. We had no safety net, no system of support, no community or services to turn to and say, dignity intact: "I need some help."

That night, I stayed out late. I visited my old haunts on the street. I hung out. I smoked weed. When I returned home the next morning, Mama was waiting for me. Her grip unrelenting, she shoved me into the car. She said, "Back to juvenile hall."

For a moment, I recalled the quiet orderliness of the place. And, for that moment, it seemed preferable to my current life, with a house full of people who treated me as worthless. But then I remembered how the juvenile court judge had said I was too young to be sent to Ventura—that was a couple of years ago, I was no longer too young. I knew that at Ventura, there'd be no pitchers of cold milk and Kool-Aid, no room to myself, no quiet respect. At a stoplight, I opened the door and jumped from the car.

I ran and ran, certain no one would miss me. I ran off into the underworld. For the next three years I stayed away, only returning when I knew my mother wouldn't be around to leave gifts on the porch for Toni.

7

THE LIFE

Black women comprise 40 percent of street prostitutes,
though 55 percent of women arrested for prostitution are
black, and 85 percent of women incarcerated for prostitu-
tion are black.

Two-thirds of those working as prostitutes disclosed hav-
ing been sexually abused as children—and more than
90 percent said they never told anyone. Only 1 percent
reported having received counseling.

It was around Main and 11th that I jumped from my mother's car. Wandering south, it was on the corner of 41st where I met James. Leaning coolly against the side of a building, he was a slender 6'2", his knees double-jointed so it looked like his legs were behind him. He had olive skin and long, straight hair. This man would consume the next five years of my life.

My adrenaline, my anxiety, blurred much of my memory of that day: I don't remember what James first said to me, only that we talk-ed some, and then I got in his car. I don't remember the car, but I remember the one he'd later buy—a used 1965 white Cadillac con-vertible with a red interior—after I brought in the money. I don't remember the place that, on that very night, became my new home, but I remember when we soon moved together to a rooming house off Western near the 10 freeway. James often wore a beard, and he had thick eyebrows. I don't remember how long it took until I saw the mean spirits haunting his eyes. But I remember I did what he said, or his fists would fly.

He'd sing to me sometimes, Lou Rawls's "Memory Lane." He'd recite "Street Corner Hustler's Blues, World of Troubles," which, to me, was the story of James himself. He was a smooth-talking hustler. And I, his willing prey. Forget learning to type, I would use the tool I already possessed: my body. I'd been exploited my whole life, so now, why not make this body work for me? If there was one thing I knew for sure: my body could get me things.

James secured me an ID that said I was twenty-one years old. And he found the johns willing to pay up. I entered into what we in the underworld called "the life."

We were making money. Dirty money. I was a live wire, sizzling, crackling, sparking. I didn't dare think about what I was doing. I didn't think about myself, and I didn't think about anyone else. My sense of self was so warped that I believed my ability to divorce myself from my emotions was my greatest asset.

I set my sights three years ahead, when I would turn eighteen and could get Toni without fear of Mama dragging me off to juvenile hall. Until then, I'd linger on my corner, no shortage of men who wanted to get with me, and make what I convinced myself was an easy living. I bought myself fine clothes. I bought gifts for my daughter. I bought James a guitar and he played and sang for me. Once, when he got mad at something I said or did—who even knows, it didn't take much to set him off—he swung the guitar at me. I instinctively put up my arm to shield my face, and the guitar splintered to pieces. So did my arm. I took a day away from work, and then was back out there on my corner, arm in a plaster cast.

Most of the time, I wanted to leave James. But where could I go? Purposefully, he kept me isolated. But I had isolated myself, too. I'd severed ties with everyone I'd known. My old life was a one-way ticket to someplace I didn't want to go. But this life, where was this train headed? It was a question I didn't bother—or, somewhere deep down, couldn't bear—to ask.

The first time I got picked up by the police for prostitution, I was unnerved. From then on, it simply was part of the job. My bail would be set at $500, and I'd make a phone call to George, the bail bondsman James used. George Cameron was a tall, soft-spoken black man, his Arkansas roots lingering in his voice. He was from El Dorado, but he didn't say it like the car, he said it with a long "a." "You know how we do in the South," he explained. "Down there in El Doraydo, we thought Colorado was Coloraydo."

Each time George bailed me out, he'd say, "Sue, you're smart and you're sharp. And you know how to get things done. Why are you messing around with all this?" I never had an answer.

Having recently moved to Los Angeles after years in the navy, George dealt with small timers, mostly pimps and prostitutes. He operated on a personal level bailing people out and driving them home. This way, he got to know people, and he got to know families. But it was more than just trying to get his name out then build his business; he cared. Each car ride back to James's place, George tried to guide me.

"Sue, you can remember that phone number I gave you without having to write it down?" he marveled. "You're real good with numbers. You'd be good at a job with numbers." Or, "Sue, you could get certified to become a notary. It's a good job. You'd be good at it."

But I couldn't yet see anything legitimate for myself. I was barely sixteen and was on the run. I'd nod, and the next time I'd talk to George was when I needed him to bail me out again or when I had a court date.

On it would go. He'd pick me up, drop me off, and he'd say, "Sue, you're a nice person. I'm not giving up on you."

But what did it matter if he saw something in me, when I could not?

At first, I was sentenced to fines. Then, I was sentenced to thirty days in jail. I was prepared; it was merely part of the lifestyle. I was sent to the new women's county jail, the Sybil Brand Institution, named for the philanthropist devoted to improving conditions for female inmates.

I was one of thirty women in a dorm, and we slept on orderly twin beds. We were given a nightgown and three sets of laundered prison clothes weekly, which we'd lay under the mattress to press. Visitors were allowed to bring us new underwear. A few unfortunates who didn't have visitors had to wear used underwear provided by the prison that was thick and bulky and fit like a diaper. But under my prison clothes, I wore pretty lace panties and bras, which I washed in the sink and hung to dry.

To pass the time, I went to a crafts class and knit myself a couple of dresses. At Christmas, Ms. Sybil Brand herself came to visit. A tiny, silver-haired white lady, she walked room to room, giving each of us gifts of lipstick and eyebrow pencils.

No one had any idea how rapidly conditions would deteriorate, and how futile Ms. Brand's mission would become when the War on Drugs hit its stride. Some fifteen years later, when I'd find myself back there, the dorms would be crammed with double the number of women sharing the same space, climbing up on triple bunks that we called coffins because of the mere inches between each. Whoever was unlucky enough to get that very top bunk had ceiling lights, which remained on at all hours, directly in her eyes. No longer was anyone pressing creases in their pants under the mattress—we were issued only one pair of pants and one top, for both the day and to sleep in. They got rid of forks and knives, too; we ate everything with a big metal spoon. The food, once decent, devolved to cheap prison-grade fare that might as well have been dog food. And everyone had to wear the used, diaper-like underwear.

Had I known when I was sixteen, seventeen, eighteen years old the horror story in which I'd later find myself; had I known that when the judge's gavel came down, the sentences would no longer be in days but in years, and not to county jail but to prison; had I known all this then, would I have changed my life? Could I have? Could I have gotten my head and myself together? The honest answer: I don't know. Life had stoked a belligerence in me. Combined with the invincibility of youth, I was both combustible and fiercely resilient. Had I been plunked into another environment, another community with role models and guides, perhaps I would have learned that I could make different decisions. But you had to have decent options in order to make good decisions, and from my vantage point, I saw few opportunities for my life.

My first sentence was reduced from thirty days to twenty for good behavior. James was waiting to pick me up, and I hopped in his Cadillac and went straight back to work.

At last, I turned of legal age. I reappeared at my mother's door. I wasn't sure how she would react, but relief filled her face—it hadn't occurred to me that she'd worried about me. Before her eyes, I wasn't just alive, I had blossomed into a woman. And I knew I looked good. My clothes were beautiful and expensive, my arms were full of gifts. Toni, a precocious three-year-old, ran over to see who was at the door. But she didn't know me. She turned to my mother, and called her Mama.

All those years I wanted to have my daughter, but couldn't. And now, how did I reconnect with this child who eyed me warily? Who, clinging to my mother, didn't want to come to me? I packed a bag for Toni and brought her to the rooming house where James and I lived. I wanted to build a relationship with my daughter, to take care of her, to be her mother—and I wanted to prove to my own mother that I wasn't useless. I wanted all this so badly it didn't occur to me that I was subjecting my daughter to the instability and violence of my life.

I had acclimated to the violence. It's difficult now to understand how that's possible, but at the time, I didn't think of myself as a battered woman. Getting roughed up was part of the world I came from. I'd heard my parents argue and saw the aftermath of busted lips and bruised eyes. Same with other families I knew; same with friends; same within the rooming house, the thin walls keeping all of us up on everyone's business. Why would you think anything was so wrong when all around you, this is how it was? With no other examples, it was easy to believe this was normal.

James had grown up with his sister and mother in Mississippi before they moved to Los Angeles. His mother now lived in the San Fernando Valley, and I'd make the drive north with James, leaning against the car and watching as he doled out cash to her. Only, he couldn't count well—for all I knew he was illiterate—and his mother would scam her own son before his witless eyes, saying she only needed a few hundred dollars, but counting off more for herself. When I pointed this out to James, he slapped me and said I was lying. I realized that, like his mother, I had better look out for myself. So I began skimming from him too.

James bought me a used Ford Falcon, a car that worked for local transportation and not much else, and I hid money under the dashboard and took it to my mother's house. I figured Mama had an idea how that cash came to me, but she was always good at turning her cheek; she kept the money and never said a word. For once, I appreciated her all-knowing silence. Eventually, however, I noticed the money in her safekeeping was evaporating. When I was young, she'd taught us it was important to save, and she took us to the bank to open Christmas Club accounts. Every week we deposited fifty cents, then at Christmastime, we wrote withdrawal slips to use our savings to buy gifts. Now, I took the remainder of my stash from my mother's house and opened a bank account. What far outweighed any concern over illegally gained money was watching my funds accrue, with interest.

There were flashes, things that made me say, *This time, I really got to get out.* James bought a puppy for Toni, a beautiful gray Doberman Pinscher. But when the puppy peed on the floor, James kicked him. One time James kicked the puppy so hard, its feces hit the wall. He literally kicked the shit out of that poor dog. If I intervened, I got beaten up too. Even little Toni tried to stop him, and she got welts on her legs before I pulled her back, shielding her with my own body. It was either the dog or the both of us. The dog ended up hanging himself on the leash in the yard. Maybe it was by accident, but I don't think so.

I packed a bag and took Toni to my mother's house. But in no time, James showed up there in a rage, grabbing me and dragging me to his car. My mother rushed out after us. She lunged toward James and bit him, taking a plug out of his arm. But he shook her off like a fly. He threw me into his car, holding on to my wrists so I couldn't leap out. Tires screeched as he peeled out of the driveway on what was otherwise a quiet block across the street from St. Cecilia's Church.

Some time passed before I again mustered up the courage to escape to my mother's. This time, my younger brothers sat in the picture window with their BB guns poised. But they were only scrawny teenagers, no match for James's fierceness, or his real gun. Other women—white women—might have gone to the police for a restraining order. But in my community, the police weren't who we turned to for help. To willingly go to the police, you had to believe they were on your side.

One day, Toni, James, and I were in the rooming house. He was fussing at me, and I knew he was about to turn violent. I saw his gun on the table. James watched me notice it. I lunged. He followed. We tussled over the gun. And then, it went off, a piercing sound in the small of the room. I scrambled for Toni. She was okay, but I was not. I was the one who'd been shot.

At the emergency room, my daughter was left with James while I was taken in. The bullet was lodged in my ankle, but the doctor didn't remove it, only bandaged me up, and I was too distraught and worried about Toni to question anything.

Out in the waiting room, James told Toni, "Chili Red, you better not say a thing about the gun, or any of it." He'd given her this nickname on account of what he called her redbone looks. She despised being called this, but that never stopped him.

A very savvy four-year-old, Toni gave him a steely-eyed glare. "I won't tell if you take me to my grandmother's house."

He looked at her, this girl whose birthday was one day apart from mine, who wouldn't call me Mama, but who'd inherited my strong will.

James said, "Okay, Chili Red, we have a deal." He took her back to my mother's house and never bothered her again. But he continued to come after me.

What none of us knew was that James was caught in the grip of a heroin addiction. With U.S. troops in Vietnam, drug trafficking of heroin had pervaded the West Coast. On the street, it was called smack and sold in little balloons for $20. When people who knew James began warning me, I didn't want to believe them. There weren't any obvious signs, like needle tracks on his arms, or paraphernalia to discover—but that's because James had been snorting it. But when he started going into the nods—falling asleep sitting up, mid-sentence—I knew it was true.

I had been the classic victim, exhibiting all the characteristics of an abused woman, including the denial. But learning James was a dope fiend snapped my eyes wide open. Heroin was dirty and dangerous— it was low. And *fiend* was an apt description because heroin possessed people, turning them vicious, demonic. My younger brother Marvin had a friend who'd perilously tried heroin—I learned about it when Toni, soaking up everything she overheard, parroted, "Hunky got bad smack and he died." My brother swore to us up and down that he stayed clear of smack, wouldn't touch it, didn't know why his friend had. Back then, it wasn't difficult to be objective about heroin—it was, simply, a line you didn't cross. Seeing clearly now who James was, I knew with conviction: I was done.

I left for my mother's house, and when James eventually showed up there, all my brothers showed up too. The five Burton brothers surrounded James, and they threatened him so bad he got back in his car, peeled out of there, and didn't dare show his face again. He was, at last, gone from my life.

8

FROM THE SKILLET TO THE FRYING PAN

Every year, 650,000 Americans are released from incarceration—a number larger than the entire population of Wyoming or Vermont.

Living at my mother's house, I spent as much time as I could with Toni. Still, she seemed perpetually angry at me, and I suspected my mother was tainting her. I tried hard to win her over, saying, "Hey, Toni, let's go for a walk." "Hey, Toni, let's go get ice cream." I bought her a Malibu Barbie. But she wouldn't allow me to get close to her. Nothing I could do pleased her. She threw the Barbie, like a bone, to my brother's dog. She insisted on calling me Sue. In a way, I suppose I understood—I hadn't been around, and that's who I was to her.

Through the government's Work Incentive Program, I found a job in a county office, filing probation files. I made the minimum wage, then under $2 an hour. All day long, my boss sat across from me, leering. He made me feel like I was back on the street corner. Thing was, on the corner, I made a lot more than minimum wage.

I got to thinking about that corner. There was a man I'd met back when I was with James. His name was Mark, and he passed my corner every day. I'd see him driving slow in his Cadillac, not a used one like James's, but a Cadillac that was shiny and new. Window rolled down, he'd try to flirt with me. I hadn't dared flirt back. If James got wind of it, he'd have beaten me up. I was there to serve customers, but Mark would lean out the window and say he wasn't about sharing his girl. I went back to my old corner and found what I was looking for. This time, I got into Mark's car. I was now a woman who worked in an office, not someone working the street and living with her pimp.

Tall, slender, and brown skinned, with a short, close haircut and a thin mustache, Mark Hamilton dressed conservatively and always looked well put together. In his thirties, he was fifteen years older than me, a real man. And his attitude was all Romeo. Mark and I began seeing each other, and he soon made it clear he wanted to take care of me—and that he had the money to do so. I was used to being treated like a dishrag, but here was Mark, telling me a woman should be adored and honored. James used to tell me about the Garden of Eden, and how all women, maybe with the exception of his mother, bore the punishment of Eve's betrayal. He used the Bible to hit me. But Mark told me about the preciousness of a woman, and he made me feel beautiful, even cherished.

Mark moved me into his apartment on Broadway and Slauson, above a barbershop he ran as a part of his business. Although Mama tried to convince me to stay with my county job, Mark assured me I'd want for nothing, and neither would Toni. With no doubt in my head, I quit my job. My final paycheck went to my mother's house; I didn't even bother picking it up.

Toni was fascinated by the electric hotplate at Mark's place; she'd never seen such a thing. I was fascinated by other things about this suave, cultivated man. Mark introduced me to Courvoisier and Dom Perignon. And, before long, to cocaine.

It was the early 1970s, and cocaine was expensive and seemed sophisticated and elite. On occasion, Mark and I did lines. Along with a glass of fine champagne, it was an enjoyable way to spend an evening. It was purely recreational, we weren't addicts, we didn't *need* it. Only, Mark did need it, in a different way.

I'd catch a glimpse sometimes, in the offices behind the barbershop, of stacks of cash and mayonnaise jars filled with white capsules.

People who weren't there for haircuts or shaves came and went. But I pretended I didn't see. Having learned well from my mother, I convinced myself I didn't know.

Mark was kind to Toni but, no surprise, she didn't like him much. She still didn't like me, either. Though I kept trying. I'd put on my brightest voice, "C'mon, Toni, let's go to the movies." "Hey, Toni, what are you reading?" "You sure you don't want to walk with me and get an ice cream?"

At best, she'd brush me off with chilling politeness. "No, thank you, Sue." But more often, she was bull-headed. "Sue, I want to go home."

"You are home."

"I want to go to Mama's."

"I am your Mama."

Many years later, Toni would tell me she felt I'd chosen Mark over her. But Mark was a calm presence, a father figure, and he provided very well for us. I wanted both of them. I wanted us to be a happy family.

A few years went by, and then a woman began calling our home, saying she was Mark's wife. I had no reason to believe her. Mark and I lived together, and I prided myself on having developed a keen instinct, and of being able to decide for myself what I'd entertain and what I'd overlook. But it was true.

All this time, he had a wife, another home, and three sons. All this time, I'd been duped, thinking Mark was all mine, thinking we'd get married. I'd touted Mark as so much better than James, but I'd only jumped from the skillet to the frying pan—I was still being lied to and still being used.

The calls from Mark's wife became irate and threatening. Even when Toni answered the phone with the unmistakable voice of a child, his wife would question her and call me names. Mark suggested that, for our safety, we move out of Los Angeles and set up a new life. He painted a picture straight out of *Better Homes and Gardens*. What other choice did I have? How else was I going to be taken care of like this? In Mark's magical way, he kept me entranced, and he made it all come true.

We moved just outside of Dayton, Ohio, to a lovely townhouse in a pristine neighborhood called Knoll Ridge. Every day, Mark headed into Dayton for business. I happily spent my days taking care of our home, shopping at the mall, cooking dinner. Although I had wanted Toni to move with us, she stayed on with my mother and visited Ohio during school vacations. I could have insisted she live with me, but she pleaded, and I didn't want to argue. Her attitude reminded me of how I'd been with my mother, a dynamic I didn't want to reinforce. Besides, Toni was doing extremely well in elementary school in Los Angeles, having been chosen to be in the Young Ambassadors program, a prelude to Upward Bound, which was a federally funded program for low-income kids who'd be the first in their families to go to college. I knew Toni was smart and on the right track. She made good grades, was a good reader, and was very talkative and inquisitive. She asked a question about everything. Every single thing. *Why?* and *Why not?* and *How come?* and *How long?* and *How does the washing machine work?* and *What makes the honking noise on the horn?* and *Why is it humid in Ohio?* and on and on and on. It could wear a person out.

In 1976, I learned I was pregnant. Mark and I were overjoyed—even Toni seemed happy about it. Going on nine years old, she was excited to be an older sister. I gave birth to a baby boy and named him Marque, after his father. The baby resembled us both, though he was slim like his dad. We called him K.K. for short. With my son, I had a clean slate. I was twenty-five years old and thought I had the maturity to be a good mother.

For business Mark often traveled back to Los Angeles, and that's where he was early one morning when I was in bed and heard the lock turning in the front door. The next thing I knew, the police were in my house, their search warrant having required the landlord to hand over the keys.

Toni had arrived in town only a day earlier, and she jumped from bed, eyes wide with fear. I took the baby from his crib, and we watched helplessly as the police combed my home—which I let them think I shared with my husband, though Mark and I weren't married.

"Where're the drugs?" an officer said.

"I don't have any." I glanced at Toni, standing there silently.

Eventually they found something: residue of cocaine in a sifter. I said, "I don't know what that is, but it isn't mine. I don't pry into my husband's business."

But one of the policemen turned and looked me straight in the face. "He's not the only one doing it, you are too."

To me, it was solely Mark's business. Maybe, sometimes, I'd go along for the ride. But the policeman's words were a like an electric shock, jolting me. My role in Mark's business had, indeed, subtly grown over time. And with him gone more and more, I would deliver, I would pick up, I would meet airplanes. When Toni accidentally had knocked over a plate of powdered sugar, I'd shouted like hell at her. She didn't say a word, but her eyes said, *I despise you, I despise what you're doing. If it's powdered sugar, why don't you just vacuum it up?* I hadn't bothered to notice I'd become entangled. I'd been walking around in a fog, only it was I who wielded the fog machine. I wasn't a drug dealer, I was a suburban housewife and mom. Who also made a fine living in cocaine.

I called one of my friends who lived nearby to pick up Toni and K.K., and I was taken to jail. From there, I called Mark. He said he had to stay away but told me to inform on people, that he'd give me names. But I couldn't bring myself to do that. Instead, my next call was to George, the bail bondsman in Los Angeles. I knew I could count on George, though, for the first time, he sounded uncertain. "I don't know if I can post bail being so far away," he said. "I'll try, but it might take some time."

The jail in Dayton was like a dungeon. I was locked in a communal cage, and all around me women were kicking heroin—dripping sweat, throwing up on the floor, moaning, violently shaking.

Every day I called my friend's house and Toni was handed the phone, but she refused to offer more than one-word replies. Years later she revealed that she knew I'd hidden a baggie of dope in K.K.'s diaper because she saw it when my friend went to change the baby.

I remained in the cage for a week before George came through. Out on bail, I packed up the townhouse and moved us from the suburbs into a house in Dayton. I didn't bother telling Mark. I knew where the cash was, and I emptied our accounts. By this point, I'd become savvy; I knew the right people and how to ask the right questions. I retained the top lawyer in the city. This time, when the gavel came down, it was clear the difference having money and a good lawyer made: I walked away with no time, only a fine.

A free woman, I returned to my house, to my children, and to work. Like the policeman had said, it *was* me: I knew everything about the business, and I carried on. It had become a way of life, and I'd become accustomed to the spoils.

One evening I was coming out of a restaurant, a bag of barbecue takeout in my arms, when someone grabbed me and tried to push me into a waiting car. But I wasn't about to go. I fought with everything I had, and flung myself from the grip of a man whose face I couldn't see. And then, I heard a sharp *pop*.

A pain seared through my middle. I fell to the ground.

Then, sirens. An ambulance. I'd never been in an ambulance before. A hospital corridor, an operating room. Then, blackness.

When I came to, I was informed the bullet had penetrated to my liver. I vowed that if I survived, I'd clean up my life. I'd be done with Dayton, and done with cocaine.

I called my mother's house to talk to Toni.

"Now what happened?" Toni asked, as dryly as if she'd heard the story a hundred times. Then it occurred to me: she *had* heard this story before, she'd seen me shot before.

After two weeks in the hospital, I called Toni again. "I'm coming back to Los Angeles," I said.

I could almost hear her shrug. "Okay" was all she said.

My mother was now living in a house off Highland Avenue that Mr. Fisher had bought her, and it had rental properties around back. Toni and K.K. stayed with my mother in the main house, while I took one of the bachelor apartments.

From a Help Wanted sign in the window of a nearby realty company, I got a job soliciting housing loans. I made minimum wage, but received a bonus for every signed loan. This was very different from how I'd been living, but I was getting by. Periodically, I'd see Mark. We'd have a glass of champagne and, for a moment, I'd dream of how things could have been. But he soon stopped coming around to visit K.K., which also meant he was no longer giving me money for child support.

My savings from Dayton were running out, but I focused on the children and on parenting the best I could. I desperately wanted to learn how to be a good mother, and I didn't want to default to the way I'd been raised simply because that was what I knew. I didn't want my children to fear me, didn't want to be a mother who barked orders or walked around with an extension cord, dangling her power. I also didn't want secrets filling the house, suffocating us as silently as carbon monoxide.

Years later, when I traveled to Ghana, the place of my people's origin—and from where my ancestors were taken—it was striking to see how differently children were raised. For the first three years, Ghanaian children are wrapped close to their mother's body, fostering a deep sense of well-being, community, and safety—feelings I'd never known growing up. I had been searching for where I came from, needing to know my roots back before the plantations had starved and mangled them. But on my return home, I felt even more acutely that I'd been robbed. The beautiful culture of my ancestors had been stolen from me and from so many generations of us.

Toni silently scoffed at my intentions to do better. I'd cook a nice dinner and say, "At five, we're going to sit down and eat." She'd say, "Sue, they only do that on TV."

She'd fold her arms, find a spot on the wall, and stare at it: that was her pose. It was as though she didn't need me. There was some truth to that; she was thriving all on her own. When we found out Toni got into Granada Hills High School, it was a time for celebration. Though she'd have to be bused an hour to the San Fernando Valley, this excellent school in a wealthy neighborhood meant opportunity for my daughter. I bought her a bunch of new clothes, but she looked at them funny and told me how corny the polo shirts with the little alligator were. I promised her that's what the kids at Granada Hills were wearing. I wanted her to have nice things, and to fit in. I wanted her to have the best chance at the life I didn't have.

To my mother's credit, she, too, was doing things differently with Toni, as though my daughter was an important second chance to her. I saw my mother patiently answering all of Toni's questions. I saw how she listened to and respected my daughter. But I suspected Mama was also dripping poison into the well—which Toni would confirm decades later. *You don't want to turn out like your mother,* Mama would tell her. *Susan, she's a bad seed.*

It didn't come as much surprise to me that my mother felt that way; if I was nothing but a bad seed, then Mama was absolved. She didn't have to take responsibility for the present, or the past.

Perhaps K.K. was my second chance. I was a different person than I'd been at fifteen, when Toni was born. K.K. was friendly and sweet, though he had a mischievous streak. When he behaved poorly, I sat him down and talked with him about it. And when he began school, I walked him door to door.

9

NO JUSTICE, NO PEACE

*The majority of incarcerated women are mothers of
underage children. Over 40 percent of these mothers
report that, upon incarceration, they were the only parent
in the household.*

K.K. and I walked home from school. It was April 1981. He
was complaining that he didn't like his kindergarten teacher,
something my mother never would have tolerated. Children weren't
supposed to complain about a teacher, or any adult for that matter.
Teachers were always right, especially if they were white—and even
if they weren't right, you most certainly didn't say so. But I let K.K.
talk, and then told him I'd arrange to visit his classroom. He seemed
happy about that, and when we returned home, he brought me a
chrysanthemum. "For you, Mama."

Then the world spun.

My son was pronounced dead at the hospital. Guilt consumed
me—I had escaped the police so many times, and now it was a police
officer who'd taken my baby.

Toni looked at me with an eye of accusation. She and my mother
were the last to find out what had happened. Toni had been at school
in the Valley and, after the hourlong ride home, she was walking from
the bus stop when a paperboy told her. My mother was in Malibu that

day, cleaning the houses of actress Louise Lasser and musician Neil Sedaka. She was driving up our street when she saw Toni's school bus go by. They both, unknowingly, rode past the spot where the accident had occurred hours earlier.

A week later, I was in a white lace dress. The door of a limousine closed then opened again at the cemetery. A photographer's camera flashed for a story the newspaper would run about the accident. Flowers were everywhere. I'd never seen so many flower arrangements. I saw Mark there, staring far into the distance.

From the hearse came the tiny casket, decorated with white roses dipped in baby blue paint. A lone rose dropped in the driveway, and everyone drove over it. Toni watched, tissues pressed to her face, as the photographer snapped a picture of the crushed rose.

Toni later told me that L.A. police chief Daryl Gates showed up, wearing a tan suit. She said she knew exactly who he was from watching local TV news, reading the newspaper, and, she added, having a criminal family. I don't remember seeing the police chief, even though he would have stuck out with his pale, freckled face. Toni insisted we spoke, that he'd approached me at the hearse. If so, I must have told him I couldn't afford to pay for my son's funeral. But there were no offers from the city to pay. At the burial, my relatives passed a hat. I don't remember that either, but, later, my mother gave the funeral home a stack of crumpled bills.

When we returned to my mother's house, my rage propelled me into the street. I stood at the corner where K.K. had stood, the corner over which repeated requests for a stoplight had fallen on deaf ears. And then I stepped into the street. I planted myself at the spot in the crosswalk where it had happened. There I stood, wide-stanced, in my white lace dress. Horns started up—little nudges, *C'mon, lady,* that quickly turned into angry blares, *Get the hell outta the street!* Unflinching, I refused to move.

Then, my brother Melvin walked into the street and joined me. My other brothers followed, then my mother, and cousins, and neighbors. For over an hour we marched back and forth across that busy corner, chanting about getting a stoplight, chanting about justice. Someone went and Xeroxed K.K.'s obituary and passed it out, and my brother Marvin's girlfriend, Marva, started a petition for a stoplight, collecting signatures from people in cars and on the street. We backed up traffic from the 10 freeway all the way to Hollywood.

When the police showed up, they were in riot gear. Scared, Toni hurried to her friend's house a few doors down and watched from there. With the police's threat to arrest us for not having a permit to demonstrate, we finally dispersed.

I went home and crawled into a bottle of booze. It was all that I could do to quell the shaking, heaving, sobbing.

Marva had collected over a thousand signatures on the petition for a stoplight, and it was delivered to the county courthouse. But, still, that stoplight didn't happen, some guff about it not being feasible, and that five accidents would have to occur there before a stoplight would be considered. We knew of two other accidents, including a mailman who was hit but survived. So, according to the city, three down and two to go?

Our community newspaper, the *Los Angeles Sentinel*, ran a story on the front page, "Family Ask End of 'Cover-Up,'" detailing the difficulty we had in obtaining a copy of the police report, and our demand for a full-scale police investigation.

At my mother's house, the phone rang. Lawyers had read the article and wanted to represent me. They offered to send cars to bring me to their fancy offices. They tossed around words like *settlement* and *seven figures*.

Some of my brothers began scheming. Michael said, "Sue, if you got a payout, you could buy each of us a car."

I shook my head in disgust. "You're talking about blood money." But my solution was no better: I was trying to drink away the pain.

The police must have been nervous that I'd file a lawsuit because squad cars slowly drove by my mother's house, trying to intimidate. It was haunting, seeing them lingering at the corner where the accident had occurred.

Eventually, Marva convinced me to meet with a lawyer she knew, and I agreed to file a lawsuit. It then dragged on and on, and I was too mired in pain and alcohol to involve myself in the process or to question my lawyer's intentions and missteps. He became yet another untrustworthy person in my life. Another person failing me. In the end, there was no seven-figure payout, and the finality of it all only deepened the ache for my son.

Unbeknownst to me, when the police report was finally released Toni managed to see it. Without telling anyone, she took a bus to the police station and asked for the detective listed on the report as having hit K.K.

He wasn't in, she was told.

"I have some questions about a case," Toni said. "My brother Marque Hamilton's case." The people behind the desk looked at each other, then quietly suggested Toni leave her phone number.

The detective never called, though Toni played over and over in her mind what she'd say if he did. She wanted to ask, *Why?* Why, according to witnesses, did two other lanes of cars stop for K.K. but the detective barreled through the crosswalk? Why had the detective not gotten out, but instead, as the report stated, stopped a full block away?

The report also described that K.K.'s fist was balled around a note folded over a dollar bill. The note said, *Eskimo Pie.*

A neighbor who'd witnessed the accident said the market on our side of the street had closed early that afternoon, so K.K. made a split-second decision to head to the convenience store across the street. The note for ice cream—I must have written it, though I didn't remember. But I must have. I sent my son running to his death.

Toni spent that summer overwhelmed with frustration and sorrow, looking at me with that eye of accusation. She entered the school year in a state of disarray. I was too checked out to notice.

Then my daughter made up her mind to do something I could not: she somehow found peace, deciding she couldn't ruin her own life too. Another decade and a half would pass before I could realize this for myself.

Alcohol had been numbing me, but it wasn't enough. A hundred proof couldn't seep as deep as my pain. Wandering bleary-eyed onto the street, I found cocaine, and that took me into total blankness. A place devoid of thoughts, empty of feelings, a respite from the debilitating anguish. My rage at that detective, at that corner without a stoplight, at myself, at the world—cocaine sucked all that up. It allowed me to function even though the depression and anxiety made me unable to stomach food and unable to sleep. Night after night, when it was too quiet and when I was terrified of the images that came when I closed my eyes, it was cocaine that made the world seem a little less unkind.

Cocaine was a brilliant lie. Though it allowed me to go on living when I didn't want to, life then became about how to get more cocaine. I had no way to fund my self-medicating. That is, no legal way. K.K.'s death left me with a lack of regard for the law. So in my warped thoughts, avenging my son's death meant defying the law any way I could. A foolhardy plan, of course, one that would only continue to hurt me and everyone I cared about. But a cyclone of emotion whirling with alcohol and cocaine didn't exactly create a rational line of thinking.

No one does dope to get addicted. But you use it, and then it uses you. I had an addiction to feed, and it made me do hideous things. In the blindness of my depression and rage, I felt I was owed. It wasn't difficult to find the people breaking the law, an underground world of hustlers and frauds. They had their own pain, their own addictions, their own warped logic. They supplied me with stolen credit cards, and I used them.

I closed my eyes and put my finger on a map, and that's how I ended up in Alaska. I was thirty-two years old, and Alaska seemed just as good a place as any to spend my days. I bought my ticket under a stranger's name. I wanted to become someone else, and I did. I became Linda Taylor, Susan Holland, Tasha Lashan James, Carla Thomas, Linda Jean Robinson. All of whom—I convinced myself—in their privileged, good-credit lives didn't know pain like the pain I had endured. In my mind, these strangers owed me, too, and I'd fund my heavy-hearted life with what I imagined were their easy lives of American Express and pay stubs and fancy signatures on fat checks.

I landed in Fairbanks, Alaska, on a dark, snowy April day, and the first thing I did was go buy myself a white fox fur coat and matching fur hat. Three days later, I sauntered out of a bank, having just cashed a check I'd forged. The police were waiting for me.

I was far, far from home, and while I'd come to Alaska seeking escape, now all I wanted was to be back in Los Angeles. I called George, and it was good to hear his gentle, reassuring voice. By this time, George had gotten to know my entire family well, bailing out my brothers right and left. He also, in a way, had come to trust me. He remembered how I'd pay for my boyfriend James because I couldn't stand the thought of anyone jumping bail on George. Over the years, if someone I knew was jumping bail, I'd put out some feelers, then I'd call George and report where that person was. In my neighborhood that's called snitching, but the way I saw it, George was kind and caring, and if he bailed you out he deserved to get paid.

I told George I'd been arrested for forgery.

"You always did have that talent for picking up things easily," he said. "I remember how you watched me sign my name and then you signed it identical."

Only this time it was no party trick; this time I was in deep. My bail was set at $5,000, but when George tried to post it, the bail was raised. He tried to post the higher amount, and then that was raised. On it went until the bail reached $100,000: the Alaskan court did not want to let me go. Can't blame them; I would've left the state and never set foot there again. Though George couldn't bail me out, he found the best attorney in Alaska to represent me.

My attorney believed he could get my sentence reduced from five years to one, which was good considering I'd been caught in the act. At trial, the district attorney shamed me. "You're a vulture," he said. "What you've done is like reaching into someone's grave and robbing them." As his words sunk in, I was shocked to learn I'd been posing as a deceased woman. All the while, I'd convinced myself that what I'd been doing was resourceful. Disgust seeped through me. But I quickly separated myself, deploying my great talent for divorcing my body from my emotions. When the gavel came down, I was sentenced to sixteen months in an Alaska prison.

10

A NEW DRUG

*The vast majority—75 percent—of crack cocaine users
are white or Hispanic. But nearly 85 percent of people in
federal prison for crack offenses are black.*

The prison was picturesque, and not just for a prison. Situated on
acres of wooded land near Eagle River in Anchorage, this wood-
beamed building with large, unbarred picture windows was nothing like prison in what the Alaskans called the Lower 48. There were
only around thirty-five women in my section, and I had a tiny room
of my own and carried my own keys. The guards dressed in regular
clothes, not uniforms. We ate from the Alaskan land, a nutritious diet
of salmon and bison and vegetables—nothing like the unrecogniz-
able meal trays I'd later face in the California prison system. While I
served my time, I took classes and earned my GED.

As I came to know fellow inmates, I got glimpses of occupation:
how the U.S. government had bulldozed into Alaska, imposing on the
land and the native communities. If the Eskimos didn't cooperate,
they were incarcerated. I met many natives imprisoned for practicing
generations-old customs, such as trapping, hunting, and fishing. The
motto on the Alaska license plate, "The Last Frontier," now seemed
sadly ironic. But little did I realize that, when I would return to my
own community of South L.A., I'd witness the government doing the

same bulldozing there—dominating and exploiting and locking up everyone in sight.

I wrote letters to Toni; sometimes she wrote back. Every week I phoned, but the conversations were curt. Any call from prison was a strained call. I never knew what to say. How do you stay involved when you're locked away, when the system is designed to make you irrelevant, no matter if you are a parent? In many ways, it was easier emotionally to remain out of touch with the outside world, and that's what a lot of people did.

Though Toni was detached on the phone, in her life she was all-in. Excelling in her honors courses, she was chosen for a summer program to live on campus at California State Polytechnic University and take college classes. She made it clear to me, though, that none of her friends' parents were in prison. I was a blight on her life, a life to which I could hardly relate.

My brothers weren't setting any stellar examples either. "Everybody's a drughead or jailbird," Toni said, matter-of-factly. My mother's house had become headquarters for all sorts of my brothers' entrepreneurial activity, and Toni was unfazed when colorful characters of the underworld showed up at all hours. Some pulled up in Rolls-Royces and Maseratis, others in smoke-puffing buckets. Some were dressed in Armani, others smelled like they lived on the street.

Even the police showing up no longer ruffled Toni. She and some friends from her fancy school were playing video games one afternoon when police pounded on the door looking for one of the Burton boys. Toni knew the drill: she squared herself in the doorway to prevent them from entering. "Do you have a warrant?" she asked. "No? Then I can't let you in. I'm a minor, and I'm the only one home." With that, she locked the door and went back to the video game, her classmates' eyeballs ready to pop. She advised, "Don't go home and tell your parents any of this."

One time Toni stood by as my mother answered the door to the police. Again, they were looking for one of my brothers, but they pointed to Toni and said she better watch it too, that she had a smart mouth on her. I figured if Toni had made it to her teenage years and the police were only on her about her smart mouth, she was doing quite all right.

Often, I thought Toni sounded lonely. But what I didn't know was that, in a way, my brothers' and my incarceration lifted a weight from her. She'd been shouldering the pressures of her academic life plus worrying about all of us, and now she no longer had to feel responsible for everyone else in the family. She could replace the shame and embarrassment of us with peace, quiet, and normalcy.

My sentence was reduced to a year, and toward the end I received a letter from Toni saying if I missed her high school graduation, she'd never speak to me again. It was her way of telling me not to screw this up, that when I got out, I needed to stay clean and get myself home.

I returned to Los Angeles in time for Toni's prom, then her graduation. On top of that, she'd earned a scholarship in math to UCLA. My daughter was going to a university. How prideful I felt sitting there in the bleachers of Granada Hills, watching her in a cap and gown. But it also made me feel even more down on myself, acutely reminding me of all I could've done, what I could've been. I was still messed up. In prison, the drugs had been removed but my depression hadn't. I was still grieving—and searching for relief any way I could get it.

During the year I'd been in Alaska, there'd been a major shift in South L.A.: lots of people were all about small, white chalky rocks. You could buy these rocks, wrapped in tin foil or stacked in small glass vials, on most every corner in my community. You lit them and smoked them, and it hit you fast and hard. I'd never seen this drug before—and neither had the police. Crack had come to town mysteriously and seemingly overnight. One day it didn't exist, the next it did. Like a biblical plague of locusts, like Hitchcock's *The Birds*, crack swarmed out of nowhere straight into South Central and ravaged the place.

Derived from cocaine, crack was easier to transport, easier to use—and dirt cheap. While an ounce of powder cocaine was around $2,600, an ounce of crack was $800, and you could find a single rock of crack on any street corner in South L.A. for five bucks. But the thing about crack—that very important thing no one realized until too late—was that your first hit was one too many, and after that, no amount was enough. One of the most addictive drugs in the world, crack took you hostage, and then it made you rabid.

But where was all this crack coming from? And why was it so cheap that any kid in my neighborhood who, just a year earlier, would've spent pocket cash on a hamburger and milkshake or, at worst, on some weed, was instead buying crack? None of us knew the bigger picture—and, I'd come to learn, that was by design.

More than a decade would pass before a *San Jose Mercury News* reporter, Gary Webb, reported a bizarre and devastating link between a CIA cover-up and the explosion of crack cocaine in South L.A. According to Webb, the sale of crack in my neighborhood was funding a war three thousand miles away by, astonishingly, arming the U.S.-backed Contra rebels in Nicaragua. The way it worked, he explained, was that the CIA facilitated massive amounts of cocaine to be flown into Los Angeles, with the same planes returning to Nicaragua stocked with weapons.

Webb pointed to a primary kingpin: a Contra enjoying political asylum in California. And his biggest customer: a young black man from South Central L.A., Ricky Ross. I'd never met Ross; few people had, because he kept a low, hardly flashy profile. A high school tennis star, Ross's college scholarship vanished when recruiters discovered he could barely read. But he found a new path when one of his teachers introduced him to a Nicaraguan cocaine dealer. Though illiterate, Ross wasn't lacking in ingenuity. Swearing off drugs and alcohol himself, he streamlined the mass production of cocaine into crack. And made a fortune. One of his biggest challenges became trying to hide his newfound wealth from his unsuspecting mother, so he became a philanthropist of sorts, outfitting neighborhood parks and renovating his mom's church—beautifying the same community his crack was destroying. He put cash in real estate and bought a hotel near the 110 called Freeway Motor Inn, earning him the moniker Freeway Ricky Ross, which was what I knew him by.

When demand grew too high to handle, Ross enlisted his boyhood friends from the neighborhood—who happened to be members of the Crips gang—to be his "distributors." Suddenly flush with cash, the Crips invested in automatic weapons, which were also, conveniently, supplied by the Contras. Soon, the rival Bloods gang began distributing crack too, creating the perfect shit-storm. In the blink of an eye, Los Angeles became the crack and gang violence capital of the world.

It didn't take long before the Crips and the Bloods sold to gangs in other cities, swiftly helping crack terrorize its way into poor black neighborhoods across the country.

The twisted irony is that while Reagan's CIA was flagging into the U.S. planes carrying tons of cocaine, the president and first lady were all over the airwaves ranting about the War on Drugs. Nancy implored, "Just say no," and Ronald declared drugs a threat to national security—which was also a call to militarize law enforcement. He vowed to hire more prosecutors, though he said nothing about public defenders. And he crowed about being in "hot pursuit" of drug traffickers, evoking the words of black boxer Joe Louis, "They can run, but they can't hide."

But the Contra kingpins didn't have to hide; they were living the American Dream in plain sight.

One simple way to stop an overflow is to shut off the faucet. But a Department of Justice Inspector General's report would later reveal that, although the whereabouts of Freeway Ricky Ross's major Nicaraguan drug supplier were known and tracked, the kingpin wasn't arrested. Unlike Ross, who eventually was sentenced to life without parole (though released on appeal after thirteen years, thanks in large part to Webb's reporting). And unlike just about everyone I knew from my community who'd done drug-related time. Same, too, with the massive lockup of my generation in impoverished minority communities across the United States.

The Reagans waved the American flag, but this wasn't, in actuality, a war on drugs. It was a war on people: black people. We were sold down the river by the government—yet again.

In my neighborhood, it was like the police were lying in wait. Waiting for you to have a taillight out, or to roll through a stop, so they could search you for drugs. The government had my community, like the natives in Alaska, under siege.

It was hook 'em and book 'em. Even first-time drug offenders faced mandatory minimum prison sentences—sometimes for just marijuana. But police were always hoping to hit the crack jackpot. If you were found with just one $5 rock in your possession, you were prosecuted far more harshly than if you had greater amounts of any other drug, including powdered cocaine. It was as though cocaine—the rich person's drug—was benign, and crack—the poor person's drug—was a grenade. Someone arrested for crack would need to have a hundred times more cocaine on them to be prosecuted to the same degree, even though the two drugs were pharmacologically the same.

At first, to me, crack seemed weird and strange, and I didn't like it. But in the act of consuming it, my pain was replaced with a silence more profound than anything I had ever experienced. The escape it brought was instantaneous. When it was over, I yearned for it again.

And again. And again. And again. And again.

Until I lost my ability to separate myself from it. It didn't matter what my mother said, or how my daughter looked at me. Crack made nothing else matter.

11

INCARCERATION NATION

Because of the crack epidemic and the harsh, racially discriminatory policies of the Anti–Drug Abuse Act, one in three black men will see the inside of a jail cell.

The average time served by African Americans for nonviolent drug offenses is virtually the same as the time whites serve for violent offenses.

Terror still gripped me whenever I closed my eyes, so I'd go days without sleep, getting so worn down I'd finally fall out, dreamless. One night, I was driving when I felt the precious veil of sleep coming on. I pulled into a gas station, parked off to the side by a phone booth, and drifted off. I was awakened by the police knocking on my window. They ordered me out, then searched my car.

My back-alley version of antidepressants, my search for nothingness, was sitting right there on the seat. Though the minimal stash I had made it clear I was a user, I was booked, at the whim of the police, for a more serious offense: possession with the intent to sell.

I was taken to the Sybil Brand Institution, where I'd served all those years ago. The holding room was so crowded it felt like a corral for cattle. Finding a sliver of space, I sat on the concrete, just as I'd done as a little girl in Aliso Village. But unless you're playing jacks, concrete ain't no place to be. The cell was dirty and littered with ciga-rette butts and stale cheese sandwiches. At some point a cart came around and cheese sandwiches were tossed to us new arrivals. To quiet everyone, guards tossed in cigarettes. Smoke hung thick in the air. I wondered what Ms. Brand would think if she saw the degrada-tion of her eponymous women's jail.

For hours I sat there, until a guard pulled me out of the cell and led me to the shower room. She watched as I undressed, her eyes assessing me, and it made me think of my ancestors, ordered to strip in slave pens as masters sized them up. Then, with a flashlight she inspected every crack and crevice of my body: under my feet, down my ear, bend over and cough.

I was told to shower, but only a trickle of water came out. The stiff thing they called a bath towel was the size of a washcloth. From there, I was sprayed, like an animal, for lice—a practice eventually discon-tinued because of the toxicity of the spray. If your hair was deemed too long, a blunt scissors was taken to it. If your fingernails were too long, they were clipped. I was issued my daily uniform: a starchy cot-ton top and pants; dingy, diaper-like underwear; and hard rubber shoes—to wear tennis shoes or something with support required you to petition for a court order from the judge. Fingerprinted with black ink, banded with an ID bracelet, a list of medical questions answered, I was led to another corral, this one with phones on the wall. I called my mother.

"I'm in jail," I said. By this point, she had received this call from all her children, more than once. I could see in my mind's eye how she was making her disappointed face, silently shaking her head.

"What happened?" she said.

"I was arrested for possession." I omitted the trumped-up charge.

There was a pause. "Well," she sighed.

And that was that. I knew when we hung up she'd tell Toni what she'd been saying about me for years: "My husband's daughter is rotten to the core." Then Mama would put me out of her mind and return to whatever it was she'd been doing.

I was delivered to my cell. With the War on Drugs in full force, jail capacity levels were disregarded, and each cell outfitted with bunk beds now had an additional mattress on the floor. Behind me, a lever turned, and the heavy steel door clanked shut. I turned the lever inside of me, too, sealing myself off from thoughts, from feelings.

One of the few things I was allowed to do was crochet, and I made a blanket for everybody: one for my mother, one for Toni, ones for all my nieces. It was also my way of trying to provide some reminder of my existence to my family.

A couple months later, I was woken at 3 a.m. with a pull on my leg: "Susan Burton, get up." Visions again came to me of my African ancestors bound and dragged onto slave ships. I was deposited in another cattle room and ordered to strip. The flashlight was back, making its bodily search. I was given a plastic bag, and dumping from it were the clothes I'd been wearing when I was arrested.

Crumpled in a heap on the floor was my jazzy Neiman Marcus outfit. I stared at the remnants of my former life. I had shoplifted that outfit, as though I could dress up the pain—if I looked good from the outside, it might distract from how mangled everything was on the inside. A sadness washed over me. Then I felt pangs of anger. But you couldn't get angry or sad in jail because you had no recourse, there was nowhere to put it—you couldn't talk to anyone about it, or shout about it, or eat it back, or walk it off, or punch the air. So I silently picked up the dirty, wrinkled clothes and put them on, as did the other women in the corral.

Around the waist and around a foot, the other women and I were chained together and led in a shuffling, clanging line to a black-and-white bus. The more experienced ones among us knew exactly where we were going as we traveled an hour east; they knew exactly the difference between county jail and state prison.

The gates to the California Institution for Women opened, and the bus drove past barbed wire and gun towers. This would be my home for the next thirteen months. Our chain gang was ordered inside, and we were called off by our county numbers and then assigned new state numbers, beginning with a W for a woman's criminal conviction. Orange uniforms were doled out, branded across the chest and down the pant leg: PROPERTY OF THE STATE OF CALIFORNIA.

Plastic bags came around holding more of our property. There was my purse and its contents: car keys, house keys, my beeper. If you wanted your belongings sent somewhere, you had to pay for postage. Though George had added money to my jail account, which was supposed to follow me here, it had to last while I waited to be classified, which could take some time. Did I want to spend money on postage when I also needed money for essentials, like soap, so that I didn't have to use the yellow lye-like stuff that gave you alligator skin? Or real toothpaste to avoid the gritty tooth powder? Or a comb that worked on black hair? Or sanitary pads? I told the guard, "There's nowhere to send it to."

"Then it's going to be destroyed."

I nodded.

Along with the busload of women I came in with, I entered prison the same way I would, I hoped, go out, through what's called the Reception and Release center. *Reception* sounded nice and civilized, but really it was a form of quarantine. For six weeks, I waited in R&R to be classified and assigned a work detail.

Separate from the main prison, I was confined to a small room with two bunks, a steel desk bolted to the wall with a round stool bolted to the floor, a small sink, and a toilet right in the open with no walls around it—you and your bunkie got to know each other real well. The room door remained locked, except at meal time, when it electrically opened with a loud *pop*. As each door popped on down the corridor, it sounded like machine-gun fire. This was the only time we were allowed to leave the room: to walk down the corridor to chow hall. But we weren't allowed to talk. In chow hall, you opened your mouth only to put food into it. The only sound was the clanging of spoons against trays.

Though we were supposed to be allowed outside every day, it only happened once in a while. To breathe anything but the stale air of my cell, to feel sun on my face, to sit on a little green square of grass, to have a conversation, to play a game of cards. That hour outside was the only time in prison that went by quickly. And then we were locked back in.

On Sundays, if you wanted to pray, you were allowed to go to the auditorium, where a volunteer church group conducted services. Every single Sunday I went to church. I didn't feel no spirit moving, I just wanted to get out of that cage.

Time dragged on. No one was allowed phone calls or family visits, and we couldn't receive packages—though someone could mail you paper and a pencil and up to ten stamped envelopes. All there was to do was sleep or write letters or read. A book cart came around, the inmate pushing it announcing the book titles, though you could only choose one to be slid through the wicket in the door.

That narrow wicket was your only connection to anything outside the cell. I wrote letters to Toni and my mother, balancing the envelopes in the wicket for the officers to come by and pick up. Sometimes inmates hollered out the wicket to someone down the hall, but guards would yell at you, "Shut up!" so you saved any hollering for a quick message, like "Bring Danielle Steele to chow hall to trade" or "Anyone got a postage stamp?"

One day I opened a book I'd chosen from the cart to find a candy bar in it, a note tucked under the wrapper—a kite, it was called, for how it flew across the prison. The kite was from my brother Melvin's wife, Beverly, an inmate in the main yard. She wrote, "I'll see you soon!"

After some weeks I was summoned from my cell to meet with a counselor. She explained the process of being classified, and how I could work as a porter, or on the yard crew, or in the kitchen, or in the cosmetology shop.

"Going to cosmetology school is something I always wanted to do," I said. "I'd love to be classified to the cosmetology shop so I could learn."

"I'll note this," the counselor said. I was returned to my cell, having been gone all of five minutes.

I hoped so much to be classified to the cosmetology shop, I dreamed about it. Dreamed how, with this skill, I'd have opportunities when I got out. All I had to hold on to, this dream became larger than anything in the reality of my life.

Finally, after a TB test and a physical, my red ID card indicating I was waiting to be classified was traded for a green ID card with my photo and criminal number: W-31416. That number would remain branded on my mind, no matter how many years passed or how hard I tried to forget.

I was called before the four members of the classification board. The brass of the prison system asked my name, where I was from, if I was married, did I have children. All the while, they each had printouts with all my information, and I watched them check off my answers as we went along. Still, I was giddy about being assigned to the cosmetology shop and having a meaningful way to spend my days.

Instead, I heard: "You are assigned to fire camp."

Fire camp? I was certain they'd mixed me up with someone else. "I really wanted to go to cosmetology school, so I can have some skills," I said.

"Fire camp is a privilege," a board member informed me. Indeed, this *privilege* was reserved for those who presented little threat of escape if taken off prison grounds. But being sent to the front line to fight California wildfires when you wanted to be learning how to do hair seemed the opposite of a privilege. As for my future as a beautician, fire camp burned that dream to ash. What I didn't know at the time was that, even if an assignment to the cosmetology shop had been granted, I still wouldn't have stood a chance of working in a beauty shop on the outside. Most professional licenses—whether it was beautician, barber, social worker, plumber, the list in many states was a hundred job titles long—were denied to people with a criminal record.

Now that I was classified, I was to be moved out of the locked cage to a permanent room along the main yard. But the prison was over-crowded, so around sixteen of us were instead assigned to the day room. The day room was supposed to be where people gathered to talk or play cards, but the tables and chairs were moved out and bunk beds hauled in, forcing everyone to crowd outside if they wanted to socialize.

At last, I was allowed to walk around. My sister-in-law, Beverly, and I finally met up in the main yard. It was strange seeing Beverly in the baggy orange uniform because, on the outside, she was a sharp dresser. She and I had once run fast and wild together. We had used together, and we'd forged together, and that's what she was in for.

Beverly had prepared a care package with everything I needed: soap, lotion, shampoo, ramen noodles, a can of tuna. We exchanged updates about the rest of the family, and then we made a plan to meet at chow hall.

Most of the time I didn't want to eat there. A frequent prison specialty was known as Shit on a Shingle, a brown, gooey, flour paste that was supposed to have meat in there somewhere. Chicken was the only food that looked like what it was, except we always knew when chicken was cooking by the strange, medicinal smell wafting through the building. On chicken nights, the running joke was: "What's for dinner? Antibiotics and steroids."

How clean your dorm was after the monthly double-scrub determined the order in which you'd be released for dinner, and the line into the cafeteria stretched far outdoors. Whether it was raining or blazing hot, you had to stand in line. Beverly taught me how to fold a sailor hat out of newspaper to keep the rain off my face. Beverly was always generous, but demanded a lot in return. She would look after me, but wanted complete loyalty. I had to agree with her, and if she didn't like someone, I, too, was expected not to like them. But in the cold and lonely prison, it was always good to see her, and I tried to be generous in return by buying things for Beverly when I shopped at the canteen. It worked out to be a good system, and by sharing our possessions we were rarely without.

The money prisoners made at work detail amounted to spare change, so in order to buy common necessities at the canteen you needed people on the outside to mail a money order to the prison to fill your account. One thing I can say for my family, they always pulled together when any of the Burtons were incarcerated. My brother Melvin was my main runner; sometimes, my mother would deposit money. George, too, would make sure I had what I needed. I was allowed up to $140 a month in my account, and rarely was there a month I didn't have the maximum to spend.

Four times a year, I could receive a box by mail. These days, prisoners can't get anything shipped in from individuals, but back then, everybody in my family would pitch in to fill a box. The box could weigh up to thirty pounds, but everyone knew to keep it around twenty-seven pounds in case the scale was off in the prison mail room, as it often was. If the box came in just an ounce over, it would be returned to the sender, and you'd have to wait until the next quarter before you could receive a box again. I'd open my box to find canned chicken, socks, panties, bras, pajamas, thermals, and sometimes jeans or tennis shoes. After Beverly got out, she'd put fancy things in my box, like packaged crabmeat. Liquid perfume wasn't allowed in prison, so she'd send me Donna Karan fragranced lotion. But before you were allowed access to your box, a guard inspected everything. If any item could be tampered with, the guard opened it and put it in another container. My Donna Karan lotion would always arrive having been squeezed into a plastic baggie.

To me, prison was about learning how to navigate and how to comply. I sized up the personalities—the leaders, the instigators, the troublemakers—and I became the quiet, invisible one. I kept to myself. I avoided trouble. And, likewise, avoided punishment. I never landed in the SHU, pronounced like *shoe*, the Special Housing Unit—otherwise known as Solitary. The SHU involved more than just the punishment of isolation. In there, you sometimes had to eat jute balls, a ground-up mash of beans and vegetables named for the similar look, texture, and taste of a ball of twine. Frozen and served cold, you occasionally could identify a black speck that was a bean or an orange sliver that was a carrot. A minor infraction, like cussing or acting uncooperative, could trigger a hearing to determine if you'd be further punished with jute balls. Not that you were able to attend your own hearing, you'd merely be informed of the outcome. Some of my bunkies worked in the kitchen preparing jute balls, and I found it alarming the care and packaging that went into creating something meant to choke you when you tried to eat it. A jute ball punishment might last three days, or it could last a month.

To fill the time, I visited the prison library. I watched lifers sitting behind stacks of old law books, turning the pages, trying to find their freedom. I read lots of Stephen King and anything else in which I could easily lose myself.

In order to make a phone call, you had to sign up first thing in the morning for a ten-minute slot, and you were only allowed one slot per day—that is, if the phone was even working. Seemed like America had figured out reliable phone service half a century earlier, but the prison phone would work some days and not others, and no one was ever sure why or how to fix it. The spotty service was especially surprising since the private company that had the prison phone contract engaged in some serious price gouging: all calls were collect, and the recipient was billed $15 for a ten-minute, in-state call. For that rate, you'd think someone from the phone company would be standing there to make sure that prison phone never went down. To make things worse, errors of overcharging were rampant, forcing the recipient into frequent disputes with the phone company. Lots of families simply couldn't afford to accept regular calls. Think about it—someone with a minimum-wage job had to work a few hours just to cover a ten-minute call with their loved one.

I'd call home weekly if I could get a slot on the call list, but sometimes, for no reason other than to mess with you, a guard wouldn't let you go to make your call.

Once you managed to get on the list, and were allowed to go to the phone, and the phone was, actually, in service, your call would be interrupted by a repeated recording that you were talking to an inmate in a California state prison, as though anyone needed reminding. When time was up, there was no warning, just a click, then silence. After a while my mother started complaining that week-ly calls were too much for her to maintain, and, with all the hassle and the distracting recording, I resigned myself to calling less frequently.

Once my work training began, I understood why some considered fire camp a privilege. I got to spend six hours a day outdoors, away from the barbed wire and gun towers, and was provided good, hot food, like steak burritos. I was also issued an army coat with two big pockets and a collar, which came in handy when standing in the din-ner line in the rain or the dry Santa Ana winds. But, despite the perks, there was no way I was going to be delivered to the front lines to fight California wildfires. My only hope was to flunk the physical test. That way, I'd be assigned back to training.

I made sure to flunk, falling out on the timed six-mile hike. And then, several weeks later, I made sure to flunk again, lagging on the pull-ups. With all that training, all those squats and runs and hikes and pull-ups, my body became lean and strong—but then I'd have to fake it and flunk again.

Years later, I picked up a newly released woman from the Amtrak station, and on the drive back to my house, she said she'd been assigned to fire camp. "I felt like a slave," she described. "They expect you, in six weeks, to be able to climb that wall, and if you don't, they tack on time and tack on time." With a hollow laugh, I thought back to how I'd never wanted to pass.

12

COLLATERAL DAMAGE

One in every 125 white children has a parent behind bars—for African American children, the rate is one in nine.

In the mid-1970s, an effort at prison reform inadvertently created more problems than it solved. California was one of the first states to address the arbitrariness and inherent racism in sentencing by mandating that similar crimes receive similar sentences. In theory, this was lofty, but the way it played out in reality was unexpected, and unfortunate.

The reform meant that people would no longer be sentenced to an indeterminate time, such as five-to-ten years, but rather, a predetermined sentence correlated with a specific crime. While this helped to eliminate various forms of discrimination at the sentencing level, it also eliminated the consideration of any extenuating circumstances. For example, there'd be no leniency shown to an eighteen-year-old mother caught stealing baby formula; theft was theft. Additional unintended consequences of the reform reverberated beyond the courtroom, directly affecting prisoners. No longer was a prisoner evaluated at intervals to determine her readiness to be released. Instead, the primary purpose of prison shifted from rehabilitation to punishment.

This legislation, coupled with slashed state funding and extreme overcrowding, turned prison classrooms and gymnasiums into barracks to house more and more and more prisoners. I would've jumped at the chance to take a class of some sort, but vocational training, college degree courses, and drug rehabilitation programs had all but vanished.

I knew of a few trade classes that were still offered, but it seemed the only prisoners who got into these were the lifers. It's no exaggeration that the lifers basically ran the prison. Because they typically held the clerking jobs in the sergeant's office, they were the first to know most goings on. They'd see when a slot for a trade class was opening and would quickly assign it to another lifer. From the sergeant's office, they also signed you up to see a doctor, ran the visiting room, and had the authority to do bed moves—and many were glad to accept money in exchange for a requested bed, which could get you out of a bad situation or surprise you with a worse one.

As for the trade classes, other than something to pass the time, they were mostly useless. Learning to print prison bulletins on equipment so outdated it was obsolete anywhere other than prison did nothing to prepare someone for a job on the outside. In a technological world, the prison system was like an Amish village.

Another disturbing area was prison medical care. You couldn't choose or, for that matter, refuse, a doctor, and there was no such thing as a second opinion. If you were assigned to see Dr. Advil, it hardly mattered what ailment you went there for—even if it was serious—you left with only Advil. If you were assigned to see Dr. Pap Smear, you knew, even if you went in for something as obvious and far removed as an eye infection or a broken toe, he'd give you a pap smear. Another doctor brought a fishing rod to work and wore a hat with lures dangling from it as he examined you.

For prisoners with a serious condition, it could be a nightmare of ridiculously long waitlists and misdiagnoses. If an inmate needed surgery but had a history of drug abuse—as most of us did—she was denied painkillers, which often meant the prison staff was blatantly disregarding an outside surgeon's prescription and orders. I watched many women, post-surgery, suffering in unnecessary pain. This was long after the Supreme Court's 1976 landmark decision that inadequate medical care in prisons was considered cruel and unusual punishment. But go ahead and try to assert your Eighth Amendment rights from behind bars; it was all but impossible.

Prisoners were billed for all medical services, the money automatically deducted from your account. California prisons imposed a $5 copay for each medical visit, which sounded nominal until you considered a prisoner earned merely pennies an hour. If multiple doctor visits were required, it could break you. There also was no consideration that some prisoners made eight cents an hour while others lucked into a $2-an-hour job, yet everyone was subject to the same copay. If there wasn't enough money in your account to cover your medical bill, the balance would automatically be deducted from future earnings. Some prisoners could never catch up. Other parts of the country were far worse. In Texas, copays were a whopping $100. In Alabama, prisoners were responsible for *actual* medical costs, and the balance—what could be tens of thousands of dollars—would follow you after your release. If you didn't or, more likely, couldn't pay your bill, the state could issue a warrant for your arrest.

I learned, early on, to avoid going to the doctor and, fortunately, I remained healthy enough to do so. Suffering through minor things like a cold or the flu without any meds seemed, to me, a far better option than subjecting myself to the crapshoot they called a medical system.

After serving thirteen months, I was assigned a release date. As the day neared, my excitement became overrun by a growing fear. I'd made a promise to myself that I was going to get my life together. But, deep down, I knew I was unprepared to re-enter the free world, even though it was all I thought about. I wanted to be brave, but I was coming out with no skills, no training, no job leads. I hadn't made a single decision in over a year. How was I going to walk out of there and be different, and expect my life to be different, when nothing else had changed? It was like walking into the rain determined that this time I wasn't going to get wet. But I still had no umbrella, so how the hell was this time going to be different than the last time it rained?

Release day: I rolled up my bedding and carried it with me to the gun tower. I gave my name and W-number, and the gate rolled open so I could pass through to R&R. I turned in my bedding to the inmates working there, and an officer fingerprinted me out. Of course, this simple process took over an hour. Then I perched on a bench for another hour until a guard drove up to take me and the other women getting released to the bus station.

I got off the bus. Downtown L.A., around the corner from Skid Row. I was going to try to find my way, I told myself, and told myself, and told myself. Telling myself so fiercely that after a couple weeks of trying to get an ID and trying to get a job and trying to earn some money and getting knocked down and kicked back, I felt like such an utter failure it seemed too unbearable to go through all this *and* try to stay clean. I had the desire to be productive, to be useful. But *how*? Finding a new direction seemed all but impossible. I was lugging around all the stuff of my past, and the rope to pull myself up was slipping through my hands.

At some point, you just let go.

Toni had never visited me in prison. She said it was because when she'd gone to the prison several years earlier, when she was fourteen, to visit her aunt Beverly, she'd just seen the movie *Helter Skelter* and spotted Leslie Van Houten of the Manson family sitting down the row. In a panic, Toni flew up from the bench. This called the guards' attention to her, which wouldn't have been a problem except that Toni was wearing blue jeans. Visitors had a dress code that excluded denim, khaki, and a list of other garb that could lead guards to mistake a visitor for an inmate, or the other way around. Both Toni and my mother, who was with her, had forgotten the no-jeans rule—and, apparently, so had the guards who'd allowed Toni to enter. Already spooked by the Manson girl, Toni was on edge when a guard cornered her, asking, "What's your number?"

"I don't have a number," Toni said.

The guard motioned to another guard. "She has blue jeans on."

"They let her in with blue jeans," my mother explained. But the guards weren't buying it. They cleared out the visiting room except for Toni and my mother, and then locked down the prison for a headcount.

"You can't hold me," Toni protested. "I'm underage." But for nearly three hours she and my mother were locked in while every prisoner was counted. When they finally were allowed to leave, Toni insisted she would never set foot in the place again.

Still, I imagine it was deeper than that. Between my brothers and me, Toni had been to the Criminal Courts building, to the county jail, and to the state prisons too many times, and she was tired of it. Tired of keeping track of who was about to be transferred from jail to prison, and hopping from the women's county jail and then down the street to the men's county jail to put money in our accounts so the maximum amount would transfer with us. She was tired of accepting the collect calls, tired of planning days around visiting hours. She felt her reward for being well behaved and a good student was that she had to run around and take care of all the adults who were screwing up their lives. By the time Toni got old enough to decide, she decided to distance herself.

When I was released, Toni was in college at UCLA. Though she was living in one of the efficiencies behind my mother's house, the rest of her life was separate from and unfamiliar to the rest of us. She was straddling two different worlds. And I could see the strain. Her friends from the neighborhood hounded her, saying, "We hardly see you anymore." Her boyfriend from high school—a nice kid who I'd watched grow up—became distant when Toni started college and he didn't. The rift made Toni resentful. She'd been working and going to school year round ever since she could remember—and she was burned out. I noticed signs that she was starting to rebel. For the first time, she started to hang out. She stopped showing up to class, and, unbeknownst to me, she lost her scholarship. She later would admit, "I looked up one day and had blown it all."

At nineteen years old, Toni became pregnant. She gave birth to a healthy daughter and named her Ellesse. I often screwed up the spelling, but the pronunciation was simple, *E-lease*. I dressed that baby girl up like my little doll, had her wearing designer jeans from Nordstrom's. I'd seen with my own mother how failed mothers could get a second chance with their grandchildren, but it took me a while before I could see it in myself.

Toni and her boyfriend moved in together, but he had a warped sense of responsibility, of what fathers are supposed to do. He was trying to be cool like my brother Melvin, who'd been his idol growing up, but he forgot to notice that Melvin was available to his children.

Toni, however, was determined to avoid the downward spiral. She began interviewing for jobs, and the one she wanted most, because it had the highest salary, was in the county jail. She scored in the top percentile on a mandatory entrance test, and was then brought in for an interview. They asked, "Do you have any family members who have been incarcerated?" She thought, *Where do I even begin?* Though I had just gotten out, two of my brothers were still in. Toni answered honestly, and was denied the job.

Eventually she heard that Pacific Bell was hiring, and she thought this might be an opportunity for a stable, long-term career. After she got the job as an information operator, she took her little girl in her arms and said, "This is where it begins, Ellesse. This is for the rest of our lives. I get to redeem myself, and we get to take this ride together." Toni worked as much overtime as she could get, both to save up money and to stay away from the rest of us as much as possible. She quickly moved up, getting promoted to service representative, and eventually to Human Resources. To think that my daughter had such maturity, while there I was: still lost and mired in my grief and addiction.

Any number of things could have landed me back in prison. I occasionally missed a meeting with my parole officer—which was caused by the bigger issue that I was having a tough time staying sober. But what landed me back in prison didn't have to do with my parole violations. I was in a liquor store when a man came at me, grappling for my keys. He wrestled them from me, but I went after him. As he ran outside, I latched on to him, trying to stop him from taking off with my car and everything in it. By that time I'd gotten nickelslick; people knew who I was, they knew what I had. I wasn't a random target. From the driver's seat of my car he fired a gun. The bullet went through the window and into my right shoulder.

The next day, my friend Joe from the neighborhood came to see me in the hospital. "Sue," he said, keeping his voice down. "They're coming for you."

I unhooked myself from the I.V. and snuck out. Back home, Mama told me the police had been by, bothering her with all sorts of questions about the carjacking. Figuring I'd head this off, I went by myself to the police station to make a statement. An officer brought me into a room, closed the door, and questioned me about what I was doing at the liquor store.

"I stopped in for a Häagen-Dazs," I said.

They questioned me about the shooter, and I described him as best as I could remember. When they were through, I was led from the room. But as I was about to leave the station, handcuffs were slapped on me. I was accused of leaving drugs in the room where I'd just been questioned. But I didn't have any drugs.

I would explain this to my public defender during the few minutes we had to talk before my hearing—which was a few minutes more than you often got. Most of the time, you met your lawyer as you were standing before the judge. I'd had this lawyer before, on an earlier offense, and he vaguely remembered me. "Boy, you sure have bad luck, don't you?" he said.

I told him I was innocent.

"We can't say that," he replied. "You've been convicted for drugs before. You won't be believed."

I seethed. Contrary to the core principles of our justice system, I bore the brand of a drug offender, making facts irrelevant. I was offered a plea deal of eighteen months. But it wasn't really an offer, it was a threat. And this talk with my lawyer—it wasn't for my benefit, it was only occurring because my name had been called from the docket. I asked what would happen if I refused to plead guilty and instead exercised my constitutional right to a trial. "You'll get the maximum of five years if you don't take this offer," he replied.

I was trapped, just as everyone I knew who'd stood in this spot and followed the instructions of a public defender had been trapped. But what *would* happen if everyone refused to automatically plead guilty and exercised their right to a trial? Some twenty years later, I'd ask this question to civil rights attorney Michelle Alexander, who'd detail our exchange in the *New York Times*. Over 90 percent of criminal cases close in a plea deal, she'd write. The dirty little secret was that if fewer than 30 percent of people charged with a crime exercised their constitutional right to a trial, the justice system would crash. There simply wouldn't be enough lawyers or judges or time. The right to a fair and speedy trial merely sounded good on paper.

Even if the odds were against me, there was something about standing up for myself. But when you're poor, you're relegated to being just another body passing through the system. I looked up at the judge awaiting my so-called decision, and I buckled. I took the eighteen-month sentence.

My anger smoldered, festering deeper. Several years later, in 1998, Los Angeles's Rampart police station, which neighbored the station where I was arrested, was sued over what the *Los Angeles Times* called "the worst corruption scandal in L.A.P.D. history." Officers were accused of fabricating arrests, falsifying evidence, and using excessive force, especially against minority victims. More than 140 civil suits were filed, with total settlements estimated around $125 million. I could say with certainty that it wasn't only the officers at the Rampart station who were rogue—they were just the ones who got caught. We were dealing with police who, when called to a homicide, would walk over the bodies looking for property to take—but under the country's seizure and civil forfeiture laws, this was not illegal.

Each time I was arrested, any money I had on me disappeared. The police said the cash was evidence. But none of this "evidence" would be recorded on booking slips, none showed up in court documents. This time I was going to prison not on evidence the police stole but evidence they planted. As if I'd voluntarily walked into the police station with illicit drugs and then left the drugs on the table? *C'mon, that was preposterous.*

I was now the taxpayer's problem. And the shooter—who'd been caught a few minutes after the robbery, around the corner from the liquor store—would soon be too. Early one morning, a prison guard woke me with a tug on my leg. I was taken to court, only this time my handcuffs were removed and I was led to the other side—but not really, it only seemed that way for a few moments. After I positively identified the shooter, I was escorted out, handcuffed, and taken back to prison.

The truth was: I didn't have drugs on me when I'd gone to make my statement about the shooter at the police station—but I did the night I'd been shot, and that's no doubt what the shooter had been after. At that point in my life, crack was all I could afford. Had I been arrested by the feds the night I was shot, the amount of crack in my possession would have subjected me to the mandatory minimum law. The Anti–Drug Abuse Acts of 1986 and 1988 had ratcheted up sentencing for all drug offenses, even for marijuana, but it especially singled out crack. Possession of 5 grams of crack (worth a total of around $100) would trigger the same sentence as possession of 500 grams of cocaine (worth a total of around $150,000) or of 100 kilos of marijuana (worth a total of around $20,000). These disparate and nonsensical sentences had been passed into law without any hearings, without any expert testimony from judges, law enforcement, drug policy experts, addiction medicine specialists, or the Bureau of Prisons.

Under federal law, I could have been facing thirty to forty years. Although I'd been framed, I'd also been granted the lesser of two evils.

13

THE REVOLVING DOOR

States with the toughest crime laws saw the largest spikes in prison population over the past two decades. California's Three Strikes law, one of the harshest sentencing policies in the country, sent people to prison for life for offenses as minor as petty theft. At one point, "strikers" made up a quarter of California inmates, serving extreme sentences that didn't fit the crime, on the taxpayers' dime.

With my arm in a cast and sling as the bullet wound healed, I was sent to the handicapped part of the prison. There, I met a woman who'd also been shot in the shoulder, in nearly the exact same spot. But instead of having her arm in a cast, she was paralyzed. Every time I saw her, an orderly pushing her around in a wheelchair, I was stopped cold. My shoulder would heal, the cast would come off, I'd be left with only a scar. She was in that chair for life.

The irony was that prison allowed me to heal. I had been running hard, using to numb not just my mind but also the physical pain of the bullet wound. Had I not been arrested, I don't know that my body would have held up.

When I was ready to be transferred out of the handicapped side, there was no bunk available in the main prison because of overcrowding. Women were being incarcerated at record-breaking rates and for lesser and lesser offenses. The state system ran out of W-numbers and began assigning women WE-numbers. Still under construction at the time was the $140 million Central California Women's Facility, which would hold the title of the largest women's prison in the world (and which, only a handful of years after opening, would be stuffed to double the intended capacity).

To deal with overflow, I, along with a bus full of women, was sent to Avenol, a men's prison. Not that Avenol had room for us. They'd vacated an occupied yard, and it was clear from the way we found it that the men who'd lived there had been mad about wherever they were being forced to move on to. For an entire week, we scrubbed the filth left behind, cleaning up scraps of food, even feces, to make the building habitable.

With all the shuffling around and shoving together, no wonder California's prisoners had the nation's highest suicide rate—a shocking 80 percent higher. Buses loaded with prisoners were spotted driving aimlessly around the state, stopping at a prison for bathrooms and a meal, and then it was back on the bus, driving for several hours to another prison to use the bathrooms and get a meal. At any given time, it was speculated that busloads of prisoners were living on the road in what amounted to mobile prisons, waiting for word that someone had been released or died and a bed had opened up.

Unlike the women's prison, Avenol was all concrete and black tar. There was no lawn, not even a sliver of green. There was, however, an area where chickens and pigs were raised and slaughtered, but inmates who worked there talked about how weirdly deformed many of the animals were—a chicken with one eye, pigs with crooked legs. *What's for dinner? Antibiotics and steroids!*

I'd been forty-five minutes from my family when I was at the California Institution for Women, but Avenol was 180 miles away. A six-hour round trip was a lot of time and gas money for someone to come sit on a bench and talk to me. So no one visited. As isolated as I felt, inmates several years later would have it worse when California's backhand solution to reduce overcrowding was to ship people out of state, sending more than eight thousand prisoners to Oklahoma, Mississippi, and Arizona.

After serving a year, I was released on parole, and my father took the long drive to pick me up. We were happy to see each other, though I knew he was saddened by what was going on with me, and with all his children. He preached a little about getting my life together. But then he let it go. I was no different than him, and no different than just about everyone else we knew. Our entire community had come undone. Mass incarceration was in full swing, and we were all targets.

I went to the unemployment office, I filled out applications in stores, I asked around if anyone knew of a job. But I had to check that felony conviction box, so all I saw were heads shaking no. The State Department of Rehabilitation was supposed to help me find a job, but nothing came of that. What I really needed was a college degree, but I also needed money to live. So I eliminated school as an option, and no one counseled me otherwise.

Then, a man with cream-colored skin and green eyes came by. There was something about him that captured me. He'd grown up in northern California. He dressed immaculately. He drove a Mercedes and took me on dates at nice restaurants. Everyone called him Chief, a nickname given to him as a child. So I called him Chief too, which didn't feel as off to me as it should have.

Chief had a mystery about him, and all the women wanted to get with him, but he was mine. It would take some time before his allure began to fade and I realized that what I'd mistaken for mystery was really arrogance and secrecy—and drugs. But I was to blame too. I didn't want to know, so I turned my head, yet again, repeating the same damn cycle, jumping from the skillet to the frying pan.

One day I called Toni and said, "Come to Vegas! I'm getting married."

There was a pause on the other end. "To who?" she asked, before declining the invitation.

Though I can't blame my actions on the drugs, I was high when I said my vows. I had no idea what a good man was supposed to be, but

Chief supported me financially and never raised a hand to me, and that meant something. We moved into an apartment, and I began collecting as many different types of plants as I could find. I filled that house with big plants, little plants, tree-like plants, in the bedroom, the kitchen, the bathroom, lining the hallway. The plants were alive and beautiful, they wouldn't bother anybody, and I could watch them thrive. I watered them and shined them and talked to them. When Toni came over she said, "I feel like I'm walking into the Amazon. Why am I knocking leaves out of my face?"

I replied, "I'm cleaning the air."

Toni and Chief tolerated each other and even found some enjoyment trading recipes. But Chief's aloofness began to make me paranoid. So did the drugs. The scene was no longer the high-flying, big-money 1980s; it had become sad and desperate. Dope doesn't exactly compel you to be a kind, considerate person, and I treated myself and everyone around me poorly. I was still mired in anger and filled with hurt. Hurt people hurt people, and that's the spiral in which I was trapped. Inevitably, I landed right back in prison.

The story would repeat itself. The story that, each time, I'd lay out before the judge: "My son was killed, I'm trying to numb the pain with alcohol and drugs. I'd like to get some help." But the gavel would come down with a smack, and the judge would say: "Prison."

I'd sit in the county jail, then get transferred to prison, where, for six weeks, I'd be held in R&R in that cage, taxpayer dollars paying for me to sit there all day long doing nothing. I'd get yet another physical and another TB test—one in county jail and then another in prison, even though it was only a couple of months between tests and the entire time I'd been confined to a cell. On it would go, for the next decade: sentenced to sixteen months, I'd do ten months. Two years, I'd do fifteen months. Three years, I'd do twenty months. I was a sad, lost, broken woman. I was an addict, an alcoholic. Not once in those courtrooms did it go down differently. Not once did a judge say, "Let's defer her to treatment." I didn't know to ask for anything different—treatment wasn't something offered up to people from my community. All I knew was that we went to prison for this stuff. All I knew was that it went: the gavel would smack, "Prison." Smack, "Prison." Smack, "Prison."

One time, I was in the holding room of the Criminal Courts building, waiting to go before the judge—even though the mandatory minimum laws all but rendered judges powerless—when I noticed a newspaper lying on a bench. For the past two months I'd been sitting in county jail and hadn't seen a newspaper. Flipping through, I glimpsed a photo that looked like my mother. I read the caption. It *was* Mama. She was ceremoniously activating a stoplight on the corner where, eight years earlier, K.K. had been killed.

My head reeled. According to the article, Councilman Nate Holden was holding a town hall meeting when someone stood up and told K.K.'s story. The councilman then went door to door looking for me, finally knocking on my mother's door. She invited him in.

When my name was called I took the newspaper with me into the courtroom and showed my attorney. "It's all here," I pleaded. But the gavel came down, and I was sentenced to twenty months in prison.

Six weeks later, when I was finally allowed to sign up for the phone, I called my mother and told her I'd seen the article. "Did you tell the councilman why I wasn't there?" I asked. "That I was awaiting sentencing?"

"No," she replied.

I could hear her shame seeping through the line. I hung up, knowing I'd resent my mother for this for a long time. I resented Mama for lots of things.

When I next talked to Toni, I told her I'd seen the article. "Were you there?" I asked.

"Yes," she said. "But I didn't want to be in the photo. It all seemed too little, too late. My brother's dead, my mother's in prison. So when the photographer came by, I moved to the side."

14

THE VICIOUS CYCLE

Only around 15 percent of those serving time for a drug-related offense are given access to a drug treatment program with a trained professional.

Not terribly long after serving my twenty-month sentence, I found myself back again in county jail for the same thing, a nonviolent drug offense, and was now facing five years.

In a cold cement holding cell, I shared a bunk with a white woman who had violated her parole because she hadn't stayed clean. She complained, "CRC is a trick."

"What's CRC?" I asked.

She eyed me as though I should know this. "California Rehabilitation Center," she said. "Didn't your lawyer tell you about the Civil Addict Program?"

She looked bewildered when I shook my head.

She first explained that she was on a civil commitment—not a criminal commitment like I was, even though we'd both been arrested for drug possession. "If you're sentenced to CRC," she said, "there's a class you have to pass. They call it Addicts University. And then you can be home in eight months. But these stupid parole violations keep you coming back. If you don't have three consecutive years without violations, it's like your sentence goes on and on. It can go on for the rest of your life."

But I barely heard anything she said past "you can be home in eight months." *Eight months?* The district attorney was offering me five years, and when I asked my public defender if he could get it down to two years, he bluntly said, "No," as though his job wasn't to fight for me but to merely messenger the DA's threat.

Public pretenders, that's what we called them on the inside. No more useful in court than your own shadow standing next to you. It seemed they were there solely to legitimize people throwing away their rights—to facilitate a fast track to guilt, to keep the conveyor belt to prison moving swiftly along.

Only years later would I consider the other side, that anyone who aspired to be a public defender, forgoing white-shoe law firm billable hours to instead work with the indigent and earn a government salary, entered with an ideal of reforming criminal justice. But the system flattened ideals like a shiny penny on a train track. Bright-eyed intentions were useless when the public defenders' office was so severely underfunded it was practically impossible for a lawyer to spend more than five minutes per case. It was the prosecutors who now ran the courtroom; public defenders and, for that matter, judges were virtually powerless.

Of course, it wasn't *supposed* to be like this. In 1963, the Supreme Court's *Gideon* decision granted anyone in a criminal case the right to a lawyer, even if they couldn't afford one. This landmark case promised to change the face of criminal justice. But when the War on Drugs and subsequent tough-on-crime measures duped the public into believing that more and more arrests would make our country safer, public defenders became so overloaded the office was paralyzed. What we were left with was the illusion of upholding *Gideon*, the mirage of representation. And this created a caste system, with poor people becoming notches on the DA's belt. So what that I got my few minutes with a public defender, talking to me in the holding cell of the courtroom, or as we walked into the courtroom, or sometimes not even until we were standing before the judge, instructing me, "Say yes, you understand your rights." "Say yes, you give up your rights." "Say yes, you're guilty." "Say yes, you'll enter a guilty plea."

I was hardly viewed as an American with the right to a fair trial—I was a folder on a desk that could be moved off the desk a lot quicker and cheaper if I took a plea deal. Time and time again I stood before the judge, railroaded—both my public defender and I caught in a broken system. Both of us spinning in circles, my futile cycle causing his, his futile cycle causing mine, the whole system so dizzy it was all but falling down.

This time, supplied with information from my bunkie, I decided *I* would be the bargainer. I told my lawyer, "I will take the plea of five years if I am sent to the Civil Addict Program."

And just like that, I got into California Rehabilitation Center.

It seemed too simple—there must be a catch. And there was: the game had been rigged, and I'd been caught up in it for all these years. From the moment I had entered the system, I was flagged for the criminal side, while my white bunkie was flagged for the civil side, even though our crimes were the same. The fact was, we both needed treatment and help. But the rest was full of stark irony: there were insufficient resources for help, but a concerted effort to fill prisons.

California Rehabilitation Center, located in Norco, about an hour from Los Angeles, was still a state penitentiary with barbed wire surrounding the premises, but the interior felt slightly more welcoming. Our rooms were more like barracks than cells, with doors that didn't lock, so we were free to move around. Though we still wore orange "Property of the State of California" uniforms, everyone there was assigned an N-number, indicating a Narcotics Civil Commitment, as opposed to my former criminal W-number.

The first obvious thing I noticed about my fellow prisoners was that they were predominantly white. Soon, other things became clear: most hailed from suburban areas of California, and most had been represented by private attorneys, not public defenders. No wonder I hadn't been offered CRC before. There were limited spots, and first dibs apparently went to Fresno County and Merced County and San Bernadino County and Humboldt County, even though Los Angeles County sent more people to prison than any other part of the state.

Formally, Addicts University was the Civil Commitment Education Program (CCEP). With around forty other women, I spent six hours a day in a classroom, five days a week. In order to be released, you had to pass a written test—which I knew I could pass—and then you had to go before the Civil Addict Committee and recite what you had learned—which I also knew I could do—and then, released to parole, you had to undergo routine drug testing—but that part I didn't think about, it was too far ahead.

Though the prison was called a rehabilitation center, CCEP wasn't drug rehab. It didn't include therapy, there were no group discussions, no counseling, it didn't delve into anything personal. Our teacher was a former prison guard, not a therapist. We were assigned a textbook and watched stilted educational movies about addiction. I memorized the twelve steps of Alcoholics Anonymous, but we weren't asked to discuss them, let alone apply them. I didn't have to search my character, admit my wrongs, make amends. I just had to commit lines to my short-term memory. In a way, it was akin to a sex ed class—you could read a whole bunch of textbooks about sex, but that would never be the same as doing it.

Once in a while, a passage in the textbook would nudge me, and I'd feel something. A dull pain, gnawing at an old wound. But my wounds needed to remain numb because I didn't know how to deal with things any other way. So I shut off: the words were just words, they couldn't hurt me. In addition to class, CCEP required physical fitness, and I pounded out any talk in my head with aerobics and sit-ups and push-ups.

From what I saw, most of the women at California Rehabilitation Center were medicated—not that this place was unique, I'd witnessed this in all the prisons. As for me, I'd only been prescribed antidepressants once, when I first arrived to prison in Alaska and broke out in a rash. They did things differently in Alaska, and I was put in a car and taken to a private-practice dermatologist. The doctor said my rash was from stress, and gave me a bunch of skin creams and special soap, plus 50 mg of Elavil in the morning, 50 mg in the afternoon, and 150 mg at night. A few months later a prison guard came up to me and said, "Susan, why are you taking all this?" The genuine concern in her voice made me wonder, why *am* I taking all this? It wasn't as though I noticed much difference in the way I felt. I quit the meds the next day.

But quitting your meds wouldn't have gone over in most states. Despite patients' rights policies that were supposed to prevent forcible medicating of inmates, not taking your meds could trigger a 115 write-up, denying you privileges, like shopping at the canteen. Collect enough 115s and you'd be thrown in the SHU or have more time tacked on to your sentence.

On the flip side, I watched other prisoners being denied medication. Prisons weren't well-stocked pharmacies, so if a medication you needed wasn't already on the premises, you'd be waiting a while. The worst version of this was upon arrest, when your filled prescriptions weren't allowed to follow you in. Thanks to the absurdities of the correctional system, you instead had to go cold turkey—whether your meds were for high cholesterol or AIDS—while waiting to see a prison doctor, who'd reexamine and re-prescribe.

For my work detail, I was randomly assigned to be a clerk for the Muslim chaplain. I wasn't a Muslim, and I'm sure there were inmates who were and would've jumped at the assignment, but if I didn't show up, I'd be put in the hole. Every day I reported to my job and, to my surprise, I found a comfort in the religion's discipline and teachings about the love for mankind, the need for self-determination, and being unaffected by worldly possessions. All this was in the Bible, too, but it never seemed as prominent to me in practice as this was. I began to pray, eventually praying five times a day. I observed the holiday of Ramadan, its message of self-repentance and sacrifice resonating with me.

But what didn't resonate was when I learned that women were forbidden to pray during their menstrual cycle. *God didn't hear me because I was on my period?* It didn't make sense that anything—especially something as natural as menstruation—should restrict me from feeling in commune with God. Still, I needed something to cling to, so I continued practicing.

I phoned Toni regularly. She'd been saving up money, and once she had enough, she moved out of my mother's house and into an apartment in Lawndale, a half hour away. It hadn't been an easy decision, especially since my mother watched Ellesse while Toni worked, but Toni knew she had to get out. There was too much traffic in my mother's house, what with all my brothers and their friends and wives or girlfriends and all their kids and their kids' friends, and Toni could only imagine what might be taking place under that roof. Also, my mother had grown oddly passive and distracted—what we'd later learn was the early stages of Alzheimer's. "I'd wanted to do everything differently," Toni later told me. "But how could I when I was still there?"

As a mother, Toni was beyond strict, and I knew her biggest fear was that Ellesse would stray down a bad path, like the rest of us. Or that she'd end up like K.K. After each of Ellesse's birthdays, Toni told me she breathed a sigh of relief that her child had made it another year. Little Ellesse would get on the phone with me too. She once insisted I come home, and wouldn't let up. I said, "The deputy won't let me come home yet."

"Let me talk to the deputy," she demanded.

"Sorry," I replied. "The deputy can't get on the phone."

Ellesse had been hearing Toni talk about her work at the phone company and, mimicking her mother, said, "Then let me speak to the supervisor."

I could feel bits of my heart breaking. And then my ten minutes were up, and the call automatically cut off. For a moment, I listened to the silence. Then I handed the receiver to the next prisoner in line.

———

I passed the written CCEP test, then went before the board for the verbal test. Right on schedule, I was released, having served eight months.

Chief picked me up. Since I'd last seen him, I'd converted to Islam, but here I was going back to a Christian husband, which was forbidden. Had it been the other way around—a Muslim man with a Christian wife—that would have been permissible because of the double standard that a husband can lead the wife, but not the reverse.

My father had taken ill while I was gone and was in a convalescent home, so that's the first place we went. When Chief tried to touch me in the elevator I jumped back, cringing. But it wasn't because of Islam, it was because I knew he wasn't good for me.

I was relieved to see Daddy, and the staff told me he'd soon be able to move back to his home. I didn't process that he was sick with alcoholism and that cirrhosis would continue to ravage him. It only sunk in several years later, when, despite his objections, I called an ambulance. "Susan," he said mournfully. "You called the meat wagon on me."

Chief and I returned to our apartment filled with plants, and it was too easy to revert back to old ways. Drugs were everywhere: in the drawers, hidden in the closet, with more for sale just down the block. It hardly mattered that I refused the first time, the second time, even the third time. I didn't stand a chance.

This went on for a couple of years, until I got pregnant. I vowed to myself not to use anymore, but I couldn't stop. I'd heard about a nearby recovery home for alcoholics, and I showed up there, desperate for help and claiming alcohol was my only issue so that I'd be allowed in.

Located in a two-story house on a residential street, the program was heavily structured with lots of rules; for example, you couldn't go back to bed if you got up, and you had to participate in all group meetings even if you were sick. It didn't feel like home, it felt like red tape. One night I cooked everyone dinner. Thanks to Daddy, all us Burton kids were good cooks, and I whipped up some beans, chicken, and cornbread. Everyone liked it so much they had me in the kitchen all the time. They insisted I break the rules and miss group meetings to cook for them. For a month, I went along with it; I was staying sober, and that's what mattered most.

But then I got my period. If I wasn't pregnant after all, I certainly didn't need to be in their kitchen.

I went back home, walking into my apartment with the goal of staying clean. But there was cocaine, and just about everyone I knew was waiting for me to cook it into rocks. No matter who I was cooking for, there was no way out.

On my rap sheet the following year, it would list my stint in the recovery home. But instead of indicating that I'd checked myself in, it recorded that a deputy parole agent—citing a man I'd never heard of—had placed me there. It also stated that I'd left before completing the program, absconding from supervision. Despite what my paper-work claimed, no part of the justice system ever put me anywhere other than behind bars.

15

HURT PEOPLE

It is estimated that as many as 94 percent of incarcerated
women were victims of physical or sexual abuse.

As my father's health deteriorated, my brothers and I found him a little apartment, and I volunteered to move in and take care of him. Now it was my turn to cook good meals for Daddy. But I didn't realize that also allowing him to continue drinking wasn't taking care of him.

One day I was gone for an hour or so, and when I returned home, Melvin was there. He said, "Daddy's dead."

He explained that he'd stopped by to find me gone and Daddy passed out. An ambulance had come, but it was too late. The ambulance left, and my father's body stayed, supine on the couch. All I could do was stare. I couldn't allow myself to feel. All I could be was detached, hardened, numb.

As the rest of my family showed up, everyone gingerly stepped past Daddy and huddled in the kitchen, waiting for someone from the morgue to show up. Only Mama, having come from the era when people died at home, seemed fine with Herman Burton's body there. She straightened up the living room around him, calling to us, "Come sit down, there's plenty of room in here." But no one moved, even though we were all squeezed shoulder to shoulder in the tiny kitchen.

I soon escaped to my bedroom and locked the door. Noticing I'd left the phone in there, I envisioned Daddy suffering in the living room and unable to call for help because he couldn't find the phone. I felt sick. But I quickly pushed it all away, far, far away. Not even at his funeral could tears penetrate my veneer.

It had been some thirty years since my mother had put my father out, but all that time she'd steadfastly refused to get a divorce, always claiming she wasn't ready to let go. Still, Mr. Fisher had never stopped waiting for her, continuing to provide for her. He'd also bonded with Toni in a way he never had with my brothers or me, taking her to church, cooking nice meals, letting her know how much he cared about her. After my father passed, none of us were surprised when Mr. Fisher asked my mother to marry him. But we all, including Mr. Fisher, were surprised by her response. Offended, she snipped that it was too soon after her husband's death.

But Mama hadn't bothered with Daddy in ages, so I doubted that was the real reason. Only later would I learn what was behind her refusal: when Mr. Fisher had bought her the house on Highland Avenue with the rentals around back, he'd inserted a clause in the contract prohibiting her from using the house as collateral to get any of her children out of jail. With this, he'd made it crystal clear: he wanted my mother, just not the rest of us. Deep down, Mama knew that wasn't okay.

I moved back in with Chief. Maybe I took my hopelessness out on him, but it felt as if he was trying to control me. I wanted him to stay away from me, and I went so far as to drill a security bar across the bedroom door to barricade myself. Looking back, he *was* trying to control me, but so were the drugs. And that's what drove me right back to prison.

It was 1996 and President Bill Clinton was in the oval office. While Nixon, Carter, Reagan, and Bush had hit line drives with tough-on-crime initiatives, it was Clinton who hit it out of the park. His policies put even more people behind bars, and kept them there longer. Two decades later, speaking at the NAACP's national convention, Clinton would apologize for his anti-crime legislation. "I signed a bill that made the problem worse," he said. "And I want to admit it." The thing was, I couldn't turn on the heat in winter or run water from the faucet on sorry. Sorry wouldn't bring back those years.

This time, though, just as my white former bunkmate had described, when I was arrested for possession, I was booked under my Civil Commitment classification and N-number, not my previous criminal number. Automatically, I was sentenced back to California Rehabilitation Center and Addicts University—with the potential of being released in eight months.

Though recidivism rates were typically lower for those who completed CCEP class, it wasn't uncommon for people to return, and return again—what my bunkie had complained was the "trick." Even if it weren't so much a *trick*, it certainly seemed a *trap*. Having technical violations, such as not passing a drug test, or even something as minor as not reporting an address change or not showing up on the right day to your parole officer, could land you right back there, though no new crime had been committed. I met women who were in their tenth year of CCEP.

Once again, I memorized the lessons in the textbook and watched the same slides and stilted movies. And, just as before, old wounds were prodded. But, this time, something unsettling happened: I couldn't automatically shut myself down. When one of the movies described dysfunctional family roles, such as the perpetual caregiver or the scapegoat, something in me began to stir. At night, as I tried to fall asleep, scenes of my childhood flashed before my eyes. I thought I'd buried these memories too deep to unearth, but the images continued to grow more and more vivid. As the months went on, emotions that I didn't want to feel flooded me. I was hurting like hell and had no idea what to do about it.

Ms. Tucker was my CCEP teacher and was known as the toughest on the yard. You couldn't crack a giggle in her class or she'd dismiss you. She was infamous for having flunked her entire class—which meant that each prisoner had to wait months to get reclassified, and then wait months for a new session of CCEP class to begin, only to then repeat the entire six-month course. One day, as I was walking down the sergeant's hall, I saw Ms. Tucker walking toward me. In her late forties, a short black woman with a round face, Ms. Tucker had a fierce command that made her nearly impossible to approach. My instinct was to get out of her way. But something compelled me, a yearning I couldn't hold back. "Ms. Tucker," I said, "could I speak to you for a minute?"

"You're in my class?" she asked, sizing me up. "What's your name?"

"Susan Burton."

She tilted her head, which I took as an indication that I could continue. "I'm having a lot of stuff coming up, a lot of memories from my childhood, and about my son, and I'm really troubled by it and don't know what to do with it all." Before I realized the words were leaving my mouth, I told her about my aunt's crazy boyfriend, and then about Mr. Burke. Never before had I breathed a word about what they'd done. And I didn't stop there. I told her about the rape and my pregnancy. I told her about K.K.

Ms. Tucker looked at me for a long moment. I feared she was going to tell me I was out of line. She said, "I don't want you to worry about passing my class. You have enough to think about."

I will never forget that moment as I watched her continue on down the hall. For someone notoriously uncompromising to ease the pressure on me, that meant something. This was an official indication that things had gone very wrong in my life. Her validation caused me, for the first time, to cry my heart out.

Ms. Tucker and I didn't have any individual interaction beyond that. I passed her class, went before the board, and was released after eight months. I had served six sentences over the past seventeen years and was returning to the same dead-end environment, still not knowing what to do with my feelings, with my life, with myself.

With $100 of gate money in my pocket, I stepped off that Greyhound bus around the corner from Skid Row. Again. No one was there to pick me up. Toni was now thirty years old and busy with her daughter and her job at the phone company. Her distance made it clear she wanted little to do with me. How could I blame her? It's difficult to keep trying to love someone when they keep dragging you through the mud. She was disappointed by my wasteful existence. So was I.

Chief was in prison, on a drug conspiracy charge. No drugs in hand, he'd been arrested based on a telephone conversation. I tried to bring myself to write him, but I couldn't. I was dealing with my own demons.

Mama let me stay in the efficiency behind her house. It was empty but for a daybed and a lamp. Searching for something to ground me, I visited a mosque. But that no longer fit.

From prison, Chief sent me divorce papers, and I signed them.

It started with Courvoisier, which seemed fancy and innocent. What was the harm in a nice glass or two of cognac to relax? It soon devolved, and before I knew it, I was caught up all over again, digging in my mother's couch for loose change. It wasn't even a decision, it just happened because there was nothing else that was going to happen.

Toni cut me off from spending time with Ellesse. She was right; I couldn't be a responsible grandmother. Not when two-for-a-dollar cans of beer and crack were my most reliable companions.

I laid around on the daybed of that little efficiency, staring at the blank walls. Not only had my talent for divorcing myself from my emotions disappeared, but the drugs that used to turn me into a virtual statue no longer hardened me. Ms. Tucker's response had awakened feelings too alive and too persistent. Scenes played in my head, incessantly, all pointing to the fact that, throughout my life, my family had little care for my well-being. One night, my oldest brother, Michael, was over, and I confronted him about how he'd treated me when we were kids. He pushed me out of the apartment and locked the door—just as he'd locked me out when I was a little girl.

I went in the front house and found my younger brother, Marvin. I was looking for his memories and seeking some clarity, but he took it wrong, yelling at me and acting like I was accusing him. Maybe I was. At that point, I didn't know how to take any personal responsibility— it was everybody's problem but mine.

The next night, my friend Joe and I were sitting in the little efficiency, drinking cheap beer. I knew Joe from years back, and he was also friends with Melvin, my brother closest in age to me, and the only one who'd been good to me. Back in the day, Joe, Melvin, and I ran together, and got high together. We were a wild bunch. All three of us had served time, but I was still doing the same thing, going nowhere, stuck in the same cycle.

"I can't keep on like this, Joe," I confided. "I'm forty-six years old, and my life is a big sum of nothing."

Joe put down his beer and focused on me as if to gauge how serious I was. He always had sad-looking eyes, a sadness I suspected his military-style father had beaten into him. "If you really mean it," Joe said, "I know of a good place you can go." He wrote down the name of a treatment program.

The next morning I went into my mother's house. She was cutting quilting patterns on the dining table. I'd watched her quilting ever since I could remember, and so did Toni, though we didn't inherit her stitching talent. Mama made beautiful quilts and sold them to the people she was a maid for in Beverly Hills and Malibu. A Hollywood studio even bought some, and we'd glimpse her quilts in scenes of soap operas.

"Mama," I said, "you remember Mr. Burke?"

She glanced up at me. "Of course I remember Mr. Burke." She said his name with the brightness of thinking about an old friend.

"Mama, did you go out with Mr. Burke?"

"No, I never went out with Mr. Burke."

"You weren't seeing him?"

"He didn't like me, Susan." This time she didn't look up. "He liked you."

A tingling shot through me. I'd always suspected, but had never before wanted to be certain: my mother had known exactly what was going on.

I went out the back door to the little apartment. Later, I returned and again stood in front of my mother. Sitting on the living room couch, she was quilting her specialty, the Double Wedding Ring, a pattern of intertwining circles.

"Mama, about Mr. Burke," I said. "I was just a little girl."

Her face hardened. "Don't try to run no guilt trip on me, Susan. You did what you did."

"But, Mama, it was illegal. Why did you keep letting that happen?"

"Susan, you never learned." She shook her head. "You just cross your legs, and you lock them. That's what I always did." She then paused from her quilting, as though exasperated. "Look, I could not help you as a little girl, and I cannot help you now. Why don't you just go away?"

I went out back, the abused little girl now a mangled, broken woman. The pain was more than alcohol or drugs could smother. I called the place Joe told me about.

The man who answered the phone apologized and said they were full. He suggested I try a different facility downtown, so I got on a downtown bus. The rehab center was in Skid Row, but they said there was no curtain to create a private area for women, so I couldn't sleep there. I knew if I was going to do this I needed to be away from everything familiar. Helpless, I returned home, though my mother's place hardly felt like a home.

Later that day, my brother Melvin came by to visit Mama. Two years my junior, Melvin and I were always the closest. I loved Melvin, but the truth was *everybody* loved Melvin. He was pure charisma, the type of person who made everyone he encountered feel special. He had thirteen children from nearly as many women, and every so often he'd bring all the women and all the children together and, miraculously, it all worked out. No jealousies sparked, no tempers flared, and no one thought anything but the best of him. Everyone just wanted to be a part of his life. He was, after all, a professional connector. He connected people with lawyers and doctors and bail bondsmen and other specialties, and he billed both sides for the referral, taking only cash payments. He had a huge appetite for life. He drove Rolls-Royces and Lamborghinis, and, in an off year, he'd settle for a Mercedes. He always had the best of everything—art, clothes, women. The best of everything and a lot of everything, that was how Melvin rolled.

When I heard him pull up, I went out front.

"Sue," he said. "I hear you're trying to find some help."

Joe must have told him, and it touched me that either of them cared enough to talk about it.

"Listen," Melvin said, "if you find a place to go, I'll pay for it. But I won't do anything else for you. Don't ask me for any money, Sue. Not a single red cent."

I looked down at my feet. All I could do was silently nod. Melvin went inside my mother's house, and I went around back to the efficiency and cried for an hour. I cried both from the compassion he had showed me and also because he knew my game—I *had* gone out front because I wanted him to give me money.

The next day, I again dialed the number Joe had given me for the treatment program. The man on the phone sounded relieved to hear from me. "Someone in the program left, and I heard in your voice how you needed to be here," he said. "Come, we have a bed for you."

I went inside to pack a suitcase, but my clothes were gone. My brother Marvin was there, and I asked what happened to my clothes. "They were in the way," he said, apparently still sore at me. "So I threw them out."

I called George, and he picked me up and drove me across town to Santa Monica, pep talking me along the way. "You've always been tough. You've always been a fighter," he said. "As I understand from your brothers, you could hit pretty hard, even as a little girl. I know you, Sue, and there isn't a whole lot you can't do, once you make up your mind to do it." George had been encouraging me for some thirty years. Maybe I was finally ready to listen.

I arrived to the treatment program, the CLARE Foundation, with nothing but the clothes on my back.

16

A TALE OF TWO SYSTEMS

Though drug use and selling occur at similar rates across racial and ethnic groups, black and Hispanic women are far more likely to be criminalized.

Black women are more than twice as likely to be incarcerated for drug offenses as white women.

When I showed up in Santa Monica, I had doom all over me. My once-muscular body was skeletal. My hair was falling out in patches. A rash inflamed my skin. I shook and trembled. My brain was so rattled, I could barely finish a sentence, and my stutter had returned. Entering CLARE, I felt all eyes on me. I can only imagine they were thinking, *Can we really help this one?* But they took me in, they fed me, they sent me across the street to the thrift store they ran and had me pick out clothes. The next morning I woke up hysterical, but Jan, the drug counselor, reassured me. "Honey, you're detoxing," she said. "If you just stay, I promise it will be all right."

It was clear I did not fit in with the others at CLARE. People laughed and mimicked my halting, self-conscious speech. We all had assigned chores, and when my roommates swept, they dumped the dustpan on my bed. Toni visited and brought me bra and panty sets, but the other women stole them. Yet I didn't respond. I knew how desperately I needed to be there, and something in me kept saying, *Down, girl*. Even Jan asked, "Susan, why are you taking all this shit off these women?" and I was so struck by the compassion she showed me. Soon, two of the main bullies were booted from the program because of their conduct. As I stayed on, I felt for the first time in my life that I was protected, and that I would be okay.

Only several miles down the 10 freeway from where I'd grown up, Santa Monica, one of the country's wealthiest cities, with white sand beaches and the roar of the ocean at the end of every major street, might as well have been a world away. That cheap beer I bought in my neighborhood, you couldn't even find it in Santa Monica. Here, a soda cost more than a can of that beer. In my neighborhood, the blocks alternated: two churches and one liquor store on one block, two liquor stores and one church on the next. And there were lots of storefronts for loan sharks. Here, you could go blocks without seeing a church, and a mile or two without encountering a liquor store, and I didn't see a single billboard for payday loans.

Most of the people in the program had never been arrested, but those who had described an entirely different criminal justice system. Able to afford good attorneys, they avoided incarceration altogether. Instead, they were assigned a court card, requiring that they complete a diversion program, which was either an individualized recovery program like CLARE or community AA meetings. Once the minimum requirement was met, they returned to court with their signed card and charges were dismissed. In this alternate world to the one I'd known, where I was always steered down the same dead-end road, the people here had been diverted away from prison and directed toward opportunity. Why hadn't the justice system ever invested in me with a court card? Why had it been up to me to fight my way here, to beg, borrow, and practically steal my way into recovery?

One of the men shared that he was here because he'd been driving drunk and hit a police car. In my neighborhood, that'd be called attempted murder. But this man, white, living in Santa Monica, was sentenced to community service, which entailed painting a jail. He complained that he'd hated painting that jail, that it had been the ugliest shade of green, and now he couldn't stand the sight of anything resembling that color. I listened silently, thinking about my brother, Michael, who'd been sentenced to eight years in prison for falling asleep at the wheel—with no alcohol or drug involvement—and he still had to serve the full sentence even after being diagnosed with narcolepsy.

Across the street was a designated Alcoholics Anonymous meeting space and, with others from my program, I walked over to attend my first meeting. People stood up and shared their stories. Some had been to very low places, but they didn't look like it, didn't talk like it, dress like it, or smell like it. This sparked something in me, something I'd never felt before, and I was moved to speak. I rose, took a deep breath. "Look what drugs and alcohol have done to me," I said, my voice quivering. My hands were shaking so much the styrofoam cup of coffee I held was wasting on me. But no one seemed to judge my piteous condition. The immediate compassion, the empathy, the love that rolled off these strangers was enough to put a sizable dent in my pain, my shame, my guilt, and all that sorrow. In that room, I found hope.

Someone passed me a newcomer chip. Someone else gave me the Big Book of Alcoholics Anonymous. On the walk back after the meeting, I held both close to my heart.

I soaked up everything. I learned about being useful and about showing up—and showing up on time to someplace other than the liquor store when it opened, or by 2 a.m. when it closed. Women and men were separate during the day except for meals—and I loved that it was the men who were responsible for cooking and washing dishes. Never before had I experienced men cleaning up for women. I learned how to meditate, and to not be afraid of being alone with myself. I spent time at the ocean, and we held meetings on the beach. I at last gave myself permission to open the door in my mind and to start reflecting.

Every morning we gathered for readings and discussion and to set an individual goal for the day. It was the first time in my life I'd deliberately set a goal. I began with meager goals, like doing sit-ups, things I knew could achieve if I tried. Through this, something amazing happened: I felt a sense of accomplishment. Incrementally, my confidence began to build, and I began setting more lofty goals, such as create a résumé.

One task I had was to find someone who'd been in recovery a while to be my sponsor. At AA meetings, I twice approached women to sponsor me. But one lived too far away, and it was a long-distance call to talk, which I couldn't afford. The other shied away when it quickly became apparent how much I needed.

In my third week, I attended a panel about the twelve-step program. One of the panelists, a tall, blond, white woman, began reading from the Big Book of AA. "If we are painstaking about this phase of our development, we will be amazed. . . ." *Painstaking*: it was a word I hadn't heard before, but it struck me. "We are going to know a new freedom and a new happiness," she continued. "We will not regret the past nor wish to shut the door on it. No matter how far down the scale we have gone, we will see how our experience can benefit others. That feeling of uselessness and self-pity will disappear. . . . Our whole attitude and outlook upon life will change." It all sounded like a beautiful symphony. But could that really happen for a person like me, who'd been the places I'd been and done the things I'd done?

After, I mustered up the courage to approach the woman who'd read. "Those words landed on me so clearly," I told her. "But is it true?" She looked me in the eyes. "Yes," she replied. "Just keep coming back. Life shows up if you do." She said this with such conviction that I'd never have guessed she was there that night because she'd felt herself slipping. I nodded gratefully and was about to turn away, when she said, "If you want, I can give you my number. You can call me if you need to talk." She wrote *Leslie* and her phone number in my notebook. But she didn't stop there. "How about tomorrow I pick you up and take you to my meeting in the Pacific Palisades?"

The next evening, I waited at the door for Leslie to arrive. I'd never been to the Pacific Palisades, a neighborhood even more affluent than Santa Monica. "Look at the similarities of everyone," Leslie suggested on the way over. "Not the differences."

Lit by candlelight, the room was full of professional and polished-looking white women. To my surprise, they immediately embraced me. I wasn't used to being welcomed like that, but, unlike the world outside this room, it seemed no color or class barriers existed, and I'd come to find this true of every twelve-step meeting I ever attended.

We went around the room, the women telling how they'd hit rock bottom, losing things I'd never even dreamed of having. Their "bottom" was much different from mine, but when my mind tried to conjure up how these people couldn't possibly know my world, I heard Leslie's instructions and steered my thoughts in another direction. Though we didn't come from the same place, we were all seeking the same thing. All of us were there with the same deepest desire.

Leslie told her story: she was eight years sober. From Michigan, her parents were teachers. "They were good people. So good, there was no alcohol in the house," she described. "But at fourteen years old, I found alcohol, and it allowed me to be someone I didn't believe I could be without it. And then, drugs followed." She spoke of how she managed to function, putting herself through college and graduate school, all while under the influence. But as she was building her career as a set designer for movies, she knew she was going to lose it all if she didn't quit using. "For three years, I tried everything listed in the Big Book of AA and nothing worked," she said. "I was living in a dingy basement apartment in Hollywood, my very own alcoholic hovel, and I was trying to hide the state of my life. And then, a friend took me to a twelve-step meeting, and that changed everything." Squeezed into her story, she mentioned that she was currently in between jobs. What she didn't mention was that she was growing depressed and getting stuck in her thoughts. Her sponsor had advised her to be of service, to reach out to a newcomer, to say yes to an opportunity. And that was how she'd wound up on the panel where we'd met, and why, when I approached her, she took me in.

On the ride back, Leslie volunteered to be my sponsor, and I eagerly accepted. Years later, when I asked Leslie what compelled her to be so devoted to me, she said, "It was a little voice in me saying, if you don't take aggressive action, this woman is going to fall into the cracks. You were like a little bird who'd fallen out of the nest. I'd never heard that voice in my head about anyone else."

As my sponsor, Leslie was patient and kind, leading me to find the answer rather than trying to answer for me. That was exactly what I needed to build my confidence. Little by little, I allowed myself to open up to her. And she did the same. "It's a precious thing to have someone trust you to be their guide," she told me, though I thought that I was the lucky one. I got to soak up Leslie's wisdom, and to know there was someone out there who didn't need to care about me, but who did. Leslie insisted I was helping her, too, that watching me be willing and open, despite my fear and the many roadblocks, compelled her to quit feeling sorry for herself and to work on transforming her own life.

Every Friday night a huge AA meeting was held at St. Augustine's church in Santa Monica. Hundreds of people from the West Side community, mostly white, filled the room, and it had never occurred to me that so many people were dealing with addiction issues. Someone gave me the book *Twelve Steps and Twelve Traditions*, but Leslie stepped in and instructed me to bring 25 cents every week to pay for it. For a moment, I was put off, *Why doesn't Leslie just let me take the book?* But I did as I was told, and the instruction to bring a quarter every week became my first commitment.

After a few weeks Leslie gave me my next commitment: stand at the front door of the meeting as a greeter. Her own sponsor had asked the same of her, and for three years she stood at the door and greeted people. The simple act, she told me, had manifested positive energy. Putting myself front and center was the last thing I wanted to do, but I followed what I was told. I stood at the door, and I smiled, and I welcomed every single person who walked through. I shook hands, some people hugged me.

Then an interesting thing happened: I made friends. People invited me places. I went to the beach, I went to art shows. I didn't know anything about art, but there I was at a gallery.

Leslie and I went to meetings in the Palisades and in Beverly Hills and to retreats in Palos Verdes. Before my eyes, my life got better and better.

One day, I was doing my program assignments when Leslie saw my notebook. "Is that your handwriting?" she asked.

I nodded.

"It's beautiful." She didn't say anything more, but, years later, told me, "Seeing your handwriting was like glimpsing you as a child. You had obviously taken such effort and pride to make your writing so beautiful. It gave me insight into a person who cared, who had dreams."

As part of the program, I worked in the CLARE thrift store, sorting and hanging clothes. People in Santa Monica had some fine clothes they were donating, and I knew fine clothes from my earlier days when material belongings held a lot of importance to me. Christian Dior, Valentino, all the top labels made their way in, and a perk of my job was that I had first dibs. Thing was, the more together I began to feel on the inside, the less I felt the need to dress up the outside.

When Toni visited, she looked at me funny. "What?" I asked. Though she brushed it off, she later said she couldn't believe the transformation, that in front of her was a kinder, gentler, more thoughtful person than she could have imagined.

Every week, Melvin visited me, bringing snacks and always leaving me with spending money. He rooted me on, saying how proud he was of me. Sometimes his girlfriend, Veltra, joined him. She was a nurse, and as she talked about her work for a home health care agency I became inspired to go into nursing. One day, Melvin came to tell me that Beverly—who was still his legal wife, though they lived separately—had been arrested. With Beverly going back to prison, he was concerned about their daughters and asked if I'd move into his house to take care of the girls. Melvin had a big house in Baldwin

Hills, L.A.'s black Beverly Hills, and I'd be living in the lap of luxury, driving around in one of his fancy cars. But he was in what I called the "cash economy," and that scared me. I was indebted to Melvin, he saved my life by paying for this program, but as much as I wanted to reciprocate his kindness and support, I knew if I left CLARE and went back into that environment, I wouldn't make it. I looked in his eyes. "I can't."

"Okay," he said, and gave me a hug. He understood without me having to say anything more.

To keep moving forward, I knew I had to be honest. But there was something I was hiding, as though it would magically disappear, but I knew it wouldn't. Before I came to CLARE, I hadn't shown up for meetings with my parole officer—*absconded* was the official term. My next parole meeting was approaching. If I went, I'd be thrown back in prison for parole violations. If I didn't go, I'd be evading getting caught until the day they did catch me, and I'd be incarcerated just the same. I knew I couldn't keep hiding; I had to come forward with the truth, even though that truth could take from me everything I'd been working toward.

When I told Leslie I needed to see my parole officer and that I was scared, she said she'd drive me. I didn't let on that I'd been crying for a week, preparing myself to be taken from all this. I doubt Leslie had ever been to the parole building before, a place I'd been in and out of most months of my adult life. Each time I reported to orientation after being released from prison, a photo was snapped, and somewhere my file was like an album of me through the years, with more photos of me here than at my own mother's house. I'd been with the same parole officer—I'll call her Ms. B—the entire time. You'd think we'd have gotten to know each other pretty well by now; yet each time she saw my face for another orientation, she barely blinked. Robotically, she'd go through the motions: reading the conditions of parole, how I wasn't supposed to break any laws, how I was supposed to find a job, and supposed to find housing. She made it all sound like I'd simply walk out the door and, if I wanted it bad enough, all that would magically happen. Ms. B had a way of talking that made me feel put down, as if she needed to remind herself that, although she and I were both black women around the same age and from the same community, she was different. I likened her attitude to how many of the black prison wardens acted—different and apart from you.

Only with some years of distance would I come to understand that they, too, were caught in a system and a culture. Their culture was power. Ms. B had bought in to the idea that punishment was always the answer and was always deserved, that getting tough would solve everything. Most of the country had bought in to this, too. After all, it was the rhetoric being spewed from the White House and amplified by the media with slogans, crime initiatives, and praise for officials who were the toughest on crime. But along with all this came the demonization of urban communities, and the painting of black people as the criminals.

Ms. B was what the system fed on: someone content to be a gate-keeper. She filled out my paperwork, shrugged her shoulders when I relapsed, and collected her very decent paycheck. How many times had she asked me how I was doing?

"I'm not doing so well," I'd sometimes admit.

"You need to get it together," she'd say, then lead me into the bath-room to watch me pee in a cup. One time, I'd gained weight from inactivity and a lousy diet in prison and I couldn't afford new clothes. Ms. B laughed at me in the bathroom as I struggled to pull my pants over my hips.

Leslie and I sat in the parole building lobby, and I warned her it might be a while. I'd spent so much time waiting in that lobby and wondering how you were supposed to keep a job when every month you had to take half a day to get downtown and wait an hour. The parole office had all these expectations of you, but then treated you as though your time wasn't of value. When your officer required a home visit to verify your address, you could be waiting all day, and sometimes the officer would never show up—no call, nothing. But if *you* didn't show up, you had violated and were re-imprisoned.

When Ms. B finally appeared, I watched how, as she noticed Leslie, her face hardened. "Susan, follow me," she ordered, then pointed at Leslie. "*She* can't come in."

I followed Ms. B into her office, and as soon as the door closed, she scowled, "How dare you walk in here and bring that white woman with you."

I wanted to explain it wasn't like that, I hadn't brought Leslie to try to persuade my officer. "I'm sorry," I said. "She's my sponsor. I'm an alcoholic and an addict, and I'm in the program. I couldn't report to you like I was supposed to because I'd been under the influence. But I'm living at the recovery center now. I'm no longer under the grip of drugs and alcohol. It's my responsibility to be honest, and I came here to tell you the truth and turn myself in."

For the first time in all these years, the look of contempt faded from Ms. B's face. She studied me for a long moment.

"Go get your sponsor and bring her in here."

When I returned with Leslie, Ms. B asked her, "Are you going to be responsible for Susan?"

Leslie replied, "No."

Ms. B's head cocked; this wasn't the answer she expected. Leslie said, "Susan's going to be responsible for herself."

I saw the words sinking in as Ms. B looked from her to me. Finally, she said, "Susan, I will give you a pass. But this will be your only pass. You better get it right."

As Leslie drove us back to Santa Monica, we barely said a word. She was digesting the severity of what could have happened. I was still processing what *had* happened, knowing that parole officers weren't in the business of giving passes. Before me was an opening, a first glint, that, this time, it all could be real. This time, my life could change.

Leslie dropped me off, leaning over before I closed the car door. "Okay," she said. "Now we can really get to work."

After one hundred days at CLARE, I at last felt ready to leave. But

I needed a safe place to go. I called my daughter and asked if I could come live with her and Ellesse.

There was silence at the other end of the phone. Toni was thirty-one years old, and we hadn't lived together since she'd been fifteen. She said, "Let me get back to you."

She'd later tell me her first instinct was that I'd gone crazy. She thought she'd be the last person I'd ever ask. But then it occurred to her: maybe, this time, I was dead serious about keeping myself together.

She broached it with Ellesse. At eleven years old, Ellesse was surprisingly wise to the world, soaking up everything around her, just like her mother did as a little girl.

"We can't say no," Ellesse said. "Grandma's a different person now."

Though she thought it nice that Ellesse believed this, Toni wasn't so sure. She prayed about it. And then she took her jewelry out of the house, counted the VCRs, and prayed some more, before finally calling to tell me okay.

Neither Toni nor I knew what to expect. We'd never thrived as mother and child, could we survive together as adults? When I stepped into her townhouse in Lawndale, I sensed Toni had little faith in me. And why should she? I'd never before stayed clean and sober for very long. Toni often retreated to her room, her aloofness letting me know I was an imposition. But I responded by trying to respect her space, by taking whatever she was dishing out and agreeing, not arguing back.

I stayed in Ellesse's room, sharing her bunk beds. She put on a good face, not letting on that she complained to her mom how the sage I burned during my morning meditation was smelling up her room. I tried to be a support to my granddaughter. I told her she was smart, beautiful, and that I loved her. These weren't words I'd heard growing up, and I doubt I said them to Toni, though I wished I had. One day, Ellesse said to me, "Grandma, I know you did some bad things, but you're not a bad person." Her words, and the beauty of a child's lack of judgment, meant everything.

I kept myself busy attending AA meetings at 7 a.m., noon, and 7 p.m. "Why are you always going to meetings?" Ellesse asked, and I explained how important it was to be healthy emotionally and to have a good environment. But the other part was that I was terrified of being alone in the real world, and the meetings felt like a spiritual armor. I was making all new friends, had daily responsibilities, and even felt inspired to give back. I picked up a commitment to conduct a twelve-step program at juvenile hall, where, all those years ago, I'd been taken.

As I drove to Eastlake, the official name of juvie, I also had to pass Aliso Village, where I'd grown up. Now gated and decrepit, with weekly gang shootings, it was on the brink of being torn down, and I wondered where the current inhabitants would go. Flooded with memories, I stood before the girls at Eastlake and saw my younger self in their eyes. I told them I'd been where they were, and I hoped something I could say might make a difference. Week after week I returned to Eastlake, passing Aliso Village on the way. Feelings came up, and I pushed myself to acknowledge them and move on, determined not to become mired in thoughts of the past.

Each day, I put in complete effort. Ellesse noticed, and one day announced, "I'll never do drugs. I want to be successful, and I don't want to go to jail." I replied that she had an excellent plan.

Little by little, I saw hints that Toni was realizing that, this time, I wasn't just pretending to myself and everyone else that things would change. I truly never wanted to go back down that old road again.

17

A WAY OUT

*Being abused or neglected as a child increases the likeli-
hood of arrest as a juvenile by nearly 60 percent, and
the likelihood of adult violent crime by approximately
30 percent.*

I was moving along through the twelve-step program when Leslie
got a set-designing job that would take her to Germany for several
months. I'd been praying for her to get a job, but I didn't want it to
be all the way in Germany. I was in my Fourth Step Inventory, a step
where you go real deep, and I was terrified about Leslie being so far
away. Selfishly, I didn't want her to go. She assured me I'd be okay and
arranged to leave me in the hands of her friend Diane.

I knew Diane from meetings. A white woman in her sixties, Diane
worked as a technical writer and lived alone in Santa Monica. I liked
her, but for the Fifth Step, where you admit your wrongs to yourself,
to God, and to another person, I'd intended Leslie to be my other person. But Diane let me know it was okay to tell her things, that she'd
done things too.

I had written a description of events in my life where I'd caused
harm, and of the times where harm had come to me and what my
responsibility had been. There were a lot of times. As I read my list
to Diane, she listened quietly, without judgment. We continued on

together and, for Step Eight, I made a list of the people I had harmed. Again, mine was a long list. In addition to people I knew, I had many people I didn't know, including those whose identities I'd stolen. I even added the courts—I had stood in many courtrooms because I'd broken the law, and I was now holding myself accountable.

Diane looked at my list and thought for a moment. "Because it isn't possible for you to reach out to everyone, there is something called Living Amends. It's where you live a new way, with purpose, each day thinking about other people and helping people and bringing goodness into the world." This resonated so deeply with me. And, eventually, it would change the course of my life.

"You can't force anyone to believe in you," Leslie had told me before she left. "All you can do is show by your actions." I played her advice in my head as I went to Mama to make amends. I apologized for being defiant and disrespectful, and for the hurt and worry I'd caused. She listened, then nodded. I didn't have expectations that we'd forge a new bond, but I left feeling relief, and that was something. I had said what I needed to, and had done so without pointing the finger back. Some weeks later, when I went to visit Mama, she asked, "Susan, you don't mess with that white stuff anymore, do you?"

"No, I don't."

"Just don't ever do it again," she said. On my next visit to her, I was sitting on the couch when she called to me from another room. The way she said my name, her voice didn't have that edge, that resentment that usually cut into her tone. Maybe the difference was, in fact, the way I heard it. But it didn't matter if it was her or me, because in that moment I believed something had been restored in her mind and in her heart.

I went to Melvin next to make amends. Years ago he'd accidentally left a diamond-covered Baume et Mercier watch in my car, and I took it and sold it. After all this time, I finally admitted this to him, and said I was saving up to pay him back.

"I always knew you'd taken it," he replied.

I felt like a rat. Of all people, Melvin had always been there for me.

And I especially felt bad because he'd recently furnished me with a used car.

"Sue, you don't need to pay me back," he said. "Just keep doing what you're doing."

George was next, and we met for lunch at a Chinese restaurant. Openly, there was no sign of hard feelings but, just because he'd never expressed it, didn't mean there wasn't hurt lingering deep down.

"George, I am sorry for the times I lied and the times I didn't show up and the times I let you down. You spent over thirty years believing in me, despite the many disappointments. There's a lot of stuff in that thirty years. You let me know that in the pit of the pits, I was still a good person. When no one else had compassion for me, you did."

He teared up, something I'd never seen him do before. "I knew you'd be all right one day, Sue. And you're all right. It just took a little time." And then he changed the subject, and we ordered lunch. A decade later, when I was honored as a CNN Hero, I'd thank George Cameron on international TV for standing by me, his devotion proving that anybody can be that one person who believes in you.

I now needed to turn my attention to Toni. The twelve-step program instructed that you were not to make amends if it could harm someone. I visited the therapist I'd seen while at CLARE as I tried to work out if I should tell Toni she had been conceived from an act of violence.

"What are your motives for telling her?" the therapist asked.

"I don't know, but I don't want to hurt her," I said.

"Are you trying to get her sympathy?"

"I don't know. It feels really complicated."

We went back and forth before I came to the decision that Toni was an adult, and she was owed the truth. She deserved to know why I hadn't been there the way I should have been as a mother, how the torment within myself kept me at a distance. She deserved to know what she meant to me.

But getting Toni to sit down and talk one on one proved difficult.

She was always on the move, as though she didn't know how to be alone with me. One night, I cornered her.

"I really need to talk with you about something," I said.

She looked at me begrudgingly. "All right. I have to take my braids down, why don't you help me and we can talk." She sat as I stood over her, using a safety pin to undo braids as tiny as strands of yarn.

"I want to talk to you about something important," I began. But I didn't know where to begin. I'd been weaving this lie since before she was even born. When I'd been pregnant with her, I had a boyfriend, Robert Carter, who offered to give his last name, though he knew the baby wasn't his. I figured it would stop questions and give my baby legitimacy—really, I don't know what I figured; I was fourteen years old and scared and angry and hurt. After Toni was born, Robert went into the military, and I ran away from home, so contact was lost. Yet Toni grew up with his name, Carter, and the story my family and I told her: that I'd lost touch with her father because of the service.

I took a braid of her hair in my hand. "Toni, something happened a long time ago. December 24th of 1965. I was raped, and you were conceived. Robert Carter isn't your father. I don't know who is."

She barely moved. I continued, describing how I was going to give her up for adoption, but couldn't. "I knew I had to keep you."

I could see, behind her eyes, she was putting it all together.

"So that's why my birth certificate says father 'Unknown,'" she said, her voice surprisingly even.

Thirty-one years ago someone at Booth Memorial had written that. I hadn't realized Toni ever saw it, but of course she had. Not much escaped her. I searched her face for a sign of what she might be feeling, but she was emotionless.

"Are you okay?" I asked.

"I'm okay," she said.

"You sure?"

"What do you want me to say?"

"Shit? Damn? *Something*. You angry at hearing this? Mad? Sad?"

"Who else knew?" she asked.

"My mother, my brothers."

"All these years, and no one told me?" Abruptly, she stood up. "So, it's like, joke's on you, Jack?"

"Wait," I said. I wanted to talk more, wanted to hug her, and desperately did not want her to leave angry. But she stormed off.

For the next couple of days, she did her best to avoid me, and I knew enough to leave her alone.

When she was ready, she sent Ellesse off to the movies and came back to me.

"I've been thinking a lot," she began. "At first I thought, okay, so now I know this, but it really doesn't change anything. I'm not gonna wake up tomorrow any different. But I *did* wake up different. I had a weight lifted. For all these years, I wondered if Robert Carter was ever going to walk back into my life. I've been holding a grudge against him. Wondering who he was, wondering where he was. Where was he when I was little? Where was he when I had my high school graduation? I've fielded so many questions from Ellesse about when was she ever going to meet her grandfather. For so long I've been telling myself to go to the VA and try to look him up. I wanted to find him, and ask him, *Why?* But now, now I can stop being mad at him." Relief filled her face. "I can let Robert Carter off the hook."

Still lingering was the question of whether she could let me off the hook, too. She continued, "I've been asking myself, how do I forgive my mom for this? But the real question is, how do I not? I can release you for at last having the courage to tell me the truth. Those circumstances became my blessing. I can't say anything else, because that would mean I don't belong here, and that my daughter doesn't belong here. I'm not owning that negativity. All I can I do is process the positive."

It was then my turn to feel relief.

Toni and I continued talking, the most open and honest conversation we'd ever had. I told her I was so concerned about leaving her at my mother's house with all my brothers around. I asked if anything had ever happened, if she'd ever been molested or beaten. She assured me she hadn't.

"As much criminal activity as my uncles did," she said, "they were good to me and looked out for me, always telling me, 'Get to your homework.' They had me reading from their high school dictionary when I was still in elementary school."

I laughed, now understanding why Toni made Ellesse lug around a dictionary and read from it. I was so grateful she was never harmed in my mother's house, though I couldn't help but wonder how most of my brothers could have been so cruel to me, yet so kind to Toni. Then again, why did I think being "kind" meant not laying a hand on her? It wasn't just lack of abuse that made someone kind. The truth was, Toni had been their little tool. My brothers would give her piles of cash to hold for safekeeping. She'd tape thousands of dollars to her stomach, under her clothes, and wear it to school. She'd been in the house, afraid, when arrests had gone down, and she'd watched the police cart off my brothers.

Not that I'd been much better toward her. As the amends process opened the door for Toni and me to begin knowing each other anew, she recounted a day when she and I, along with some of my brothers, were in a motel room and the police burst in, shouting at us to get on the floor. Though only five years old, Toni knew the drill: don't say anything, don't cry, just step to the side. But this time, the police yelled at her to get down, too. Terrified, she started crying as she got down, the motel's musty shag carpeting in her face. As my brothers and I were arrested, Toni overheard the police deciding to drop her at MacLaren Hall.

In our neighborhood, you knew about MacLaren, the children's center where neglected or abused kids were taken. Toni crossed her arms and insisted she be taken to her grandmother's house. She recited the address on Highland Avenue, saying it over and over and over, until the police finally pulled up at my mother's if for no other reason than to get this stubborn kid out of the car before taking the rest of us to the station.

I didn't realize Toni remembered that day, she'd been so young. Or maybe it was that I hadn't wanted her to remember. As she recounted it with a surprising level of detail, shame rushed over me. I had subjected my young daughter to that? She'd seen me and her uncles treated that way? And, if she hadn't known my mother's address by heart, I could have lost her to the system. "I was scared and sad for a long time after that," Toni said. "That was the day that made me stop trusting the police."

It occurred to me she'd lost her trust in me long before.

18

FINDING PURPOSE

In large urban areas such as Los Angeles and San Fran-
cisco, up to half of those on parole are homeless.

Melvin's girlfriend, Veltra, who worked as a nurse for a home
health care company, came to me with a job opportunity. One
of her patients, an elderly woman, could no longer afford a nurse after
reaching the maximum that insurance coverage allowed for home
services. "Ms. Andrews just wants to live out the rest of her days in
her own home," Veltra explained. "But she needs some help getting
by. Would you want to care for her?"

Not only was I grateful for a job, but I eagerly approached this as
the beginning of my Living Amends: helping another person.

Ms. Andrews was a sweet lady, and I bathed her, did her laundry, cleaned the house, grocery shopped, cooked, and picked up
her prescriptions. Appalled at the cost of some of her medications,
I discussed with the pharmacist how I could petition the insurance
company for cheaper options—which I then did with success. When
Ms. Andrews had to trade her walker for a wheelchair, I ordered an
electric wheelchair so she could scoot around the house and ride
alongside me when we walked outdoors. She told her friends about
me, and they began calling me too. I saw firsthand how poorly most

seniors are treated—how lonely and scary it is to grow frail, and how ill equipped we are as a society to provide care. Each time I walked through the door, I watched Ms. Andrews's face fill with joy and relief. She soon asked if I could move in. Never had I experienced validation like this. Ms. Andrews not only needed me, but she wanted me there. I'd come into this job focused on my Living Amends, not anticipating that it was I who'd get so much in return. I had been given a sense of purpose.

After six months living at Toni's, I moved into Ms. Andrews's home. Though Toni never asked that I pay rent, I had offered, and when I left I gave her what I had. It was the first time I had been honorable with my agreements. Before that, drugs hadn't let me. Some time after I'd moved out, Toni was at work and opened a bottom drawer in her desk to find her jewelry. She'd forgotten she had hidden it there, in an unlocked drawer in her office—a place she'd once deemed safer than in her own home with her mother.

Ms. Andrews paid me $8 an hour, but couldn't afford to pay overnight hours, so we arranged that I would make up the difference by also working for some of her friends. My schedule was busy: in the morning, I made breakfast and got Ms. Andrews up and in her chair before leaving to care for another client. I returned for Ms. Andrews's lunch, then left again to care for a third client. During the night, I was on call for when Ms. Andrews needed me. She and her friends continued referring me, and before long, I was caring for seven clients, visiting different homes on alternating days of the week. I was accountable, and I was building self-esteem. People needed help, and it felt so good that I was someone who was able to help.

Soon, I had more clients than I could handle, so I brought on my friend, Mitzi. Short, with long, wavy hair and a bubbly personality, Mitzi also had a sharp mind. We knew each other from the neighborhood, and she had been my entrée into the world of forgery. We'd been in and out of prison together, and now we were both on the path to turn around our lives. As I divvied up the clients, I began to envision how I could build my own agency to care for seniors. I even came up with a name: Susan's Angels.

When I'd been at CLARE, an inspirational speaker, Dena Crowder, offered a class about finding your life's work. At the time, the idea of a *life's work* seemed frivolous—work was where you could get it; the job that paid the most was the job you took. But now, I was thinking differently. I enrolled myself in the class to learn how to make Susan's Angels a reality.

A third-generation Angeleno, Dena was glamorous and vibrant, wearing a cocktail dress the way others wear jeans. Though black, Dena seemed to defy ethnicity—you couldn't easily put her in a box by looking at her. The class went far deeper than mere job skills. As Dena had me plot out the steps to starting my home care agency, she brought up things I hadn't considered: licensing requirements, insurance coverage, incorporating as a business. Overwhelmed, I realized I wasn't yet ready for this path. But I soon came to appreciate having learned early on what I was up against, rather than finding out after having sunk a lot of time and hope and money. Still, I stuck with the class, even though the others who'd abandoned their business ideas stopped showing up. I was learning about seeing things through, that it wasn't about what you started, but what you finished. At the end of the session, Dena offered me a scholarship to continue on with her private class, called Essential Woman, which she taught from her home.

Dena lived in a beautiful old mansion in the Hancock Park area of Los Angeles. The other women in the class were highly successful—movie producers, doctors, attorneys. When they discussed their everyday issues and problems, it often sounded like a foreign language to me. But with this exposure, my mind expanded. Dena encouraged us to set not just daily goals but big life goals, and I felt myself moving from a place of impossible to *anything's possible*. After each class, I'd drive back to Ms. Andrews's house and my senses were heightened—colors looked brighter, food tasted better, I was aware of the fragrance of foliage and the sight of a beautiful moon. I was finding a connectedness within myself.

But as my world was awakening, Ms. Andrews's was narrowing. Her diabetes worsening, she had a wound on her leg that wouldn't heal. One day, I unwrapped the bandages to discover maggots infesting her leg. I called her doctor, who said to bring her to the hospital. "No matter what, Susan," Ms. Andrews said, "I don't want to lose my leg. I'd rather die than have my leg cut off." I felt helpless, wondering whether I could have done something earlier if only I'd had more skills.

There was a community college I often drove by, with a banner out front that promoted their nursing program. I stopped in to ask about applying. I was directed to a counselor and told him about the caregiving I'd been doing and how I wanted to advance my skills. He asked about my background, and I stumbled through some answers, which prompted him to ask if I'd ever had a felony conviction.

"Yes," I said.

He put down his pen. "You are not eligible to take nursing courses," he said. "You can't be licensed as an RN or certified as a home health aide with a criminal record."

I felt like the air was knocked out of me. I wanted to say, *But Ms. Andrews might lose her leg, and maybe I could have done something.* I asked, "Can I take nursing courses just to learn?"

"You should forget about being in health care," he said. "But you could take a computer course or a business class."

I walked out with a receipt for two night classes, Intro to Computers and Business Math. When I returned to Ms. Andrews's, I closed my bedroom door and cried. I'd naïvely thought that if I got my life together, things would manage to fall into place. Like Leslie said, *When you show up, life shows up.* I was showing up, more than I ever had, and feeling, for the first time, that I was putting something good into the world by helping people who were helpless. Only, it hadn't occurred to me that my path to advancement couldn't go much further, that I'd be denied the opportunity to learn, to gain skills, to better myself. Would Intro to Computers and Business Math take me someplace I wanted to go? Where would I find myself in ten, fifteen years? Were my dreams not meant to be bigger than minimum wage, Section 8 housing, and a Social Security check?

I began to read. In prison, I'd read thrillers and romance novels to escape. Now, I was reading to learn. I had collected books that passed through the CLARE thrift store, and I read *Diet for a New America* about how food choices affect your health, which opened my eyes to corporate greed and taking a stand for what you know is right. I thought about how the prison system was a part of corporate greed, too. I read *Alcoholics Anonymous Comes of Age*, about the two men who founded the movement in the 1950s. I read *The Road Less Traveled: A New Psychology of Love, Traditional Values, and Spiritual Growth*, which got me thinking about the importance of living a more principled and less materialistic life. I read *Feelings Buried Alive Never Die*, and as I did the exercises in the book, another layer about how I saw myself and the world was revealed.

The books prompted me to consider other ways to help people. I thought about women like myself, cycling in and out of prison. I thought about my Living Amends. An idea began to take shape. I envisioned a recovery home for women getting out of prison who, like me, needed a safe, sober place to live.

I talked about the idea with Mitzi, and then with Beverly, who was herself newly out of prison and trying to start over again. She and Melvin had gotten back together, and Beverly and I were trying to support each other, going to AA meetings together and holding each other accountable for staying clean. "What if," I posed, "we pooled our money to buy a house? I could live there, and we could take in ten other women whose contributions would cover the mortgage and expenses." Profits weren't a part of it—at least not for me. They eagerly supported the idea, and we began looking for a house.

As Ms. Andrews grew progressively worse, her son made plans to transfer her to a nursing home. In the nine months I'd been living with her, I'd managed to save $11,000. But more than that, I knew I had made a difference—and I now knew what it was like to feel valued.

Beverly and Mitzi and I found a house in Watts: a three-bedroom, two-bath bungalow, complete with a lovely yard and a lemon tree, on a residential street lined with trees shaped like gumdrops. Though Beverly had more money to put toward the down payment, I would be the one to live in the house with the women. Mitzi didn't have money, but she would cook for everyone—something I felt passionately about since that time I got stuck in the kitchen when I should've been focused on my recovery. There was one problem: none of us had the credit to get a mortgage.

We went to Melvin's son, Lamont, my nephew and Beverly's stepson, and asked if he would sign for us. Lamont had gone straight to work from high school, never having gotten caught up like the rest of us. He had a good job with the Department of Water and Power, was married, and had learned well from Melvin how to be a good father. Only years later, once I had signed for other people, did I fully understand to what lengths Lamont had gone to put up credit for us.

Beverly and I purchased five sets of bunk beds from Ikea, and I asked some men I knew from my twelve-step meeting if they'd help us assemble them. I wasn't used to asking for help, but I discovered that when you're trying to do something good, people want to help. My niece Tamara, Beverly's daughter, and I brainstormed a name to call the recovery home. In the Big Book of Alcoholics Anonymous a line is often repeated about finding a new way of life. We decided A New Way of Life was exactly right.

Ms. Andrews and I said a sad goodbye and, as she moved out of her home, I moved into mine. It was 1998, and I had no idea I was on the brink of something that would become larger and more meaningful than I could ever have imagined. My first night in the house in Watts, I stared up at the ceiling. I was alone, but the least lonely I'd ever felt.

Part II

MS. BURTON

19

A NEW WAY OF LIFE

At least 95 percent of state prisoners will be released back to their communities at some point.

Our first referral came from a friend I'd made in my local AA meeting, Stan Dowells. Stan worked for a social service agency then called the Homeless Outreach Program, HOP for short, which had been founded by a homeless Vietnam War veteran who was living out of a cardboard box in Skid Row.

Stan was, himself, formerly homeless. A black man from Chicago, he'd been arrested for a murder he didn't commit and was imprisoned for two years before being proven not guilty at trial and, at last, released. But in the years he'd been locked up, he lost everything—work, his home, his family. He left Chicago and wandered west, hoping for a new start. In Los Angeles, he found good jobs, in aerospace manufacturing and for the Sanitation Department, but drugs and alcohol had followed him west too. "I kept on picking up," he said. "One morning, I just stopped going to work." Eventually, Stan wound up homeless in Skid Row. One day, he was sitting on a box outside a rundown hotel on 5th and Main, when a baby fell from an upperstory window.

"I saw that poor baby and thought, why did it have to live down like this?" Stan said. "And then I looked at my own self, how hopeless

I felt. I thought, *you* don't have to live down like this. I started to cry. And that's when I surrendered. I didn't quite know at the time I was running up the white flag, but that's what I did." He hobbled to the nearby Weingart detox center where, he said, "They saw something in me that I didn't see in myself." A few days later, he picked up a newspaper and read that the baby had lived. "It shot a spark through me," he described. "I wanted to live. God works through people— God saved the baby, and that baby saved me. And that started me on this journey." Stan went on to earn a degree in drug and alcohol counseling. When I met him, he'd just been named director of HOP's Community Resource Center.

Stan's referral was a fifty-five-year-old woman named June. The only thing, he said, was that she needed transportation. I didn't realize most recovery homes wouldn't do pick-ups, and Stan seemed relieved when I said, "No problem." Though June had never been incarcerated, she had mental health issues and a history with drugs and alcohol. She also had a daughter who'd pay $500 a month for room and board. Quiet and sweet, June enjoyed doing art projects, and her daughter's reliable monthly payment helped bridge the gap while I worked on filling the rest of our beds.

Our second resident came by happenstance. Linda Washington hadn't been to prison either, but addiction was getting the best of her. She'd lost her apartment, knew her job as a nurse's assistant would be next, and even felt her own life was on the line if she didn't get help. A bed was supposed to be opening up at CLARE, but when Linda showed up, the space wasn't yet available. Told to come back in an hour, Linda went for a walk along the beach. When she returned, I happened to be in the lobby, dropping off a flyer for A New Way of Life. I overheard the conversation with Linda—the person who was supposed to leave still hadn't, and no other beds were available.

I handed Linda a flyer and said, "I have a bed."

At first she looked perplexed, then a smile spread across her face. "I'll never forget looking over and seeing you," Linda later told me.

"You didn't know me from diddly-squat. But your hand was extended to me."

One day, when I returned home from running errands, Mitzi popped her head out from the kitchen and said, "The court called you." The court? I didn't have a clue what the court would be calling about. But I knew from personal experience that a call from the court was never good. I ignored it, knowing if they wanted me bad enough I'd be hearing from them again. Five days later a woman named Wanda called. "When are you coming to get me?" she said.

"Where are you?" I asked.

"In county jail. The court released me to you. They tried calling you."

I couldn't believe it. The *court* was releasing someone to the care of A New Way of Life? All those times I went before the court, and now I was a person the court was relying on? Never before had I driven to the county jail with a smile. I had no idea how the court had learned about A New Way of Life, and I never questioned it. I chalked it up to a "God-shot"—what would be the first of many.

Wanda wasn't able to pay our suggested $500 a month toward rent and expenses. But I wasn't about to turn anyone away. Eventually, the county granted Wanda General Relief of $200 a month, which helped, but we still had half a dozen empty beds, and it was becoming clear that covering the mortgage and expenses was going to be much more challenging than we'd thought.

I went to the bus station around the corner from Skid Row. I didn't know who'd be getting off the bus, but I knew that, every day, women released from prison were on it. I showed up there because I wished someone had been there for me. Sometimes I saw a familiar face get off the bus, someone I'd served time with. "I have a house in South L.A.," I offered. "There's a bed if you'd like it. It's drug and alcohol free. You don't have to go back to the streets if you don't want to."

Some women looked wary and said no. But some said yes.

Still, we had empty beds, and bills to pay.

There was talk in the community that a social services agency called Walden House was looking to contract with local organizations. I knew about Walden House because, when I was in prison at California Rehabilitation Center, they were creating a comprehensive drug rehabilitation program for inmates—I'd tried to get in, but only a handful of slots existed, and I was shut out. Now, Walden House was looking to continue services for people after release from prison.

On a whim, Beverly and I flew to the Walden House headquarters in San Francisco. We didn't know where to go or who to talk with, so I stopped someone in the hall to ask who was in charge of contracting with community organizations. As I explained about A New Way of Life, a man stepped out of a nearby office. Little did I realize, I'd stopped to have this conversation in front of the door of the executive director, Demetrius Andreas. Having overheard everything, he said, on the spot, that he would authorize Walden House to issue A New Way of Life a contract for housing. Another God-shot.

Walden House funded $35 per woman per day, to be used for shelter, transportation, and meals. Also, through Walden House, I was granted special clearance to go into the prison system to give presentations about A New Way of Life and recruit future clients.

Prison was the last place I ever wanted to return to. But there I was, in street clothes, walking into the California Institution for Women, knowing I'd be able to walk out. As I passed through the doors into the yard, I felt a rush of emotion. I was here with purpose, in possession of my dignity, my individuality, my own power—all the things that had been stripped from me the last time I stood in this yard. Thoughts of Harriet Tubman and Sojourner Truth filled my head. In some small way, I hoped my presence and my voice could offer women a way out of the cycle, could help them find their own lasting freedom.

The first woman I saw—she was tough to miss—was Cherelle, nicknamed Six-Two, for her height. We'd known each other from the neighborhood, long before prison. "Girl, I got a house now," I called to her. "And I'll have a bed for you when you get out."

Her face turned sad. "I'm a lifer," she said. She'd been involved in a drug transaction that went very bad, and someone was killed. I knew how easily that could have been me. How easily I could've ended up just like Six-Two. Or wound up dead. I thought of my Living Amends and made a commitment to myself to keep coming back here to provide what support I could to these women.

One of the guards came up to me. "I remember you," he said.

"I remember you, too," I said. No longer having to keep my head down or my mouth shut, I continued, "I remember how you tore up my locker. For no reason."

His eyes narrowed. "It must have been good for you," he replied. "Because you didn't come back."

I wanted to get into it, to talk about the abuse of power, but I was here for a different reason. I gave him a look that said, *You still don't get it*, and walked on.

Walden House's drug rehabilitation program, called Forever Free, was held in a trailer. I spoke to the class about my journey and about A New Way of Life, and then asked each person what she wanted to do with her life. I could see the pain all over the women's faces and the fear in their eyes. I could hear their bewilderment about what might be in store for them on the outside. Many said they could only dream of walking back in here to help as I was.

I'd served time with one woman there, Mary. She had the voice of an angel and I got chills just remembering how I'd lie in my bunk at night listening to her sing "Amazing Grace." I asked when she was getting out.

"I got caught stealing two sweatsuits, and struck out," she said, referring to the Three Strikes sentencing law. "I'm a lifer now. I'm not coming home." Nearly half the states in the nation had some type of three-strikes law, though, in California, the name was a misnomer because it also hit "two-strikers," automatically doubling the sentence on a second offense, regardless of the crime. While curbing repeat offenders had been the goal, the result was that prisons were filled with people serving inordinate sentences for low-level offenses. Mary was doing twenty years to life for petty theft. Rather than striking out, I had lucked out because the law wasn't enacted in California until 1994. It was only timing—not lack of offenses—that had me on this side.

At the end of the day, leaving the prison grounds, getting in my car, and heading home felt surreal. The full circle of my life was drawn so completely it hardly seemed possible.

Over the following weeks and months, when many of the women I'd spoken with were released, they called me. I'd drive up to the prison gates and holler to the gun tower the name and number of the person I was picking up. "She'll be right out," they shouted back, which meant I'd be waiting at least an hour.

First thing, when a woman got in my car, I asked if she was hungry. We often stopped at McDonald's on the drive to A New Way of Life. I listened if she wanted to talk, but I never asked what she'd done. She had paid her debt; I was only interested in what she wanted to do from here out.

After several months, all ten beds in the house were at last filled. I slept on a cot in the dining room, next to the fax machine. Within the walls of A New of Life, a beautiful community of women helping and supporting each other was blossoming. Together, we were healing. Never again would I feel like it was just me; it was *us*. I watched bonds form, like a family; not without ups and downs, but with support you could count on in a way you couldn't with most people.

I'd spent much of my life so caught up in my own head I wasn't able to care about anyone else. But I remember the moment that began to change: it happened at CLARE, while I listened to a man sharing his story, and all his feelings jumped out at me. Concerned, I found Jan, a counselor, and told her, "I'm feeling so deeply what this man is talking about. I'm feeling his pain, and feeling his joy." Jan looked at me knowingly. "Susan, that's what connecting with your feelings is about." This was the first time I really understood empathy.

Now, it was my goal to live with unwavering empathy for the women at A New Way of Life. I began to view this as my talent: I could connect with people and feel something. I could see the hope and possibilities in everyone. My job now was to value each and every woman, to cast aside my doubt and to believe in them—and to teach them to cast aside their own doubt and to hold themselves and others to a standard of accountability, integrity, and respect.

Toni and Ellesse came by the house, and, at the end of their visit, Ellesse looked at me and I could see the pride in her eyes. I picked up Mama and brought her to visit the house. She took a good look around. "I like these women," she said. "They're liberated."

I set a schedule for A New Way of Life: 8 a.m., we did a morning meditation together to start each day with positivity and reflection, and to set a personal goal. Then, the women made their own breakfast and completed their assigned household chores. After that, we went our separate ways for the day. I chauffeured women to jobs or to look for a job, to mandated parenting classes, to report to their parole officer, to twelve-step meetings, to social worker appointments, and to courtrooms as they tried to regain custody of their children.

In the evening, Mitzi cooked dinner, and we all ate together, going around the table to hear about each other's day. Maybe, to some, having a cook seemed excessive. But I believed coming home to a meal set a warm foundation for the household and eliminated a worry many of us knew all too well: that we might go to bed hungry.

On weekends we did errands together, like grocery shopping. Some women were eligible for food stamps, though it didn't matter who was or wasn't—everyone contributed what she could. Somehow, we always managed to cobble together enough to cover our bills. We were just getting by, but I wasn't looking for anything beyond getting by.

As the months passed, I watched with pride as women made enough strides to begin to transition out of the house. Seeing them go on their own, into their own apartments, some reunited with their children, was victorious. Often they were scared, crying as we hugged goodbye. "Just because you're leaving," I said, "doesn't mean we aren't still here for you." But I knew their fear—in the house there was a cushion of stability, the lights would be on, food would be there. Leaving meant the responsibility was now all on them.

To continue filling the beds as they became available, the women and I wrote to imprisoned women we knew who were approaching the end of their sentences. Our letters said: If you need a safe, sober, women-only environment, call A New Way of Life.

The phone rang. "I got your letter. You said to call."

"Where are you?"

Their voices trembled. "I just got off the bus."

I'd say, "I'll be right there."

As word about A New Way of Life spread, prisoners began writing us. When I was behind bars, I'd written letters to treatment programs asking for help, but I never got any response. Which is why I personally answered every letter we received, even when letters began arriving daily.

"Dear Ms. Burton," they'd write. *Ms. Burton.* It was a title that conveyed a level of respect. It was also, to me, my mother. But here I was, becoming a kind of surrogate mother to others in need—and, in a way, making amends for those years I wasn't the kind of mother my own children deserved.

"I kept on, kept on, kept on," Dana said when she phoned A New Way of Life from the street. "I'm tired, and I don't want to wind up back in jail. I need a place to go, but I don't have any money."

I told her to come over.

"Thank you, Jesus," she exhaled.

Dana thrived at the house. She was able to reunite with her children and received permission to spend weekends together at A New Way of Life. I took Dana with me to the Cocaine Anonymous Convention in Palm Springs. "I've never been anywhere," Dana said when we arrived at the hotel. She even mustered the courage to stand before a large group and speak about her experiences. Because of Dana, I started taking all the women to the annual Cocaine Anonymous Convention to meet people and see a world of recovery. Often, this was the first time the women had gone on a trip, and I instructed them to pack for a formal dinner, a swimming pool, and a nice hotel—though they kept calling it a motel.

When Dana began experiencing health symptoms, her skin itched horribly and she always felt like she needed to use the bathroom, I pestered her. "You going to get to the doctor?" For weeks I bothered her. "You going to get out of here tomorrow and go to the doctor? You going to get up in the morning and make an appointment with the doctor?" Finally, she went and was diagnosed as severely diabetic. "I don't want to think, Ms. Burton, if you hadn't seen me out there to the doctor," Dana said, her head shaking with gratitude.

By the time Dana had been in the house for six months, her health had improved and she was in the process of gaining full custody of her children. But her subsidized housing—which was so difficult to get when you had a criminal record—hadn't yet come through. She came to me, asking if she could stay longer.

Initially, Beverly, Mitzi, and I had intended A New Way of Life to be active, with each woman staying up to six months, at which point she'd ideally have enough elements in place to transition out on her own. But Dana risked losing her children if she didn't have a permanent address, and she'd worked too hard to have everything jeopardized, so, of course, I told her she could stay.

Beverly saw things differently. She insisted that Dana leave, that a maximum of six months was what we'd decided at the beginning. But, in the beginning, we didn't know what we were doing, and we thought we needed to impose some type of structure. Now, things were real. These were real people, real lives. Enforcing arbitrary rules that disregarded an individual's needs would make us no better than the senseless system we'd all been trapped in and were still trying to escape. But Beverly held firm against me.

Though she tried to hide it, I knew Beverly had become addicted to Vicodin. I was deeply sad and concerned about her. I was also disappointed. We'd been in this together, and I felt hurt and let down. It was clear Beverly wasn't ready to confront things, and I knew, from

being on the other side, how quickly entangled and dangerous inter-
fering could become. My only choice was to distance myself. Though
my pulling away also succeeded in angering her.

The local news was on TV one day when a picture of Beverly
appeared on the screen. She was on the run after having robbed a
jewelry store in Redondo Beach. Horrified, I raced through the house
cutting off the TVs, hoping none of the women had been watching.

Not long after, Beverly showed up to the house, demanding that
Dana had to be out.

"If you want to get a place and put people out, go get a place," I said.
"But I'm here to help people."

At that, Beverly pushed me. I was holding a mug of coffee, and it
spilled everywhere. There's a line in the Big Book of Alcoholics Anonymous that came to me, "Half measures availed us nothing. We stood
at the turning point." Beverly was family, but Dana was a woman who
needed help. I saw Dana, cowering in the corner, feeling awful that
she was the cause of such friction. But the decision to let Dana stay
or not was the difference between Dana's life falling apart or coming
together. This was a turning point. I took the turn. I pushed Beverly
back.

She punched. I punched back. One of the women called the police.
With the threat of the cops arriving, Beverly ran.

I was shaken, but relieved. I didn't see or talk to Beverly until eight
months later, when she sent a message asking me to appear in court
on her behalf. She was being prosecuted for grand theft. I showed up
to her trial, and I made a statement to the judge about how difficult
life experiences can be and about the opportunity to give someone a
chance to recover. But, hooked on Vicodin, Beverly had committed a
string of thefts. The judge commented that she'd been apprehended
at the high-end store Barney's. "I can't afford to shop there," he said.
Beverly was sentenced to eight years.

Dana stayed on at A New Way of Life; when she left she had her
housing and full custody of her kids. She started her own cleaning
service, and remained sober, productive, and happy.

20

THE WALL OF NO

*Sixty-five million Americans with a criminal record face
a total of 45,000 collateral consequences that restrict
everything from employment, professional licensing, child
custody rights, housing, student aid, voting, and even the
ability to visit an incarcerated loved one. Many of these
restrictions are permanent, forever preventing those who've
already served their time from reaching their potential in
the workforce, as parents, and as productive citizens.*

*"The result is that these collateral consequences become a
life sentence harsher than whatever sentence a court actually imposed upon conviction." —American Bar Association president William C. Hubbard*

The more women who came through A New Way of Life, the
more I saw the same story played out again and again. I watched
women being excluded from public housing; I watched them being
denied private housing, unable to rent an apartment when faced with
the box indicating a felony conviction. I waded with them through
the paperwork and bureaucracy of the L.A. County Department of
Children and Family Services as they tried to reunite with their kids.
I saw them, morning after morning, iron their sole business outfit,

and then I dropped them off and picked them up from job interview after job interview, the outcome of rejection almost always the same, despite their capabilities. Capabilities didn't matter; neither did skills, past experience, or aptitude. The sum of everything else was blotted out by a criminal conviction.

No surprise, the parole office wasn't giving people any type of real assistance. Out of desperation, some women tried to get Social Security disability benefits, pointing to how they'd been heavily medicated in prison so they must have a mental health issue, right? To me, this was no solution. These were people with abilities. To have them strung along on a meager payout was basically relegating them to a life of poverty and uselessness. Naïvely, I had thought that if I could provide shelter and a nurturing environment, everything else would fall into place. But many days it felt like A New Way of Life was base camp at Mt. Everest.

For so many years, I, too, had come up against these seemingly insurmountable barriers. But I'd done a good job of convincing myself that my failing was personal, that it was all on my shoulders. Now, a larger picture was emerging: if you got locked up, you get locked out. It didn't matter that you'd paid your debt to society. Nor did it matter how hard you were trying to get your life back together. A criminal history was like a credit card with interest—so what if you paid off the balance, the interest still kept accruing. And accruing and accruing and accruing.

Yet I remained determined. All over the city, I drove women looking for jobs, or tracking copies of their birth certificates, or filing for Social Security cards. With all this running around, gas and upkeep on my old Ford Escort was expensive, and I soon began doling out bus fare. Which led to a bigger issue: I was running out of money.

When Stan from HOP told me that the First African Methodist Episcopal Church in South Central gave bus tokens, I showed up there right away. But before issuing me tokens, they asked if A New Way of Life was a 501c3.

I paused. "What's a 501c3?"

They explained it was a nonprofit organization, and that they could only issue bus tokens to nonprofits.

I went home and began making phone calls to figure out how to become a nonprofit. Eventually, I found my way to Mr. Malone, who worked with a religious-based recovery home in South L.A. If Mr. Malone had a job title, it was lost on me back then—to me, we were all like-minded people struggling to improve the community. He knew how to become a 501c3, and he graciously helped me through the application process so that I could file without having to pay out.

In record time, state nonprofit status for A New Way of Life was approved. But all that meant, really, was I then had to fumble through the federal filings. Back and forth I went with the IRS until, finally, my application was ready to be submitted. And then, I waited.

During this time, I was invited to speak at CLARE's annual fund-raising dinner. I had no idea I'd be speaking to a roomful of some of the biggest power players in Los Angeles. I stood at the podium, looking out over tables of people dressed in the most beautiful clothes. But I was wearing fine clothes too—fine clothes from the CLARE thrift store. I probably had on the discarded dress of somebody sitting in the audience.

I spoke about my past, comparing what life had been like to what my life was now. I expressed gratitude for the help I received. "If there'd been a CLARE in my community," I said, "I could have found intervention and a different outcome sooner." I described my dream of creating a safe place for women getting out of prison, and the creation of A New Way of Life. And I explained how my current goal was to obtain nonprofit status so we could get bus fare for the women's commutes to their jobs.

When I was done, chairs screeched against the floor as people rose to their feet. Never before had I experienced anything like this. *A standing ovation? For me?* In that moment, I flashed back to when I'd first walked through the doors at CLARE, the condition I was in— pain to the point of incapacitation, despair, sorrow, grief, addiction— and how restoration seemed all but impossible. At once, the image seemed both alarmingly stark and like an old, brittle photograph. It was me, and it wasn't. It was where I'd been, and why I was here. I put the lid on the shoebox in my mind. And returned to the beauty of the moment before me.

After dinner, a silver-haired man approached me. I didn't know who he was, but he had a commanding presence. He said he wanted to learn more about A New Way of Life and that he'd be in touch. A few days later, I received a call from the office of Theodore Forstmann, instructing me to make a list of things A New Way of Life needed. I still didn't know anything about this man, but I knew we needed a lot of things. We needed cleaning items and toilet paper and, of course, bus tokens. When Leslie saw the list I was making, she looked me square in the face.

"Susan, ask for what you need."

"We need toilet paper and bus fare," I said.

"You need a washer and dryer," Leslie countered. "You need a van to drive the women around."

"I can't ask for things like that," I balked. "I don't even know this man." And wasn't that the truth—I had no idea Mr. Forstmann was a billionaire, with companies like Gulfstream and Dr Pepper to his name.

"Susan, you need to think big," Leslie said. "He can always say no." Following her advice, I took toilet paper off the list and replaced it with a van.

Even though we didn't have 501c3 status yet, Mr. Forstmann bought us that van.

Ever since I'd conducted the twelve-step panels in juvenile hall, I wanted to continue working with young people, and Mr. Forstmann provided funding for me to work with Youth Opportunities Unlimited, a high school in South L.A. for at-risk kids. I talked with the students about my own path, describing how, if I'd known at their age what I knew now, I'd have done a lot of things differently, I'd have planned for my life. I gave each student a leather-bound daily planner, plus a T-shirt that said, "If you fail to plan, you plan to fail." I watched them excitedly write in their planners, and I hoped, in some small way, that I was helping to break the school-to-prison pipeline.

On the morning of Christmas Eve, 2000, I went to the mailbox and there was the certificate of our federal nonprofit status. I mailed Mr. Forstmann a copy, and he mailed back a $10,000 check with a note that said, "Keep up the good work." His encouragement meant as much if not more than the money. For the next decade, until his death from a brain tumor, Mr. Forstmann quietly and steadily supported us.

I was still on parole when I returned for my monthly check-in with Ms. B and handed her a flyer about my nonprofit organization. She looked intrigued. But our meeting went as it typically did: she filled out paperwork, I peed in a cup, she watched, I left. In 2001, I showed up for my check-in and Ms. B handed me a discharge card. I hadn't known to expect it—your date of discharge depended on the slow wheels of government, so there was no predicting the week, the month, sometimes even the year. When I left the parole building that day, it was the first time in two decades that I was no longer in the clutches of the U.S. justice system.

One day, Ms. B dropped by the house. The only other time I'd seen her outside the parole office was when, decades earlier, she'd visited my mother's house to verify I was living at the address I'd provided. We sat in the living room. I still referred to her as *Ms.*, though I hoped she'd tell me to call her by her first name, a gesture acknowledging that the past was finally behind us and we were now peers. But that didn't happen.

She looked around, noticing the women coming and going. I could tell she was impressed, but she soon changed the topic to complaining how she wanted to retire but still had kids in college. I thought about our women's kids, most in the custody of relatives or relegated to foster care; some, permanently lost, having been adopted out. Each time one of our women attended a custody hearing or spoke on the phone with the children she couldn't be with, my heart broke. I wondered if Ms. B thought about any of this, if she ever stopped to consider how far the inefficient and punitive parole system had strayed from the original intent of successfully reintegrating people back into society. Did she, I wondered, ever allow herself to feel others' pain? Or would that make it too difficult to do her job?

To my surprise, Ms. B referred a few women to A New Way of Life. Some years later, I would see her again. I was at an Erykah Badu concert and the odor of weed was wafting from the group in front of me. I looked over, and there was Ms. B. I watched her notice me. Then I wondered how many people she'd sent back to prison for marijuana offenses. After the lights came up, she turned to me and said, "Don't mention this."

21

WHO'S PROFITING FROM
OUR PAIN?

*More than twenty new prisons opened in California from
the mid-1980s through the mid-2000s—compared to a
total of twelve new prisons from 1852 to 1984.*

It began when I saw a flyer for a group called the Community Coalition, looking to organize leaders of nonprofits in South L.A. The year was 1999. I showed up to their meeting—and my life's path was changed forever.

The Community Coalition was founded in the 1980s when Karen Bass, then an emergency room physician's assistant—she'd go on to be elected to California's state legislature, followed by the U.S. House of Representatives—gathered in a living room with a group of action-oriented residents of South L.A. Alarmed by the carnage of the crack epidemic and the increasingly violent response of law enforcement, the coalition organized residents who felt helpless and in despair to work together to build up and strengthen the community.

Now, more than a decade later, I sat in a meeting room hearing that, sadly, not much had improved. Incarceration rates in our community had increased astronomically, especially for women, and especially for poor black women. It lit me up knowing I was in those statistics. I should have been an activist in that living room with Karen Bass, but instead I'd been caught in the vicious cycle.

Leading the meeting was Saúl Sarabia, a twenty-nine-year-old recent graduate of UCLA School of Law. It was as though Saúl was speaking directly to me. He discussed the barriers and lack of services for people coming home from prison, a topic, of course, that I knew all too well. But then he added something I'd never heard anyone talk about before: that the barriers were by design.

"In this country, there's a public policy commitment to incarceration," Saúl said, explaining how those in charge had made a conscious decision to treat addiction and mental illness not as the public health problems that they were, but as criminal justice problems. "What does it mean that the number-one funder for political campaigns in our state is the California Correctional Peace Officers Association, which is the prison guards' union? It means that law enforcement organizations are deciding who will be our governors and our state senators, who in turn write laws to expand prisons. What does it mean that recidivism rates are at an all-time high? It means that, rather than create more mental health treatment centers and hospital beds, there's an incentive to create more prisons and prison beds. The State of California profits from the expansion of incarceration. It benefits from repeat customers. Our state's coffers are being bankrupted to create the most well-funded prison system in the world."

My eyes were popping. I knew the phrase the forest for the trees, but now I got it. Could it be that I'd been barking up a single tree, when all around me a wildfire was raging?

Saúl explained that the first goal was to expand the Community Coalition's Prevention Network, a collaboration between nonprofits and community residents fighting for a stronger social services safety net. "We need to utilize the power of those who are directly affected, and give community leaders and the people in South L.A. a voice," he said. "Welfare recipients fighting the injustices and inefficiencies of welfare reform, young people working to improve their schools, neighborhood residents fighting to shut down liquor stores that profit off addiction by selling drug paraphernalia, ex-offenders advocating for sentencing reform. We're also specifically committed to building black-brown unity."

I was so inspired I could barely sit still. After the meeting, I approached Saúl and told him about A New Way of Life.

"Are you a 501c3?" he asked.

At that point, I was still waiting for the approval to come through.

"Not yet," I said, worried he might turn me away.

But he didn't. He said that if I was interested in becoming a member of the Prevention Network he would need to do a personal visit to my organization, agency, or home. In my case, A New Way of Life was all three.

When Saúl arrived, I gave him the grand tour of A New Way of Life: the women's rooms, each bunk bed made up pristinely; the dining room that doubled as my bedroom and office; and the kitchen, where I introduced him to Mitzi, who was cooking the evening's dinner.

"How do you recruit residents?" he asked.

I explained how I'd visit prisons, that we wrote letters to women in prison, and that I'd go meet the bus in Skid Row.

"Wow, Susan, that's such a direct and obviously effective approach," he said, then gave me a warm smile. "It's also an act of love."

Before Saúl came to the Community Coalition, he was doing welfare case management in the basement of a church in San Pedro, California, trying to help eligible families actually receive their welfare benefits and medical coverage. In 1996, President Bill Clinton had signed the Personal Responsibility and Work Opportunity Reconciliation Act—otherwise known as welfare reform—but it was riddled with barriers, and as Saúl saw family after family come through that church basement, he grew increasingly frustrated. He used his own sick days to attend L.A. County Board of Supervisors' meetings to advocate for sorely needed welfare policy changes. But change wasn't happening.

When Saúl went to his boss to discuss how the group could advocate for policy changes, she told him, "We don't do organizing here, that's left to the flamethrowers." He was shocked that his boss didn't realize that the only reason they were doing welfare case management was because of the original flamethrowers, who fought for the strong safety net for Americans. He soon left to work at the Community Coalition.

As we sat in the living room of A New Way of Life, Saúl described how he envisioned starting an Ex-Offender Task Force, equipping people like me to lead action campaigns and engage in policy advocacy. I'd never heard anything like this—most everyone who hadn't been incarcerated thought *ex-con* was a dirty word, and I was used to being perceived as someone lacking. This was in the years before we had the language for what would come to be known as *re-entry*. Yet here was Saúl, saying formerly incarcerated people should be viewed as a population with something to offer, whose collective voice deserved to be cultivated, valued, heard. But, he cautioned, it was a stigmatized issue, and most in the political arena wouldn't give the time of day to a group with no political presence. Especially because this was also a group with restricted voting rights. Most states banned the right to vote until your sentence plus parole or probation was complete.

"There's this book I read as a child," Saúl said. "It was called *The Little Red Hen*, where a hen finds a grain of wheat and goes around asking all the other farm animals to help make it into bread. But no one will help. Finally, when the hen manages all on her own to make the bread, everyone who wouldn't help shows up to eat the bread. This is not unlike what I see when I advocate for the needs and rights of people who've been incarcerated. Even within organizations created to defend civil rights, the responses I often get are, 'There are so many needs in black and brown communities, we don't have the resources to advocate for the criminal element.' And yet, everyone wants safer communities and low unemployment. People don't realize these things go hand in hand. I believe that when formerly incarcerated people flex their political muscle, we will change the skeptics' hearts and minds. We will also possess the power to impact laws and policy. People lead, politicians follow."

Then Saúl took a deep breath. "Susan, I'd love for you to be part of the Prevention Network and the Ex-Offender Task Force." I nodded eagerly, but he gave me a hesitant look.

"Since we're dedicated to forming an independent organization that's not solely dependent on foundations for support," he continued, "we're asking residents to become dues-paying members." Some years later, Saúl admitted I was his first ask—and that he'd been so nervous and conflicted about asking for money, especially from a small organization like mine. But I thought it an honor to be asked to take ownership and to be invested in this movement as a card-carrying member. I got my checkbook and joined both as an organizational member and an individual member.

Though Saúl wasn't from South L.A., our lives weren't as far apart as I'd otherwise have thought. He grew up poor in Cypress Park in northeast L.A., a high-crime area of predominantly Latino and Chinese immigrants. When he was fifteen, his family moved to Baldwin Park in the suburban San Gabriel Valley, which wasn't as rough—the working poor versus abject poverty was how he described it—but, still, a lack of decent wages coupled with the availability of the underground drug economy made for limited choices. "Many of my family members were drawn into the web," he told me.

"One relative, who wasn't doing or selling drugs, still wound up arrested after her boyfriend had been stashing drugs in the walls of her apartment, without her knowing," he described. A law student at the time, Saúl was in Washington, D.C., doing a summer clerkship and didn't know what was happening in his family until it was too late. "A lawyer told her that if she agreed to a plea bargain, she'd only be sentenced to a year," Saúl said. "The bigger problem was that, because she'd been born in Mexico, she only had a green card. When she accepted that guilty plea, it transformed her from a 'bystander' into an 'aggravated felon,' a conviction that could get her deported." He detailed how, in 1996, President Clinton passed what was commonly known as immigration reform, broadening the criteria for deportation and solidifying it as a major collateral consequence of the War on Drugs for legal immigrants. Even misdemeanor drug offenses could lead to deportation.

"Here I'd been thinking the War on Drugs was really a war on black people and on poor people," I said. "Now I've got to add a war on immigrants to this list."

Several of Saúl's family members had been incarcerated or deported, or both. The region his family hailed from in Mexico was controlled by some of the most powerful drug cartels and, from the outside, it seemed like his extended Mexican family was part of a vicious cycle destroying the lives of so many. "But people in that part of the world aren't in the drug trade by choice," Saúl described. "They are poor peasants living in the mountains. What are they supposed to do? Tell the cartels they want to grow coffee beans instead of drug crops? Not everyone is allowed to make such decisions about their lives."

I knew what he was talking about: the chasm between making a decision and winding up someplace. The truth was, your decisions hardly mattered if none of your options were any good to begin with. Like Saúl's family: be involved in the drug economy or starve to death? Like the women I knew: stay with an abusive spouse who at least provided for the family, or take your children onto the street? What kinds of decisions were these?

The youngest of five, Saúl had been the only one in his family to finish high school. He'd never met a lawyer when he set his sights on law school, but he knew there was power there, that a law degree could be a tool for change. When he graduated UCLA Law, he decided to work in communities like his, where most people hadn't interacted with lawyers before—or, if they had, they'd come away feeling exploited.

"Living in a household ravaged by drugs," Saúl said, "I wasn't supposed to end up here, an attorney, a community organizer. I was supposed to be in a gang, or in prison, or dead. We should be participating in making the laws that are about us. We, the people who aren't supposed to be here."

As part of the Prevention Network, Saúl began a study group, populated with social services providers from around the community. Within that group, I found people with a vision broader than just themselves. Now, I was standing with them.

"Any successful movement has a combination of social services and organizing," Saúl taught us. "But where do we start? How do we find the people who should be here with us? How do we create a plan to go from fifteen to five hundred to five thousand of us? There's a science to building community power. You build a base with outreach and recruitment, then you sustain that base by developing leadership skills from within."

Saúl taught us how to analyze community conditions and services and ask, "Who's profiting from this?" He taught us to know our audience. "Everything I'm sharing with you, I also lived through," he said. "It's scary going out there and recruiting. It's scary being told no over and over, but you get good at not taking it personally."

I soaked up every bit. And by doing that, I also began to develop a level of forgiveness for myself. All this time I'd lived with great sadness and disappointment over what I'd thought was my own inability to pull myself up for all those years. Only now did I see all the ways these barriers had affected me, pushing me back into the prison system. I'd been considered a throwaway. And this oppression caused me to become depressed and aggressive, ruthlessly seeking what I thought I needed. The more my understanding of these social and political structures deepened, the more I was able to release myself.

So many people in communities like mine were caught in the same vicious cycle of desperation and punishment. Only to be subjected to continued punishment and exclusion even after paying their debt to society. Able people wanting to work who were shut out from jobs—that shouldn't be the norm. Parents who served their time, but still lost their children even when their parenting had never been in question—that shouldn't be the norm. Saúl had sparked something deep and vital in me. I needed to raise my voice. We all deserved an opportunity—not just for a second chance, but for a first chance.

I accompanied Saúl to meetings, to service providers, to church groups, to local and state government hearings. "Who's working for brown and black people who've made mistakes?" he'd say. And soon, I was echoing him. "Where's the elected official who's going to embrace this issue?" "Who's working for us, the throwaways?"

Back in our study group, Saúl spoke about the generations of children left behind because of the War on Drugs, and the lack of assistance for relatives raising children when one or both parents have been incarcerated. "Children's group homes and private foster agencies receive thousands more dollars in monthly funds per child than does a relative who steps up to care for a child," he said. "The truth is, most relatives receive no funding at all, even though, by law, they should."

He explained how a 1979 U.S. Supreme Court case ruled that child welfare agencies must provide the same compensation for relatives approved to care for a child as for unrelated foster parents. "But what's really happening," he continued, "is that relatives get strong-armed by the system. Most people are so scared, so they end up saying, 'I don't want money, I just want to take care of these kids.' I saw it happen in my own family. When my uncle died, my mother wanted to care for his son but was bullied by the system." He described a social worker questioning how some of his siblings had turned out and insinuating his mother had nothing much to offer the child. Then, the social worker, noting that Saúl's parents lived with his sister, said there were too many people in the house. "What this really was," Saúl said, "was an interrogation about poverty. There's hard-core evidence of far fewer instances of incarceration or homelessness for children in the care of relatives as opposed to a group home. Children have a legal right to be with relatives."

Saúl had been in Central America doing human rights work when the custody battle over his cousin began. Realizing there was a human rights violation happening right in his own family, he returned home. He filed a civil rights complaint, claiming his mom was suspect based on the fact that she was poor. The next time the social worker visited the home, Saúl was there. He offered a seat to the social worker, and watched her notice his UCLA diploma, crookedly hanging on the wall. A few days earlier, his cousins had been roughhousing and cracked the diploma's frame. You couldn't help but notice it.

"Is that yours?" she asked. Saúl nodded and added that he'd just finished law school at UCLA as well. At this, the social worker's demeanor changed, and she listened. Saúl said, "My cousin lost his father, and he needs to be in a home with people he feels close to, not taken from us and given another reason to be angry at the world." After the meeting, the social worker requested that the judge make a discretionary decision to let the child stay. At last, Saúl's mother was approved to care for her nephew. Even still, it took eight months before his mother saw a single payment to cover the child's needs, bringing to light another major challenge, another so-called decision with no good options: low-income families are often forced to choose between going broke or losing the children.

Saúl passed around to our study group a sheet with columns of numbers—numbers I'd soon grow accustomed to studying—detailing payment rates for foster care. Group homes received the most, several thousand dollars a month per child, though the group home system was riddled with documented cases of severe neglect and abuse. And, once children turned eighteen, they were automatically booted from a group home and expected to somehow possess the know-how and resources to create a productive life on their own. *C'mon, now.*

"We can't sit here and talk about trying to keep kids with their families without talking about the whole political equation," Saúl said. "So many children are relegated to the foster system because of tough-on-crime initiatives. We need to be talking about how, the tougher politicians are on crime, the more they are applauded, and that's because the media and political rhetoric has caused this country to wrongly believe that locking up more people for longer is the right and only answer."

My perspective continued to expand, my mouth filled with new words. At night when I came home, it was no longer enough that ten women were sleeping soundly in their bunks. I'd lie on my cot in the dining room, staring at the light of the fax machine, and think about how much more there was to be done. And then, one night, I heard rocks.

Someone was throwing rocks at the window. I turned on the lights but saw nothing. The next morning, I found the rocks on the ground. Not pebbles or small stones, but palm-sized rocks that should have broken the window, but, miraculously, didn't. Night after night, I'd hear the rocks, and I'd hold my breath, waiting for the sound of shattering glass. In the morning I'd clear away the rocks and wonder how it was that the windows never broke. One of the women in the house quoted a Bible passage to me, "No weapon that is formed against you will prosper." Just as inexplicably as the rock throwing had begun, it stopped.

If, indeed, someone, something, was watching over me, then this was also my chance to do more. A New Way of Life was about individuals; but helping woman by woman wasn't going to fix the broken and discriminatory system. What if we could have a system that wasn't about chaining people and throwing them in cages? What if the general public understood that prison was a tool of social control, and that locking up more people did little to enhance public safety? What if our country could adopt a holistic approach that helped both the individual and the community? What if the massive amount of money spent on prisons was put toward education, so that our country was no longer a leader in the prison business, but in the long-term venture of providing urban schoolchildren with more opportunities than just drugs or crime?

Fixing the system *had* to be a part of A New Way of Life. As Saúl taught me: a component of helping people was getting them involved and invested in the larger movement. This shift, this new and broader commitment—this is what would truly make my mission unique.

Some months later, the *Los Angeles Times* wrote about the Community Coalition's tenth anniversary conference: "With a passion reminiscent of the 1960s, residents and social service providers vowed to organize themselves and push to change public policy and laws detrimental to residents of South Los Angeles—such as those pertaining to the current foster care system." Saúl was quoted about our "Family Care, Not Foster Care" campaign and conference, which I and the study group helped spearhead. I was quoted too. "'We have a voice,' said Susan Burton, a member of the coalition, echoing the theme of the conference. 'I can't do it alone, you can't do it alone, but together we can.'"

Saúl eventually left the Community Coalition for a professorship at UCLA, believing he needed to involve students in his mission. "Legal education normalizes everything," he said. "We're not talking about these issues to aspiring lawyers, and we need to be."

Several years later, in 2010, as if Saúl hadn't already done enough for me, he filled out an online nomination form: "Courage. This is the word that ran through my mind when I first met Susan ten years ago," he wrote. "She did not know how to incorporate a non-profit organization and had no financial grants or donations. She just knew she was going to provide a high-quality environment to support women who had been exactly where she had once been." I was driving down La Brea, not far from where K.K. was killed, when my cell phone rang. A voice said, "Are you sitting down? You've been named a Top Ten CNN Hero."

22

WOMEN AND PRISON

The majority of offenses committed by women are non-violent drug and property crimes, motivated by poverty and addiction. Most women offenders are under thirty years old, and are disproportionately low-income, black, and didn't complete high school.

The lifetime likelihood of imprisonment for white women is 1 in 118; for black women, it's 1 in 19.

Now that I'd begun seeing the full picture, I couldn't keep silent about it. I went around disrupting meetings, fussing at anyone and everyone who had some power. I'd jump to my feet, shout out the uncomfortable truth. I had no desire to play nice or polite about issues that were crushing people.

When I showed up to the Watts Labor Community Action Committee for a "Day of Dialogue" program about police and community relations, my hand was soon waving in the air. "We need police accountability," I called out. "All of us here in South L.A. know police misconduct isn't a new thing. It's never *not* been happening."

This was in the early 2000s, before everyone had a cell phone with a camera or video recorder in their pocket. The brutal 1991 beating of Rodney King had exposed to the world American police acting with impunity. But, unlike the way it was portrayed by the media, this wasn't a rare occurrence. Something as minor as jaywalking routinely landed a black man facedown on the street, his hands slapped with cuffs. Power was a beast, and it was hungry, especially in poor communities where citizens had little recourse.

"The equipment at their disposal could decimate an entire neighborhood," I continued, in front of the full meeting room. "It's frightening to think what they're capable of doing to us at the drop of a dime." The militarization of police weaponry had started in L.A. with the creation of the first Special Weapons and Tactics (SWAT) unit in reaction to the Watts riots. But it didn't stop there. Under the nearly fifteen-year reign of Police Chief Daryl Gates, the War on Drugs became literal, with officers in war gear, busting through houses with the infamous armored B-100 battering ram. "It's like state-sanctioned murder," I said.

At this point, I sensed others in the crowd getting riled up too. I continued on, mentioning K.K.'s death, but one of the facilitators interrupted me.

"Ma'am," she said. "That doesn't matter."

"How dare you," I said. "How can you be a conflict resolution facilitator and say my son's death doesn't matter?" I rose, slinging my purse over my shoulder. "I'm not going to participate in any sham-ass meeting," I said, and marched out. To my surprise, more than half the crowd followed me.

But a bespectacled man trailing after us wasn't happy with me: City Councilman Mark Ridley-Thomas. He'd founded this "Day of Dialogue" event several years earlier, after watching the verdict of the O. J. Simpson trial divide his city and the nation.

"We have some simple rules of the road here," he called after me. "Everybody listens to everybody else, and everybody has an opportunity to be heard. I know that can be frustrating for those who are a bit more . . . spontaneous."

I turned to face him. Mr. Ridley-Thomas was a rising political star—he'd go on to the state assembly and then to become L.A.

County supervisor—but I was frustrated by some of his tough-on-crime stances. Just like most every policymaker and elected official, he knew it was political suicide to be soft on crime—though I wondered if that put a black man such as himself, born and raised in L.A., at odds with his personal beliefs.

"You mentioned you have an organization?" he said.

I told him about A New Way of Life.

"Where is it?" he asked.

"Right here in Watts."

"Well, I'm coming over there. I'm going to do to A New Way of Life what you've done to my meeting today. I'm going to tear it up." But his voice was chiding, not angry. And, together, we laughed. Some years later, he'd tell me he had sensed something about my spirit that day. That, alongside my nonconformity, he saw a goodness in me, and that's what had compelled him to follow me out of the meeting room.

Mark Ridley-Thomas would, indeed, visit A New Way of Life, though he'd do the opposite of tearing things up. "What you're doing here grounds my perspective," he would tell me. "This makes it clear what the issues are, what people's journeys and struggles are, and roots the policies that we're trying to advance. It keeps it real." He would go on to put solid and heartfelt action behind his words.

While I saw firsthand the power of my voice to inspire, I also realized I was raw, and my words were crude. If I was going to continue speaking out, I needed to get myself a better vocabulary. It wasn't as though I had extra time on my hands, but I knew that continuing my education was crucial. I enrolled in Southwest College in psychology and chemical dependency counseling.

Sitting in a classroom brought back memories of when I was a little girl and school was my safe place. I wasn't only learning about psychology, I was learning about myself. I delved further into the study of family dynamics, noticing similar dynamics in the lives of most of the women at A New Way of Life. Like me, they'd been conditioned to have low or no expectations of themselves or others. Also, like me, they'd turned to using. When all around you life was hard and unfair, when you were filled with rage and you didn't know where to put it, why wouldn't you seek a way to numb yourself? But what started as an attempt to find some relief went on to become an illness. Because it's what they saw, the next generation followed your lead, and then the next. And, now, generations in, it had become just the way things are, a treacherous form of normal.

For three years, I took night courses, lugging my textbooks all around town, studying at the kitchen table of A New Way of Life, reading by my mother's bedside when she took ill. At last, I completed my certificate. Though I had dreams of going on to a university and pursuing a degree, my advocacy work had taken over. A Ph.D. wasn't going to happen. But that was okay; life was earning me a Ph.*Do.*

When the Little Hoover Commission, an independent state over-sight agency, released a 2004 report entitled "Breaking the Barriers for Women on Parole," a photo of me, in cap and gown, at my gradu-ation from Southwest College, appeared on the cover.

Spurred on by this report about the unique issues affecting women in the correctional system, Governor Arnold Schwarzenegger creat-ed the Gender Responsive Strategies Commission and appointed me one of ten commissioners. Among the state and local officials, crimi-nologists, and a seemingly disproportionate number of people from the California Department of Corrections and Rehabilitation, I was one of only two formerly incarcerated women on the commission. We were tasked with addressing the unique issues of female prisoners in an environment designed, structured, and programmed for men, despite the massive increase of women behind bars. It was, of course, a dubious distinction that Schwarzenegger's own state was home to the largest women's prison in the world, the Central California Wom-en's Facility, a full square mile in Chowchilla, about four hours from Los Angeles—filled to over 180 percent of its intended capacity.

Our Gender Responsive Strategies Commission met quarterly, each time in a different county in California. I identified many issues affecting women behind bars, such as the shackling of women during labor, a routine and often mandatory practice. Though a handful of states had guidelines against shackling, it still continued, unchecked. As did the ruthless practice of separating babies from their mothers immediately after birth.

I brought up the more routine issue that women in jails were not provided sanitary napkins or tampons; in prisons, women were required to purchase sanitary products at two to three times the market price. The only time an incarcerated woman was provided sanitary napkins—but only a maximum of five pads a month—was if she was declared "indigent." This distinction spotlit yet another issue: it used to be that having less than $5 in a prison account qualified an inmate as indigent, but the amount had been updated to $0. So, if you had a nickel in your account, you weren't considered indigent, but you certainly couldn't afford a package of ten tampons for $2.70. Even if you had several bucks in your account, you still could face precarious decisions—see a doctor, or buy tampons? Sadly, it wasn't uncommon for women inmates to resort to bartering sex acts for basic necessities.

I was eager to get to work on these pressing issues but, for reasons unexplained, the commission wasn't pursuing any of them. It was becoming clear to me that, although the commission sounded great on paper, we weren't accomplishing much of anything.

When I hosted one of our meetings, in Watts, the most important thing to come out of it happened by chance. As an official from Valley State Prison spoke, she casually mentioned that they ask pregnant women going into labor if they want to get their tubes tied. The meeting room fell silent. Performing sterilizations in prison for any reason other than medical necessity was a violation of state law—likewise, it was illegal to seek a woman's consent for a tubal ligation while she was in labor.

But the comment was brushed off by the commission heads, assuring us that nothing like that *ever* happens. Still, the scene harkened back to California's dark history of eugenics—what historians cite as a model for Nazi Germany—targeting the disabled, the mentally ill, criminals, minorities, and the poor. Though thirty-one U.S. states practiced eugenics in the first half of the twentieth century, California was the leader of the pack for the number of forced sterilizations on men and women.

Unlike our commission, a women prisoners' rights group called Justice Now did not disregard the prison official's comments. The group opened an investigation and managed to obtain prison records, which indeed revealed a practice of tubal ligations, beyond the amount that, statistically, would be deemed medically necessary. The baton was then passed to Center for Investigative Journalism reporter Corey G. Johnson, who, after years of research, broke the story in 2013 that sterilization procedures were occurring in state prisons without proper approval.

His reporting painted a picture of the women being coerced into surgery, each fitting a strikingly similar profile: repeat offenders who already had children and who had low levels of education. Firsthand accounts revealed inmates who'd been unaware what "tubal litigation" or other sterilization procedures were. Others described being pressured for consent on the operating table as they were about to undergo a C-section. Also documented were various other surgeries resulting in sterilization, such as hysterectomies and ovary removals, most of which were not demonstrated to be medically necessary. Resulting from this investigation, a 2014 bill was signed into California law banning sterilization as a form of birth control for all state and county prisoners.

As for our Gender Responsive Strategies Commission, the only progress I could point to that was a direct result of our years of meetings was the passage of a 2006 bill, spearheaded by Assemblywoman Karen Bass (who'd founded the Community Coalition), to remove restrictions so that a cosmetology or barber license could be earned by someone with a criminal record.

This was certainly a step in the right direction, and yet, when our commission visited the California Institution for Women, a cosmetology teacher there told me that even though her students were now able to obtain licenses, they still were falling through the cracks upon release, unable to get placement in salons. We decided I would return and spend some time with her cosmetology class to gather more insight and provide some inspiration and information about finding jobs and housing on the outside.

A few weeks later I drove back to the prison. But I was denied entry. Apparently, my clearance as part of the Gender Responsive Strategy Commission meeting didn't apply to my solo visit. I returned home and reapplied for clearance. After some months of waiting, my clearance came back denied. I called the cosmetology teacher and asked her to advocate for my clearance. But she was scared to intervene, even though we were trying to help her students.

I never did end up visiting the cosmetology class. Sometimes you get too tired of having to walk that same extra mile over and over again.

23

A KINDRED SPIRIT

*Over 70 percent of Americans in prison cannot read
above a fourth-grade level.*

*When inmates are provided literacy help, the rate of
recidivism drops to a 16 percent chance of returning to
prison—as opposed to a 70 percent chance for those who
receive no reading help.*

At a meeting with the Community Coalition, I met a formerly
incarcerated man, Dorsey Nunn, who ran a San Francisco–based
nonprofit called Legal Services for Prisoners with Children. While I
was still naïve and idealistic, Dorsey had been working in the nonprofit world for many years and had a broad understanding of the
way things really worked. Right away, we hit it off, and I invited Dorsey to visit A New Way of Life. After I led him through the house and
he met some of the women, he turned to look at me.

"Sister, do you understand the impact of what you're doing right
here?" he said. "I think a chicken's gonna fall out of a tree right into
your lap."

I thought, what does he mean a *chicken*? Is this man crazy?

But he knew exactly what he was talking about. The chicken—the sustenance, the meat—turned out to be a $50,000 fellowship from the California Wellness Foundation. Dorsey had nominated me.

With the fellowship money, I replaced the bunk beds in the house with single beds because bunks were reminiscent of prison. This brought the number of women who could live in the house down from ten to seven, but the funding meant I no longer had to rely on residents' unpredictable income to cover the bills. Also, from the grant, I drew my first salary: $800 a month.

At Dorsey's encouragement, I moved out of the house, folding up the cot I'd been sleeping on in the dining room, and rented a match-box of an apartment down the block. At first, it seemed a waste to have my own apartment when I wasn't returning there until 9 p.m., up again at the crack of dawn. But I quickly grew to appreciate the quiet of my own space, with no TV, no stereo, no half a dozen people around. I'd never before lived in my own place by myself, and I began to revel in it.

Now that we had the fellowship, I needed to bring A New Way of Life to the next level. I hired a bookkeeper who kept our records and set up payroll—my first time on a payroll. I was fifty years old and it was the first time I was living within the constructs of society and being totally legitimate. While I took pride in this, Mitzi, who earned $500 a month to cook, wanted to remain part of the cash economy. Mitzi was my friend, but I couldn't jeopardize A New Way of Life by paying her under the table. We parted ways, though we kept in touch, and I visited her in the hospital when she took ill. Several years later she passed away from liver damage. At her funeral, I spoke of what we'd started, and the legacy she left.

In her place, I hired Ruth, a former resident of A New Way of Life and someone I'd known first from the streets, then in prison. Ruth had been volunteering, helping the women who were trying to get housing, and I was proud to make her our first salaried employee. Like everyone who'd come to work with us, her job encompassed doing what needed to get done. She continued working on housing, and she also cooked.

Dorsey flew me to San Francisco to meet his staff at Legal Services for Prisoners with Children, and to see the treatment center he helped build, Free at Last. Around the same age, Dorsey and I were both from the streets. He grew up in a poor area of San Mateo County and got involved with drugs as a teenager. At nineteen, he was convicted for a liquor store robbery that ended in the fatal shooting of the store owner. Never alleged to have been the shooter, Dorsey received a life sentence with the possibility of parole. When he first entered prison, he recalled seeing more black men in one space than he'd ever before seen. He also reunited with the kids from his neighborhood he'd played Little League with, and they soon realized their whole team was there in prison—except for the one white kid.

Dorsey could barely read, but in the yard of San Quentin, he was inspired to learn. There, men who'd been in the Black Liberation Army and the Black Panthers held political education courses. "They would read aloud to us," Dorsey recalled, "and would ask others to get up and read, and we'd all talk about the readings." He respected these men so much, he set his mind to learning to read. Before long, he was devouring books. He read *The Autobiography of Malcolm X*, Adam Smith's books on economics and capitalism, biographies of Ho Chi Minh and Mao Zedong.

After reading Eldridge Cleaver's *Soul on Ice*, he got up in front of the group in the yard and debated it, though he was nervous the others would be mad at his outlier view. "I can't accept this analysis that justifies rape," he announced. "I read the book twice, and I've come to the conclusion, I disagree." When he was done, he waited for the fallout, especially from the older prisoners. "Instead," he recalled, his round face beaming, "I got a hug. And they said I was ready to read to the group."

After serving twelve years, Dorsey was granted parole in 1981. Before he left San Quentin, the president of the prison branch of the NAACP came to him. "He wanted to extract a promise from me," Dorsey described. "The promise that I would return to the community an asset, not a liability." He took this to heart.

In the free world, Dorsey got on the airwaves of KPOO in San Francisco, otherwise known as Poor People's Radio, an independent station dedicated to giving voice to the disenfranchised. There, he interviewed attorney Ellen Barry, one of the nation's leading advocates for women prisoners' rights, and the founder of Legal Services for Prisoners with Children.

"In the interview, Ellen kept saying 'O-B-G-Y-N,'" Dorsey recalled. "And here I am, thinking I'm a worldly guy and that OBGYN must be a women's prison gang, but it must be a small-ass gang because I'd never even heard of them. You've got to remember that, from nineteen to thirty-one years old, I was in prison. I didn't have exposure to women. I wasn't educated about women's issues." But Dorsey still made an indelible impression on Ellen Barry, and he went to work for her organization. Eventually, he became its executive director.

Dorsey and I spent long hours talking. "Sister, you're gonna earn your bones," he said as he mentored me. We talked about the uphill battle of starting an organization, and the sacrifices that had to be made to sustain it. "Getting funding isn't the only struggle," he cautioned. "You also have to prove the reasons your organization needs to exist, and that you, who has little or no professional track record, *you* are the one to run things. We came to our roles not knowing all the things people learn in prestigious schools. We speak from the world we knew."

He warned of not getting bogged down in the bureaucracy of your funding streams, and told me that he'd long ago decided his organization would not take any government money. "You have to be mindful about getting co-opted," he said. "Especially with the trappings government agencies can dangle." This would be sage advice that I'd be sorely reminded of some years later.

After I returned to L.A., Dorsey and I kept talking. We talked so much, he had to explain to any woman he was seeing who I was and why, no matter what, he'd always stop to take my call.

24

TAKING FOOD OFF THE TABLE

*People and their families are more likely to live in poverty
and be hungry if they have been incarcerated.*

*Just 3 percent of federal spending goes toward nutrition
programs. The average Supplemental Nutrition Assistance Program (SNAP) benefit per person is about $29.25
per week.*

E veryone I knew on welfare would tell you they'd rather have an
honest job and a way out of poverty than be in the dead-end
cycle of waiting for that monthly welfare check. From all sides, the
welfare system was riddled with issues—and had been for decades.
Back in 1996, with the clock ticking on his run for reelection,
President Bill Clinton made good on a promise to reform welfare.
Although Clinton's promise to "end welfare as we know it" sounded
lofty, the bill awaiting his signature was hardly reformative. Its harsh
and nonsensical provisions actually promised the opposite, putting even more hurdles before poor Americans who were trying to
stand on their own, and limiting benefits families relied on. "Legislative child abuse," Senator Edward Kennedy called the bill. And yet
Clinton signed it into law, which wasn't all that surprising given the

tough-on-crime climate. After all, weren't we supposed to believe that *poor, black,* and *crime* all went hand in hand?

Part of Clinton's flawed Welfare Reform Act was a seemingly random stipulation that anyone convicted of a drug felony was banned for life from receiving food stamps. Not only did this continue punishing those who'd served their time, but it let their children go hungry. Also, it arbitrarily singled out drug offenders while still permitting food stamp benefits for those with any other conviction, such as armed robbery, rape, or murder.

Food stamps, born out of the Great Depression, gained permanent status under President Lyndon Johnson in his self-proclaimed War on Poverty. So why, several decades later, was the country going backward, cutting off these benefits to people trying to get back on their feet and to children who'd already been hurt by having had a parent in prison? There were other insidious effects, which I was seeing firsthand: social service agencies sometimes utilized their clients' food stamp benefits to help defray operating costs. When convicted drug offenders suddenly and systemically got cut off from food stamps, I also watched them being denied spots in residential drug treatment programs.

Collateral consequences, invisible punishment, sanctions—no matter the term, it was interest on your debt that kept accruing.

There was, however, a caveat to the food stamp ban: individual states could opt out—and many did. But not California, even though, of the 92,000 American women affected by the ban, a whopping 40 percent lived in California.

The citizens and the California state legislature were all for the opt-out, and this was made clear: twice, opt-out bills were passed. But, twice, Governor Gray Davis creamed the bills with vetoes. "Convicted felons do not deserve the same treatment as law-abiding citizens, especially those that manufacture, transport or distribute drugs," Davis announced, in what would become his habit of thwarting his state's legislature and citizens.

In 2001, an opt-out bill was once again up for a vote of the California State Assembly. At the request of the Drug Policy Alliance, I flew to Sacramento to testify. As I sat in the state capitol listening to testimony, I realized the amount of time, the organization, and the passion that had gone into fighting for the opt-out bill. When my name was called, I told my story and described A New Way of Life. "I can tell you, firsthand," I said, "that withholding access to food for poor people isn't going to curb crime. It's real tough to go out and look for a job and to try to raise a family if you're also scrounging for food."

The bill passed.

And—again—Governor Davis vetoed it.

Hearing the news, I felt like I'd swallowed a stone. After all that work, what good was the legislative process if one man had the ability to stop everything? How was this democracy?

In 2004, an opt-out bill was back on the senate floor, and, again, I went to Sacramento to testify. "We're not talking about anything but people eating," I said. "We're talking about the bare minimum. We're not talking about a steak dinner, we're talking about meeting daily nutritional requirements." After my testimony, State Assembly Member Mark Leno, who'd authored the bill, ran down the hall after me.

"I was touched by your story," he said, shaking my hand. "Thank you for coming to Sacramento to tell it." I couldn't believe he'd left the hearing room to personally say this to me, and his gesture made me feel so valuable.

Once again, the bill passed the senate floor. But, this time, Governor Davis was out—having faced an unprecedented recall by voters, a glimpse of democracy at work after all!—and Governor Arnold Schwarzenegger signed the bill into law.

The victory, however, wasn't what it should have been: the opt-out was only partial, exempting people with simple drug possession felonies, but leaving those with "possession for sale" convictions still subject to the lifetime food stamp ban.

All I could do was shake my head. My own record had trumped-up charges of possession for sale. If I had been caught under this law, I'd be subject to the lifetime food stamp ban. It seemed an awful lot of fighting to barely solve anything. An awful lot of fighting to return benefits to some families, but not to others. America's vow not to let its citizens starve was hollow.

For another decade, the partial ban remained in California, even though thirty-nine other states had long since opted out entirely or significantly modified the severity of the policy. At last, in 2014, snuck into the budget of the State of California, was a provision to remove the entire ban. When Governor Jerry Brown signed that budget, the food stamp ban was, at long last, dead.

Now, women at A New Way of Life could get food stamps, though they still had to take a day to wait in long lines, fill out paperwork, and then wait more days for the stamps to come through. Sadly, with all the state assembly bills, all the support and pulling together and the money spent on the many attempts at the opt-out, none of it actually fixed the system. None of it actually helped anyone get *off* food stamps. It was like watching pennies being taken, one by one, out of a piggy bank and finally put back in, but so what? Even a full piggy bank of pennies doesn't amount to much.

As I became more involved in policy, I continued to return to Sacramento. But time and time again, I watched so much effort fall on deaf ears. I'd leave there and my body would be sore, like someone had been punching me. Eventually, I could no longer sit there feeling so powerless, so I quit going. I figured the best place for me was to be in my community, helping to build a powerful voice of many.

25

BROKE LEG HOUSE

Most women are behind bars for social or victimless crimes—while the real victims, which the flawed system perpetuates, are the children. The number of children under age eighteen with a mother in prison has more than doubled since 1991. Approximately 10 million American children have or have had a parent in prison.

By 2001, Alzheimer's had gripped Mama. Toni, my brother Billy and his wife, and I took turns caring for her. We enrolled Mama in a clinical trial, but she continued to worsen, and her confusion caused her to be mean. If she could get a hold of you, she had a vise grip. She scratched and bit, drawing blood.

Mama passed at eighty-four years old. At the cemetery, Toni didn't want to leave the limousine. "If I get out," she said, "it will be real. Mama will be gone."

I tried to comfort her as best I could, tried to be her support, tried to be her mother. But it was clear that she still felt Mama was more her mother than I'd ever been. "She saved my life," Toni said to me. "And that allowed me to save your life."

She was right. I swallowed back a lump in my throat and headed into the cemetery. For me, my mother's funeral was a release. I stood at her grave knowing we had healed. I had forgiven her and felt

certain she'd forgiven me, too. And I thanked her for helping to make
Toni the woman and mother she was today.

I also made a vow to myself. I knew the destructive places grief
took me, and I couldn't allow such pain to pull me under. I made up
my mind to view death differently, to make peace and accept that
death was, after all, a part of life. Pain was inevitable, I told myself,
but suffering was optional. Rather than putting energy into mourn-
ing death, I'd try to do my best with the people in my life. I prayed for
Mama and asked that she be taken to the place of her heart's desire,
wherever, whatever, that place might be. And then I let go.

The same year, I held our first annual celebration for A New Way
of Life. What would later become a formal fundraising gala in a
downtown hotel ballroom began as a gathering in the living room.
I cooked up a big turkey dinner for the women and their extended
families, and Saúl came over too. Then there was a knock at the door.
To my shock, there stood U.S. Representative Maxine Waters. I had
written to her office to tell her about A New Way of Life and invite her
to our celebration—but never did I think she'd actually show up to
the house. But there she was, with a big fruit basket in her arms. I'm
not lying when I say that was the best fruit I'd ever tasted.

Around this time, I received a call from the *Los Angeles Times*. A
reporter noticed that I'd registered myself and several women to hear
the surgeon general speak at Martin Luther King Hospital, and she
was seeking comments to the speech. I didn't end up quoted in the
article; instead, the reporter and a photographer came by the house
to do a feature about us. The *Times* article ran with the headline
"Helping Women Get a New Start After Prison: Through her sober
living program, an ex-addict offers a home in Watts for just-released
inmates who are reclaiming their lives" and delved into my personal
story and the many barriers to re-entry.

Between the calls from people to congratulate me on the article
came a call from a realtor I knew. Her voice was hesitant as she made
small talk before finally getting to the point. "Beverly got in touch
with me," she explained, "and she's having Lamont sell the house."

Sell the house? That would mean closing the doors of A New Way of Life.

I hadn't spoken with Beverly in a couple of years, and my thoughts raced in all sorts of directions before finally landing on: Beverly must have seen the article, must have gone red with lines like, "Burton's women" and "Burton's home." But she hadn't been involved in a long time, and I was the one running A New Way of Life.

Defiantly, I told the realtor, "I will buy the house." I didn't know how I'd do it, but I would find a way.

"I'm sorry, I'm really in the middle here, Susan," she said. "But Beverly has forbidden me to sell it to you."

I hung up and called my nephew, Lamont. He didn't have too many words other than how he, too, was in the middle, and there was nothing he could do. I couldn't blame him. Beverly was his stepmom, and I knew how charming and calculating she could be.

That night, I called Leslie, my sponsor, to tell her the house was on the market. She fumed, "You have worked too hard to have someone pull the rug from under you." Then there was a long pause. When she spoke again, her voice was soft, tentative. "This may sound crazy," she said. "But I do crazy things sometimes. I've had a couple of good years. I have a little money socked away. What if I could sneak in and buy the house? Would you be able to pay rent?"

I sat up in my bed. With the Walden House contract and the California Wellness fellowship we were in solid financial shape. "Yes," I said.

I slept fitfully, worried Leslie would realize she'd made a rash decision and change her mind. But the next day, Leslie had a realtor contact Beverly's realtor. The transaction was completed without anyone knowing who Leslie was.

Just about everyone in Leslie's life *did* think she was crazy. She was a single woman living in Santa Monica, and she'd just spent her savings on a house in Watts inhabited by women newly out of prison. I worried she'd have buyer's remorse about being saddled with a mortgage and with all of us. But, as soon as she closed on the house, she showed up with a tool box and got to work fixing things up. She put us to work too, assigning women to be project managers. "Your neighbors have been here thirty, forty years," Leslie said. "Look how nice they keep their homes. It's a neighborhood that cares, and I want this to be one of the nicest houses on the street."

Leslie's brothers came by too, and we all got to work, scraping old paint off the outside of the house and tending to the yard. Leslie taught the women how to lay tile. And the women who'd learned maintenance skills on their jobs in prison taught the rest of us how to work on the plumbing.

Leslie pulled me aside one day. "Susan, look at the women painting the walls. They are so proud of what they're doing. I think when people are invested in their home, they take care of it differently." She would turn out to be right. Even though this wasn't a permanent home for any of the women, I never saw anyone treating the house carelessly. It was always straightened and scrubbed, vacuumed and polished.

As Leslie told more people in her life about us, they, too, began showing up on weekends to help out. We had Hollywood movie set designers sanding and painting with us.

On the one-year anniversary of Leslie's purchase of the house, her entire family traveled to join us for a party. "This house has transformed the lives of so many," Leslie said to us. "You can't help but see the joy of what's happening here. Look, even my naysayer brother is here. It's infectious."

But a dark cloud still hung over the house—most of the women had children they couldn't be with. The vicious cycle was heartbreaking: you couldn't keep your children unless you demonstrated a safe place to live, but your criminal record banned you from subsidized housing and disqualified you from most private housing. Though A New Way of Life was certainly a safe residence, we only had room for the women's children to visit, not to live full time. It tore me up watching so many children practically held hostage in the system and knowing that I couldn't offer any real assistance.

Something needed to be done. We needed more space. But more

than that, I wanted to tackle the systemic issues, what had become the "children-industrial complex." The country was now full of agencies built on the back of the prison-industrial complex and operating under the auspices of Child Protective Services. Just like prisons, foster care and group homes were mismanaged gluts of taxpayer money. It cost up to $60,000 to incarcerate a woman for one year—but, after her release, zero was invested in reuniting her with her children and providing support for the family.

Not long after Leslie had bought the house I was at my neighborhood market and slipped on a clear piece of Plexiglas lying on the ground. I flew through the air and came down hard. I couldn't get up, although the store owner tried to make me. I asked someone to call an ambulance. I wound up with a broken ankle and a cast up to my thigh for six weeks, followed by a shorter cast for another six weeks, then a boot for three months, accompanied by physical therapy and lots of help from A New Way of Life's residents, who bathed me and drove me around. I also ended up with an $80,000 settlement from the store's insurance policy.

I took that money and I bought a house that had come up for sale a few doors down. By this time, I had good credit to my name, and I bought that house on my own. I moved the current women into what we named the "Broke Leg House." And into Leslie's house, moved six women and three children.

I had the pleasure of watching the women raising their kids. Watching both generations go to school, keep up with their daily chores, and face life's responsibilities. Watching them laugh and cry, work their way through disappointment, and celebrate success. One day, a woman ran up to me, holding a check like it was a blue ribbon. "Ms. Burton, this is my very first paycheck!"

"What are you going to do with it?" I asked.

"I'm going to put it in the bank account you taught me to open."

"Then what are you going to do with the money?"

"I'm going to get a place and pay rent and buy groceries. Eventually, I'm gonna get a car."

I smiled. Thinking in terms of *eventually* was, for many of the women, a new way of thinking. She'd heard my message: if you fail to plan, you plan to fail. She'd listened when I said: have discipline and focus with your finances. Planning for the future, setting a goal, seeing it through—these were important benchmarks for successful re-entry, and a successful life.

Sometimes, though, no matter what I tried, a woman lacked momentum or continued to pull the rug out from under herself. I watched one woman excitedly begin training to become a truck driver, but she dropped out right before getting certified. "Why?" I asked her. She had no answer. Others didn't keep up with their chores. "When you don't wash the dishes, that leaves someone else to come home from work and have to do your chore," I'd say. Most of the time, the warning from me, backed up by the rest of the house holding each other accountable, was all that was needed for someone to get back on track.

Occasionally, women would go out and use. I could look at someone and tell she'd used, it was like a veil over her face. When this happened, she started all over again with a thirty-day restriction— she could only leave the house for places relevant to re-entry, such as work, parole meetings, and AA meetings. And, if she left, she had to go straight to her destination and then come straight back. "If you go to work and come back three hours later than you should, then we got a problem. Then, we have to have a talk," I explained. "If you can't do this, I understand, but you and I have an agreement. I'm keeping my side, but you've got to keep yours, or you're out. We work on the honor system here. Integrity, discipline, honor. That's your side of the agreement."

In prison, the culture was that one person usually dominated a room. If the dominator said, "I want the light out," the light went out. If she said, "Clean the room this way," others cleaned exactly that way. I could always tell who'd been the dominator in prison because her entry into the house had everyone else scared.

"This is everybody's space, bullying doesn't happen at A New Way of Life," I'd say. Usually it clicked that the behavior that got someone through the day in prison wasn't okay in the free world. Most pulled it together and adjusted quickly, but the few times a woman didn't, I'd give her a second chance before going to talk to her parole agent. Only rarely was a woman unable to adjust, and then I'd find another placement for her. "Maybe it's not the right time for you," I'd say. "But when you're ready, we'll be here."

The Board of Prison Terms called me on a Friday and said they were bringing Annie to me on Monday. I knew Annie. Every time I was in prison, there was Annie. She was an eighty-seven-year-old white woman who'd been incarcerated for forty-six years.

Though A New Way of Life was full, I had the weekend to figure it out. I knew I wasn't turning her away. When I told the women in the house about Annie, many of them also knew her, and volunteers stepped up to share their room. I went out and bought another twin bed and, on Monday, when Annie's wheelchair rolled through the front door, we were ready for her.

Annie had grown up in wealthy and conservative Orange County, though, at this point, she wasn't from anywhere but prison. She'd been convicted when she was around forty years old of drowning her brother with a garden hose, though she maintained it was an accident. I never asked for details about the situation or her original sentence. All I knew was that her way of dealing with what had happened was to keep punishing herself. Long ago, she'd resigned herself to living out the rest of her days in prison.

Though every woman experienced some type of adjustment after being released, watching someone acclimate to life on the outside after four decades behind bars was an extreme detox. In the middle of the night, Annie went searching for toilet paper. In prison, toilet paper was coveted: prisoners and guards would snatch it, or never supply you in the first place. In Annie's prison mentality, toilet paper had become so significant, she'd wake herself to hoard it. During the day, she carried three rolls with her around the house. "Annie, this is not prison toilet paper," I explained. "Everyone can get as much as they need."

But the challenge wasn't just about breaking Annie of prison mentality—her sense of the world was stuck in the pre–Civil Rights era. Here was this white woman, in my house, calling people niggers. I had to have plenty of conversations with Annie, had to explain we don't use that word, had to explain that all people are equal, that the black women in the house weren't there to clean up or cook for her. And I had plenty of conversations with the other residents, explaining that A New Way of Life takes a person right where she's at, without judgment, even if where she's at is stuck in the 1950s. Little by little, I watched Annie improve, along with her relationships with the other women.

In 2006, Leslie decided to return to graduate school to become an architect. She said owning the house and seeing how the neighborhood was changing had inspired her to specialize in affordable and sustainable housing. But the program she chose was on the other side of the country. Since she was moving so far away, she asked if A New Way of Life wanted to buy the house from her. It would end up taking several years before I was able to amass the funds to buy the house, but Leslie patiently waited. At last, I called to let her know we were ready.

"We have to figure out the best way to work this," Leslie said. "I don't want to be negotiating with you, Susan. I once saw you negotiating for a used car, and I don't want to be on the other side of that."

I hadn't wanted to negotiate with Leslie, either. But after a lifetime of being scrappy to survive, boy, was it hard for me not to try. In the end, I researched the comps for the area, then agreed to Leslie's asking price.

It had been thirteen years that Leslie had owned the house. In all that time, she'd raised the rent only fifty bucks.

26

FROM TRASH TO TREASURE

*Among developed Western democracies, the United States
stands out for its extremely limited assistance to the poor.*

I'd been praying for a way to keep the houses nice, to have fresh
sheets on the beds, to be able to afford towels that were of enough
quality not to fray, to get shades and drapes that properly fit the
windows, and to keep the silverware drawer stocked, since it always
seemed like utensils were up and walking away. Out of the blue, I
received a phone call from Bed, Bath and Beyond. They said they had
some items for A New Way of Life and I should come to the loading
dock at the West L.A. store to pick them up. They told me to bring a
forty-foot truck.

I didn't know what this was about, but I went to U-Haul. The
forty-footer was the biggest truck they had. It was also a stick shift—I
hadn't driven a stick in twenty years. But, there I was, gripping the
steering wheel with white knuckles and grinding into gear with forty
feet behind me as I headed across town. When I arrived to the loading dock at Bed, Bath and Beyond, they told me to back it in, but
after a couple harrowing tries, I got out and turned the driver's seat
over to one of the dock guys. He backed the truck up to the dock,
and I waited, unable to see what was being loaded in. I didn't ask any
questions, just let them do their thing, and when they were done, they

locked the back door and off I drove, grinding the gears up and down the streets of Beverly Hills.

When I at last returned to the house, I unlocked the back of the truck. Top to bottom, back to front, the entire forty feet was filled. Towels, sheets, bedspreads, pillows, silverware—whatever Bed, Bath and Beyond carried, it was in the truck. Not only was this the answer to my prayer, but God had upped it. As I began unloading I couldn't believe the luxury. I'd never dreamed such things existed—memory-foam mattress toppers? Triple-milled soaps? Thread counts of 1,000?

It struck me, then, in a way that made me sad: all this was available to some people, but not others. Abruptly, I closed the truck and went into the house. I stewed on this for a while, the notion of so many have-nots and the financial divide of our society. But, there, in the driveway was my chance to make these things available to people who otherwise never could've afforded them.

The women with families had first pick of the items. From what remained, I weeded out the baby items and delivered them to the nursery at the Watts Labor Community Action Committee. The rest I donated to the Watts senior program, personally delivering a memory-foam mattress topper to an elderly lady I knew had a bad back. A few days later she called me, exclaiming that she hadn't needed to take her pain medicine since she started sleeping on the mattress pad.

Bed, Bath and Beyond then took their donations to the next level. Twice a week, I set my alarm for 5 a.m., drove to rent the U-Haul, and pulled up to Bed, Bath and Beyond's loading dock before they opened for business. I could hardly give out the items as fast as they were coming in. I began storing things in the garage, then the backyard, and when I ran out of space, I rented a storage unit. But both the storage fees and truck rental were getting too expensive, so my brother Marvin sold me a raggedy Chevy pickup for $200. It held less than the U-Haul, but would have to do. The Bed, Bath and Beyond staff loaded up that pickup with everything it could hold, tying it all down. Through Beverly Hills I drove with that beat-up pickup filled with lamps and pots and pans and furniture tied to it, looking like the real Beverly Hillbilly!

When the store called with the news that their Torrance location also had pick-ups for us, I knew it was time to formalize a way of storing and distributing the items. I envisioned a place where people moving from homelessness into permanency could pick out essentials for a new home. I contacted other nonprofits to join with me in creating a Household Goods Distribution Center. With donor support, we rented a warehouse in South L.A. People with an agency referral and proof of a new housing lease were invited to "shop" for as long as they wanted, and leave with whatever they needed.

Folks were shocked when we told them they could get a vacuum cleaner *and* a comforter *and* pillows *and* a blender. Many people broke down in tears right there in the aisles of the distribution center. Every day might as well have been Oprah's Favorite Things. Bursting with gratitude, people thanked us hundreds of times.

One of A New Way of Life's first residents, Linda Washington, whom I'd first met in the lobby of CLARE, began volunteering at the distribution center. Linda had been on her own and doing well, working as a nurse's aide, and she was eager to give back. "This place is my little piece of sanity," she told me.

But soon, it seemed Linda's tune had changed. "This place is getting so demanding," she said. And she was right. Around five hundred formerly homeless people were visiting the center annually to help furnish a new residence. But Linda hadn't meant this as a complaint, and the next thing I knew, she quit nursing and came to work full time at the distribution center. "It's my baby," she said proudly.

Year after year, Bed, Bath and Beyond continued providing twice-weekly truckloads. Other stores, including the Avenue, donated clothes that had been on clearance or were returned. A drugstore distributor donated diapers, tissues, soap, and laundry detergent. When President Barack Obama signed the American Recovery and Reinvestment Act, welfare-to-work programs enabled us to hire four employees to help Linda.

One day, I stopped by the center and saw a black man in his sixties assembling a cabinet. He looked familiar. As I moved closer, I was certain I recognized him.

"Senator?" I said. He looked up. "What are you doing here?" I asked.

Senator Rod Wright gave me what I'd come to learn was his ever-present smile. He said, "I'm doing community service."

Rod had been a California politician for nearly two decades, serving in the state assembly until he faced term limits and was then elected to the state senate. He represented my district, and I'd followed him because he made good policy. He advocated for prison and jail reform and argued that releasing elderly or ill inmates into treatment centers or house arrest would save money and have no negative impact on public safety. He advocated against incarceration for parole violations that didn't include new crimes, and he sought to eliminate the duplicate and costly medical exams administered for no justifiable reason every time an inmate was relocated. "It would be cheaper to send someone to stay at the Ritz Carlton," Senator Wright told the press. "But we beat our chest and say we're protecting the public."

But, in 2014, the senator was charged with allegations of not residing in the working-class Inglewood district he represented. Through he maintained his innocence, he was convicted.

"Who had it in for you?" I asked.

He didn't so much as flinch at my directness. "Do you know about the Book of Esther?" he said, gently touching my arm. "It's about the power of persuasion. I've been in public service since college. But I also had a lucrative consulting business for campaigns and regulations, and I've been in real estate since college, too. I own four houses. The house in Inglewood they claimed wasn't my domicile, I've owned and paid taxes on that house for nearly forty years. But they claimed I wasn't living there *enough*. Most of the time I was living in Sacramento being a state senator." Rod shook his head. "The way they came after me—they could take out half the legislature." He described scenarios of senators whose children go to school in Sacramento, because that's where Mom or Dad is five days a week. "You can't tell me they disrupt their children's lives every single weekend by putting the family on an airplane just to go spend the night in their district. There are so many examples like this. But it didn't matter, because, at trial, the D.A. showed pictures of my Maserati and showed my charge account at Neiman Marcus." Rod flashed his disarming smile. "What can I say? I like nice things. I worked hard and did well, but that didn't mean I wasn't a longtime resident of Inglewood."

He was sentenced to ninety days in jail, three years of probation, and fifteen hundred hours of community service, and he was banned from holding public office. But when he turned himself in to L.A. County jail to begin his sentence, he never saw a jail cell. Just like 13,500 low-level offenders each month in California, he was released because of overcrowding—one of the major issues he'd been working to reform when he'd been in office.

To fulfill his community service hours Rod visited a placement agency, though it was for the opposite reason that most people of means pay an agency to secure a certain placement. He *didn't* want a cushy assignment behind a desk in a county or state agency. "When I saw Watts on the list," he explained, "that's where I wanted to be. To me, this is home. I've represented this area in some way for forty years."

As Rod continued to work in the distribution center, I came to know him as a man of exquisite taste and knowledge, with a photographic memory and a connection to everything and everybody. And yet he had no airs; he was eager to roll up his sleeves—custom-tailored ones, no less.

Growing up in Los Angeles, Rod's mother had worked in the post office until the day she died. His father was a photographer for the coroner's office and, in the golden age of Hollywood, had photographed the murder scene of Lana Turner's abusive boyfriend, Johnny Stompanato; the mysterious death of the original Superman, George Reeves; and the autopsy of Marilyn Monroe. Rod's dad developed the film in a makeshift darkroom in the family's garage. "I was too young to recognize the nostalgic value," Rod said. "We had the negatives of Marilyn Monroe's autopsy in the house, and I didn't think to save them!" When Rod was eleven years old, his father quit his job at the coroner's and bought a gas station. This was Rod's introduction to owning your livelihood. Rod's political aspirations were also evident early on: he was elected senior class president in high school and then study body president of his college, having earned an athletic scholarship for track to Pepperdine University. Majoring in city planning and urban studies, he graduated in three years.

"An Afro-centric movement was taking place in Los Angeles politics then," Rod described. "And I wanted to be a part of it." He went to work for the mayoral campaign of Tom Bradley, who was the son of sharecroppers and grandson of slaves. Bradley became the first black mayor of a major American city in which the majority of voters were white, and he went on to serve five consecutive terms. Rod continued to work on successful campaigns for City Councilman Bob Farrell and for Maxine Waters's run for state assembly. And then he pursued office himself.

One day I asked Rod if he was burdened with anger about being banned from political office. "If you allow yourself to get caught up in what you were, or what you think you were, it would drive you straight crazy," Rod replied. "I've left the senate, but more importantly, I'm a cancer survivor. I had prostate cancer in 1998 and, through something like that, you realize a lot of what you think is important, ain't."

I eventually moved Rod from the distribution center to help out in the office. When I mentioned that I was trying to get silent auction items for our annual gala, Rod came in the next day with a signed photograph of Venus and Serena Williams. "It was on my wall in Sacramento," he said, proud to make the donation.

After Rod completed his community service hours, he continued showing up at A New Way of Life—every single day. Just like he was reporting for a job. By this point we had a bustling office, and Rod staked out a desk for himself. He printed business cards and hung framed photographs of Martin Luther King and Malcolm X, along with photos of his granddaughters, and a collage from his days in the legislature. A year went by, and there wasn't a day that Rod didn't come in. He was there for good.

27

ALL OF US OR NONE

In the United States, one in three adults has a criminal record—though black men are six times more likely than white men to be incarcerated.

Over 60 percent of the formerly incarcerated will still be unemployed a year after release. Those who do find employment are typically in low-level jobs, earning 40 percent less pay than adults with no criminal background.

The more nonprofit leaders I met from around the country, the more it became clear that what we were really talking about was a national problem. Individually, our groups were serving our own communities, but what about the big picture: the 2.2 million Americans currently incarcerated, and what happened when they got out?

Though a huge segment of the national population, formerly incarcerated people had no seat at the table. Dorsey pointed to the United Farmworkers movement of the 1960s and how the workers themselves organized, demanding to have a voice. In this spirit, he proposed creating a national organization of formerly incarcerated people and their families.

I heeded his call and, in 2003, gathered in the hills of San Fran-

cisco with forty other men and women who had served time for felony convictions. We created a mission statement to advocate for the
human rights of those in prison, and to demand full restoration of
our human and civil rights after release. We vowed, "Nothing about
us, without us."

Dorsey had come up with a name for the group after visiting the
San Francisco County jail and paying his respects at the memorial of
his late friend and mentor, Nate Harrington. Convicted as a teenager
for selling drugs, Harrington earned his GED in prison and, after his
release in 1976, passed the American Bar Association exam and successfully appealed to the California bar to receive a license to practice
law. Harrington then went back to prison, devoting his career to giving inmates a voice in civil law issues, such as child custody cases.
In 1997, at forty-four years old, Harrington died in a freak home
accident. The county jail's law library was dedicated to his memory,
with a memorial case featuring some of Harrington's favorite things:
Franz Fanon's book *Wretched of the Earth*; a Snickers bar; and Bertolt
Brecht's poem "All of Us or None." It was from the poem's refrain that
Dorsey drew his inspiration:

> *Comrade, only slaves can free you.*
> *Everything or nothing. All of us or none.*

Christening the new organization All of Us or None, Dorsey developed a call and response. "All of us!" he shouted.

"Or none!" we answered, our fists pumping in the air.

Through President George W. Bush's Faith-Based and Community
Initiatives I received a sub-grant from a church, which I used to turn
the garage of the Broke Leg House into an office—and it was there
that our first meeting of the Southern California chapter of All of Us
or None took place.

One of our initial goals was to hold Peace and Justice Community summits throughout California. Our first summit was in

2004 in Oakland. We taped large sheets of paper around the room, each with a major issue faced by the formerly incarcerated: Family Reunification, Housing, Jobs. We then handed out sticky dots and instructed everyone to place dots on the issues most important to them; they could put a dot on each issue, or all their dots on one. When the exercise was complete, Jobs had the most dots, which was no surprise—the effects of job discrimination extended to families, to children, and to entire communities. The correlation was crystal clear: when unemployment rates rose, so did crime and violence. From that moment forward, jobs would become All of Us or None's top-priority issue.

But we were still learning as we went along. At our summit in Compton, we were surprised when the city council welcomed the Junior Reserve Officer Training Corps. Marching into the room were children with wooden guns slung over their shoulders. The council then began the Pledge of Allegiance. I looked over at Dorsey. This was *our* summit, we didn't want to glorify guns or open the day with pledging allegiance to a flag under which we were denied our constitutional rights. From this day arose All of Us or None's Self-Determination Pledge:

> To demand the right to speak in our own voices; to treat each other with respect, and not allow difference to divide us; to accept responsibility for any acts that may have caused harm to our families, our communities or ourselves; to fight all forms of discrimination; to help build the economic stability of formerly-incarcerated people; to claim and take care of our own children and our families; to support community struggles to stop using prisons as the answer to social problems; and to play an active role in making our communities safe for everyone.

For our summit in Watts, invitations went out on the letterhead of U.S. Representative Karen Bass. Replies of attendance streamed in from officials from the Housing Authority, the state legislature, and Congresswoman Maxine Waters.

We gathered in Phoenix Hall, home of Los Angeles's Civil Rights Museum, which—like the indomitable phoenix—rose from the ashes of the Watts riots. The politicians were led to the dais, but, to their surprise, they had no microphone. The only microphone was in the audience, for the community—to amplify the voices of those typically left out.

For the first half of the day, formerly incarcerated people testified to the challenges they faced after being released. They spoke from the heart of the difficulty of reuniting with their children, the lack of access to affordable housing, and the consistent rejection from jobs because of their criminal record. I watched the officials who were unable to interrupt or give excuses or make empty promises—and I saw them *truly* listening.

We instructed the officials that, after lunch, they would have the microphone—*but* they had to return with some answers to the target issue of job discrimination. They followed instructions, and the discussion narrowed to that question on all job applications: *Have you ever been convicted of a felony?* When you automatically had to check that box, your application went no further, regardless of your qualifications. That box superseded all other job skills, experience, qualifications, and talent. It weeded out people before they even got a foot in the door.

What if, we discussed, that initial box could be eliminated so that everyone who was qualified had the chance to get to that next step? This way, you could walk in with your strengths, as a full person, with no stigma blocking you. The question of a criminal record could come later in the process—during a personal interview, most likely—after a potential employer at least had the chance to get to know your qualifications and you. From this, the Ban the Box movement was born.

The city of San Francisco was the first to vote—unanimously—to Ban the Box on municipal employment applications. Though not comprehensive, it was a step in the right direction. First Boston, then

Oakland, followed with Ban the Box legislation. These policy shifts spurred national discussion, and we saw the language evolve as a result: the word "ex-con," which unfairly defined a person for the rest of his or her life, soon fell out of use in academia, journalism, grant applications, and in the words of elected officials.

But when it came to my hometown, progress was lagging. Los Angeles County was one of the largest employers in the state—and it also had the state's largest population of people with criminal records. Despite this, it took years of clamoring before finally, in 2006, Ban the Box was slated to go before the L.A. County Board of Supervisors. Of the five members, three were Democrats. We were ready to celebrate an overdue victory.

Unbelievably, we lost. Despite other counties and neighboring cities, such as Compton, stepping up, Los Angeles failed to act. After several years, Governor Arnold Schwarzenegger at last banned the box from employment applications for all state agencies. And when Governor Jerry Brown took office, Ban the Box was further expanded to all public sector job applications in California.

San Francisco continued to enforce the broadest coverage of Ban the Box, with the law eventually applying to city contract employers, housing applications, and private companies with twenty or more employees. And it went an important step further by prohibiting employers from asking about criminal convictions during an initial interview, and from even considering a criminal history unless it had a "direct and specific negative bearing" on the applicant's ability to perform the job. San Francisco employers were also required to display in the window a poster from the Office of Labor Standards Enforcement, demonstrating compliance. To us, this was a beautiful welcome sign.

Sweeping the nation, twenty-one states and over one hundred cities and counties banned the box on government applications—some enacted broader bans extending to private employers. In 2015, President Barack Obama spoke the words "Ban the Box." To think that we, a ragtag group of people with conviction records, came up with this! When Obama banned the box from federal job applications, it was another victory, though not as wide-reaching as we'd hoped. For every stride we made, it was clear how far we still had to go.

At Christmastime, All of Us or None members stood before a San Francisco community center full of families. Dorsey called children up by name and, one by one, eager kids raced to receive gifts they'd asked for—but not from Santa. "This," Dorsey told them, "is from your dad. He loves you." These children didn't need to believe in Santa Claus so much as they needed to believe in their parents behind bars who desperately wanted to remain relevant.

For days I'd watched Dorsey running around collecting gifts, and now I stood back marveling at all the people taking care of each other, especially the men, looking out for other men's children. A cadre of volunteers, most of whom were formerly incarcerated themselves, wheeled in bikes for the kids.

"I stole a bike when I was a teenager," Dorsey admitted to the volunteers.

"So did I," a volunteer offered up. Others nodded, that had been their story too.

Dorsey smiled. "Well, now's our chance to give that bike back."

28

TREATING THE SYMPTOMS
AND THE DISEASE

Every year in L.A. County, 45,600 people are released on parole.

A survey revealed that over 40 percent of L.A. employers would not hire a person with a criminal record.

When I looked at mass incarceration and all 45,000 barriers to re-entry, the way I saw it was that the law was a major part of the problem. I also saw that the law was difficult to change. But if some laws are part of the problem, can we make other laws part of the solution?

Saúl Sarabia and I got to talking. It was 2007, and he was now the director of UCLA School of Law's Critical Race Studies program, the first of its kind in the country. His students studied racial oppression and the law, and delved into groundbreaking projects, such as filing lawsuits in New Orleans after Hurricane Katrina to prevent the city from bulldozing homes without notice.

Eager to return his attention to issues of incarceration and re-entry, Saúl began organizing campus panels on structural racism and speaking about the legal needs of people who'd been behind bars. But the response outside of the Critical Race Studies program shocked him. "It was as if I was talking about things you don't mention in

polite company," he described. Which made him all the more convinced we *really* needed to be talking about such things.

Together, Saúl and I applied for a grant from the UCLA Center for
Community Partnerships, with the vision of coupling law students
and A New Way of Life to create a prisoner re-entry initiative. I had
never set foot in a university classroom, but after we received the two-
year grant, there I stood, side by side with leading civil rights law
professors, talking to law students who were motivated to learn and
eager to make a difference.

The grant coincided with the first time the Ban the Box initiative
was going before the L.A. County Board of Supervisors for a vote, and
the students got behind it full force. It was exhilarating to listen and
watch as they held focus groups with formerly incarcerated people,
discussed employment rights law in a community meeting, and created fact sheets to illustrate how requiring a job applicant to automatically indicate past convictions had a disproportionate negative effect
on black and Latino men. Until I met these students, I doubted that
the weight of the law could be tilted in our favor, a notion that, sadly,
had been reinforced by most everything I'd seen and lived. But the
students' passion swept me up, and I dared get optimistic. When Ban
the Box was rejected by the Board of Supervisors, my shock was mir-
rored, even amplified, by the students. Young and idealistic, wanting
so badly to believe the law was just, many were devastated.

To Saúl, this was a critical and teachable moment: How can citizens actually affect change? How does a poor person or someone with
a criminal record have a voice and a presence in a democracy? From
discussions of our disappointment and defeat, a new idea material-
ized: though we couldn't—yet—ban the box, what other barriers to
employment *could* we address?

The students began researching existing policy for expunging misdemeanors and crimes that didn't culminate in incarceration. They
also learned that certain job licenses could be obtained if a judge was
petitioned to grant a Certificate of Rehabilitation, showing someone
had been law-abiding for seven consecutive years. What emerged was

the idea of a free legal clinic to assist the community in petitioning for expungements and Certificates of Rehabilitation.

But this idea didn't excite me. The public defender's office already offered these services. Sure, we'd be helping by bringing assistance directly into the community, but it was a one-person-at-a-time approach that tended to the symptoms but ignored the disease. To me, a clinic wouldn't get us any closer to preventing *why* all this was going on in the first place.

"What else can we do," Saúl asked his class, "to get at some of the core issues?" We knew that job discrimination and negligent hiring practices were rampant. We knew employers were unaware there could be incentives for hiring people with records. What if, Saúl and the students posed, we could screen people who came into the legal clinic? By surveying this target base, we could uncover large-impact issues, such as discrimination, that could be litigated—and *this* was where we could make seismic moves. Saúl then added, "Susan, we can also use the clinic to recruit for All of Us or None." Now I was excited.

We planned two pilot legal re-entry clinics to be held in Phoenix Hall in Watts. Volunteering with Saúl to supervise the students were attorneys from Homeboy Industries, an L.A.-based program providing classes and employment to people with criminal pasts; Neighborhood Legal Services, one of California's largest public interest law offices, which offered free legal services countywide; and a supervising paralegal from the public defender's office.

Amazingly, when the doors of the first clinic opened, clients were already waiting. A steady stream continued throughout the day, numbers we hadn't anticipated. We learned that, even though similar city resources existed, they were mostly self-help—*Here's the form, good luck!* With our clinic, to walk in and be able to talk, for free, with an attorney, that was a big deal—especially since most of the people showing up had only ever spoken with a lawyer when they were in orange and cuffed.

After our hugely successful launch, Saúl gathered the students. "The legacy of our grant was supposed to be Ban the Box," he said.

"But when that didn't happen, it made us think differently and deeper to make law an agent of change, not an agent of oppression." Then he turned to me. "This re-entry clinic is going to long outlast the grant." At our second legal re-entry clinic, students began to survey the clients, asking things such as *Where have you applied for a job? Did you experience any discrimination?* This approach made some of the other volunteer lawyers uneasy. Nervously, someone said to Saúl, "Your students' questions are suggesting to people that they have rights under federal discrimination law."

Through the clinic, a picture began to form of the attitudes and hiring practices of South L.A. employers. In response, we created an Employment Rights Job Fair to put employers face-to-face with people who wanted to be employed. It was our own way of banning the box. To watch people showing up flat-out kicked the myth that those with criminal histories or those on welfare didn't want to work: people were lining up around the block to find work.

The students were deeply impacted by all this, and some went on to careers in public interest or civil rights law. One third-year student, Joshua Kim, was so affected he wrote a paper about areas where the current model of law didn't address discrimination. It was sometimes over my head, but Josh and Saúl were often in heated discussion. *How can you have Title VII of the Civil Rights Act and still have an increase of racial oppression? How can we create the language for re-entry law? How can legal strategies support social movement building?*

Josh, a hippie-ish guy with long hair wrapped in a ponytail, was born in South Korea and raised in California. He had planned to become a public defender but, after the grant ended, he asked if he could temporarily stay on as an unpaid intern to get the re-entry clinic running on a monthly basis. Here was a young man with opportunities awaiting him, but if he wanted to stay on, I was thrilled to have him. "There are needs here," he said. "And I want to be where the needs are."

Josh grew deeply invested in the clinic. This was the forefront, he believed, of a burgeoning movement: creating re-entry law. He saw, in the hazy distance, an entire legal area devoted to the needs of people getting out of prison.

As I got to know Josh, he opened up about his past. In his first year of law school, he started using crystal meth. Addiction led him to fail classes, and eventually he was kicked out of UCLA. "I knew how fortunate I was to be able to return home to loving parents, and to be given the time to recover," he told me. "Which meant taking a good, hard look at my life and realizing who I'd become and how I got there." He wanted to reapply to law school, but he was detoxing, and that clouded his focus and memory; he couldn't read a page, let alone a law book. "My family was patient," he said. "And I was so grateful that I didn't have to worry about where my next meal was coming from, or how to cover the rent." Eventually, he reapplied and was accepted back to UCLA.

As Josh told me his story, I began to realize what was fueling his extreme passion and dedication—and why he'd offered to work for free. He'd had run-ins with law enforcement, but was never incarcerated, never even arrested. He'd been given a pass, and he understood that other people didn't get passes.

Josh had been volunteering for six months when he came to tell me he'd passed the bar exam and needed to look for a job. It was 2008, the first wave of the recession, and I couldn't afford an additional salary. But I didn't want to lose Josh and what he was doing in the legal clinic. I gave him my salary.

I set up a desk for Josh across from mine. Here he was, stepping out of UCLA Law and into a garage.

It didn't take long before potential cases of discrimination arose in the monthly legal clinic, some of which Josh filed with the U.S. Equal Employment Opportunity Commission (EEOC). What continued to pop up as a major issue was licensure. Josh was seeing that most jobs that paid a living wage—such as security guard, nurse's assistant, commercial truck driver—required a license, but licensing required a background check. When people were denied licensing because of their records, they were all but relegated to earn the minimum wage for the rest of their lives.

Josh grew increasingly troubled by these commercial background checks. Under California law, there was the Seven Year Rule—though it was rarely enforced—where, after seven years, a crime that either hadn't resulted in a conviction or was pardoned should not show up on a background check. But Josh noted instance after instance where this wasn't happening in compliance with the law. Because Josh wasn't a litigator and we had limited resources, he referred these cases to private firms. But the private firms rarely ended up pursuing the cases, making it clear that re-entry law and this demographic of people weren't a priority for most attorneys.

Stemming from his own frustration, Josh partnered with a former classmate from law school who was a litigator and together they took on the cases he found through the clinic—and began making small recoveries. Josh spent countless hours piecing together all the laws that could affect formerly incarcerated people. He uncovered laws that had fallen into obscurity. The more he learned, the more convinced Josh became of the potential for impact in this area of the law—which he was helping to pioneer.

Josh came to me one day with the case of a client. Her record had been expunged through the clinic, but she showed up again saying she'd been denied a job because her background check didn't reflect the expungement, her entire record was still there. Josh tracked where she went next: she applied for another job and the background check was run through the same company, IntelliCorp, that had provided her previous background check. Again, it showed her expunged record.

IntelliCorp Records Inc., a large Ohio-based company, advertised nationwide about its instant background checks. The problem with the instant background check was that it didn't allow for the time-consuming procedure of checking with the courts for any updated records. This was why recently expunged records were still showing up even though, according to the law, none should have. Since the law wasn't being enforced, instant background checks were being conducted by companies all across the country. Why was a practice that violated the law allowed to flourish right out in the open? Because it was extremely lucrative, and because the people most affected belonged to a segment of the population with little voice and no recourse.

"We found our named plaintiff," Josh said to me, and shared the details of the person he'd been tracking: a black woman in her thirties who was pursuing her master's degree in social work and had been seeking employment to fulfill her mandatory internship credits. When the results from the background checks shut her out of jobs, it also threatened her ability to graduate.

"IntelliCorp is far from the only company doing instant background checks," Josh said. "But they're the one we're going after. We only need to make an example of one for all the others to comply." Then he took a breath. "But it's going to take a while."

To keep A New Way of Life afloat, I donated my savings; it wasn't a loan, it was a gift. The problem was, I was overextended. Two years earlier, in 2006, when real estate was booming, I bought a duplex in South L.A. for A New Way of Life's longer-term residents who had gotten their lives together but still were unable to secure their own housing. But now, with the economy in the toilet, A New Way of Life was feeling it severely. For the women, jobs that were always tough to come by disappeared entirely. Donations that we relied upon had dried up. At first, I tried to remain optimistic, but as the months went on, it became clear this wasn't a dark cloud that would be lifting anytime soon. One morning, I couldn't bring myself to get out of bed. I had no salary and no savings, and the day before we'd learned that one of the women had lost her child to the system. This wasn't the first time a woman's children had been lost, and it wouldn't be the last, but each time it happened, I felt as if I were losing K.K. all over again. I was emotionally and physically spent. Everything looked bleak, and I just couldn't see how I was going to push on. Dragging myself up, I decided to do something different. I got in the car and went to the car wash, something I rarely did, especially when money was tight. As I sat in the car wash, I flipped through the day's mail, coming across a letter from Vinny Green, a name I didn't know.

"I am the principal at the Wilshire Boulevard Temple religious school," she wrote. "I teach the Jewish concept of *Tikkun Olam*, that one person can change the world through acts of loving kindness. I learned about you after you were honored as a Phenomenal Woman at Cal State Northridge. When I told my class about you, they asked if we could send *tzedakah* to your organization. *Tzedakah* is a Hebrew word meaning justice or righteousness. One of the highest forms of *tzedakah* is an anonymous donation, where lives are changed without need of credit or anything in return. Our donation is modest, collected from change brought in by the students over the year, but we hope this can help one of the women in your organization to pursue her education. As an educator, I stress the importance of education in changing someone's life. Please let her know we are behind her with our support. In turn, when this woman earns her degree, perhaps she can help another person."

Enclosed was a check for $900. I sat there in my car, the water flowing down the windows, and tears flowing out of my eyes. How could I be in a place where I wanted to give up, when these children I didn't even know wanted to support our cause? Here was this teacher, imparting to young people how important it was to look out for others, to take responsibility for your actions, to act with loving kindness. These weren't the messages I heard growing up. I folded the letter for safekeeping. Sometimes in the darkest moments, the dawn comes, and those kids were my dawn.

Josh worked around the clock to bring about the first nationwide class-action suit based on instant background checks. I moved us out of the garage and into office space, but A New Way of Life could barely afford it, and it showed. The office was stifling, and if we ran too many fans the power cut off; worse, the plumbing was always stopping up. I felt like a sweatshop boss.

After the class-action suit became known, large law firms outside of California filed similar cases. Instead of fighting to keep them out, Josh agreed to join forces with them. Ultimately, there were six law firms and twelve attorneys attached. As far as I could tell, none of those fancy firms put in as much work as Josh, even though they had entire staffs at their disposal, even though their hourly billable rates were double, nearly triple, what Josh billed. To me, those big firms were mainly out for the dollar, while Josh toiled away in hopes of restoring people's rights and removing systemic barriers. I lost count of how many mornings I came in to see that Josh had fallen asleep at his desk. For two and a half years, he litigated the case.

In 2014, a settlement was approved for $18.6 million, and background check companies were mandated to accurately report up-to-date background records. A New Way of Life received about $400,000 of the settlement money. The people who were violated received a structured settlement of $300 each—not a lot, but far more than the paltry sums plaintiffs typically receive from class-action suits. The majority of attorneys' fees went to the white-shoe law firms, though none of this would have existed without Josh. Even in the law profession, there was a class system, rich versus poor, corporate versus nonprofit. Even this was about power.

Still, I reveled in our victory, and I moved us out of the sweatshop and into new office space with reliable plumbing, heat, and air conditioning.

But Josh was having a tough time feeling satisfied with the outcome. "The big settlement number tends to obscure the relative insignificance of this win," he said. "We pushed the law as far as we could, but was it enough to make a real difference?" He estimated that it would only cost companies a couple dollars more per background check to comply with the law. "If the cost of background checks had gone up significantly," he said, "companies would start to think twice about requiring background checks for every single job, especially positions where a mistake someone made in the past would have no impact on their ability to successfully be employed."

In a way, Josh reminded me of myself. Surmounting a hurdle only seemed to provide a clearer view of how much further we had to go. Still, I was so proud of Josh. And his work put us on the map.

Never had there been any notion that a legal department would come out of A New Way of Life, but we continued to expand. Had anyone told me at the start that I'd go on to have six staff lawyers, I'd have laughed them right out the door.

29

THE MEANING OF *LIFE*

Women commit far fewer murders than men, but receive far longer sentences. A woman who kills a male partner receives, on average, a fifteen-year sentence, while a man who kills a female partner typically receives two to six years.

Flozelle Woodmore and I met when we were doing time. She was much younger than me, but we'd grown up in the same neighborhood. She was always smiley, talkative, and insightful, and she was a lifer. She had, however, been sentenced with the possibility of parole, so after I started A New Way of Life, I optimistically wrote to her. "When you get out, Flozelle, I'll have a bed waiting for you." Little did anyone know that her bid for freedom would cause a statewide uproar.

What led Flozelle to prison at eighteen years old was an all-too-familiar story. At thirteen, she'd become involved with a man five years her senior, Clifton Morrow. At fifteen, she showed up to a domestic violence shelter in Los Angeles, but was turned away because she was underage. At eighteen, fearing for the safety of her two-year-old son, she told Morrow the relationship was over. He struck her numerous times, shoved their son against the wall, and threatened to kill them both.

Flozelle fled the house. Morrow followed, wielding what witnesses would describe as an icepick and shouting, "If I can't have you, no one can!" Flozelle ran across the street to her sister's home, where there was a gun. She delivered a single, fatal shot to Morrow's chest. This was in 1986. Flozelle had no prior criminal history, and friends and family lined up to attest to the years of physical and emotional abuse she'd endured. But the jury was not allowed to hear evidence of "battered women's syndrome" because the law in California, and most states, did not recognize this as a medical condition and a form of self-defense. Flozelle pled guilty to second-degree murder and was sentenced to fifteen years to life. Wracked with guilt, shame, and fear, she shut down, unable to speak.

Her mindset changed when she learned that her thirty-three-year-old brother, a manager at Sears, had been mistaken for someone else and fatally shot. Heartbroken, and unable to console her mother, Flozelle vowed to become a model prisoner so she could get released, reunite with her family, and devote herself to working with victims of domestic abuse. Out of her newfound determination, she organized a battered women's support group in prison. She earned her GED, and then successfully petitioned a transfer to the women's state prison in Chowchilla so she could study in the computer technology program there—only to see the program discontinued shortly after her arrival.

In 2002, after serving a decade, Flozelle went before the state parole board. By this time, California law had changed, allowing battered women's syndrome to be presented as evidence during a trial. Also, in an unusual twist, the mother and sister of Morrow, the murder victim, advocated to the Board of Prison Terms for Flozelle's release. Less than 5 percent of lifers are recommended for parole, but, impressed with Flozelle's rehabilitation, future goals, and the depth of her remorse, the Board of Prison Terms found her suitable.

Enter Governor Gray Davis, who'd taken office ranting that never would he allow a convicted murderer out of prison regardless of the circumstances—and, because of an abused 1988 proposition,

California governors were granted this power. Davis overturned the parole board's recommendation to release Flozelle.

The following year, Flozelle again went before the Board of Prison Terms and was found suitable for release. Yet, again, Governor Davis shot down the board, even though it was comprised of twelve commissioners he himself had appointed. And it wasn't just in Flozelle's case that the governor brazenly exercised his veto power—of the board's 285 recommendations for release, Davis overturned all but six. Protestors descended upon the governor's office, calling for an end to Davis's no-parole stance. Painted in bruises and blood, they stood in a silent vigil, handcuffed together, duct tape covering their mouths.

The next year, Flozelle was again found suitable for parole, and this time the board's recommendation went before Governor Arnold Schwarzenegger. Tania Morrow, the victim's sister, wrote in a letter delivered to the governor, "I realize it must seem strange for the relative of a victim to ask that the person who committed the crime be set free. She has taken something very dear and irreplaceable away from me and my family. Yet I have completely forgiven Flozelle. I know because of her letters that she deeply regrets what happened."

I was shocked when I heard that Schwarzenegger, too, went against the board, deeming Flozelle an unreasonable safety risk. For three consecutive years, Schwarzenegger continued to overturn his board's decision. By this point, the judge who had originally sentenced Flozelle was advocating for her release. Newspaper op-eds had been published about the unbelievable circumstances. Trying to do what I could, I submitted petitions and hundreds of letters on Flozelle's behalf.

On the other side, the Los Angeles County deputy district attorney, David Dahle, cited that Flozelle's son—an impressionable toddler when she'd been convicted—was now himself incarcerated for murder. What should be held against Flozelle was the family's "dynamics of violence," Dahle insisted. "This is a pattern of behavior imprinted, I believe, from generation to generation."

In 2007, Flozelle's sixth recommendation for parole went before the governor. It was the fourth time Schwarzenegger had presided over her case. He waited right up until the deadline, then, for reasons that were never explained, he at last upheld the board's decision. Flozelle had served twenty-one years. Convicted as a teenager, she came out a grandmother.

At the time, most women paroled from a life sentence were released to Crossroads, a transitional facility in Claremont, about thirty-five miles from Los Angeles. Though Flozelle couldn't live at A New Way of Life, I proudly offered her a job doing administrative work. But, logistically, it was difficult: Flozelle's commute, requiring a train and a bus, took over two hours. And the rules of Crossroads were unyielding, requiring her to return by 6 p.m. for dinner, even though she wanted to work an eight-hour day. Instead, she had to pack up around 3:30 p.m. to make it back to the dinner table.

Still, Flozelle went well beyond her duties at A New Way of Life. She spoke with me about an idea: she wanted to bring the families and friends of people serving life sentences before the Board of Prison Terms in Sacramento to say they understood the extreme loss suffered at the hands of their loved one, but that it was possible for people to be rehabilitated. This was unheard of—no one from the outside went before the board except for D.A.s and victims. But I supported Flozelle's idea, and so did the Open Society Foundation, which granted her a Soros Justice Fellowship to see it through.

Flozelle filled a van with the loved ones of women serving life sentences and they drove four hundred miles to stand together before the Board of Prison Terms—an indelible image of how incarceration didn't just affect the individual behind bars, it affected families, it affected generations, it affected communities. The trip was powerful, for both sides. From that moment on, the Board of Prison Terms welcomed Flozelle and the families every quarter.

Flozelle made such an impression on me. Bursting with passion, she had the ability to organize people and advocate for change. It was important to me that a formerly incarcerated person always lead A

New Way of Life to keep it true to its mission, and I took solace knowing that when the day came that I was ready to retire, I could pass the baton to Flozelle.

Flozelle's parole was scheduled to end in August 2012, five years after her release. It was a presidential election year, and Flozelle, who'd never been allowed to vote, couldn't wait to cast her first ever vote for Barack Obama. Inexplicably, her paperwork didn't come through and, when November rolled around, Flozelle was still on parole. The election came and went, her right to vote denied.

In February 2013, I received a call from Flozelle's sister. My knees went weak. The unthinkable. Flozelle had suffered an aneurysm. At forty-five years old, she was gone. She had lived five and a half years of adult life in the free world. She died while still on parole.

I had planned to support Flozelle as she transitioned into what I had started; instead, it was I who acted upon what Flozelle had started. I got in a van with twelve former prisoners, all of whom had received written permission from their parole officers to travel outside of L.A. County. We drove six hours to Sacramento and stood before the Board of Prison Terms pinned with ribbons in memory of Flozelle. Some of the commissioners stepped from the dais, eyes red, to grieve with us over Flozelle's passing.

"She was so grateful to get to know her family again," I told them. "Thank you for releasing her." But the board knew this wholeheartedly; Flozelle had told them herself in her visits to plead for others to know the same freedom. Then, another unthinkable happened: the Board of Prison Terms thanked me.

From then on, I raised money to bring former lifers to Sacramento to thank the Board of Prison Terms for their release. Four times a year, twelve of us piled in a van. Along the way, we stopped at the beach and had lunch at a restaurant—some folks had never been to a nice restaurant. We played oldies but goodies on the radio the whole way there. Every time I planned one of these trips, we had more people who wanted to go than could fit in the van. You'd think folks might never want to set foot back in that place, but instead they were eager to go before the board as free people, to stand there and shine, to take pride in their accomplishments, maybe even brag a little. By going back, they paved the way for others who were still incarcerated.

The thousands upon thousands of others who, just like Flozelle, had hopes and dreams and so much they were capable of achieving.

30

THE WOMEN FROM ORANGE COUNTY

Women give significantly more to charity than their male peers—around twice as much—even though women generally earn eighty cents for every dollar men earn.

When I was a resident at CLARE, donors showed up at Christmastime with gifts, and I was given a cuddly teddy bear. My roommate wasn't there that day, so the program director suggested I hold an extra teddy bear for her, but then changed her mind. Later, when my roommate returned, the director asked me for the second teddy bear, but I told her I only had one. She didn't believe me, and I had to give up my own cuddly bear. Looking back all these years later, she was probably just confused, but you couldn't have told me that then. I was deeply hurt, and it was so early in my recovery that feeling like I wasn't being believed could have been enough to tip my boat.

When the first Christmas came around at A New Way of Life, I thought about that teddy bear and made a commitment that every resident would get a gift of her own. It had been a long time since I'd had any type of Christmas, but the day after Thanksgiving I bought a tree, just like Daddy had done, and we all decorated it. Then I got to work soliciting donations so I could buy gifts.

In the winter of 2002, I was asked to speak before the Orange County chapter of Women of Vision, a faith-based volunteer organization. Afterward, Nancy Daley, a petite brunette, approached me. "You are anointed to do what you're doing," she said. I chuckled, saying if only she knew how I was running around like a chicken with its head cut off making sure everyone in the house had a Christmas gift. A smile spread across Nancy's face. Then she asked if her group could be our Santa Claus.

Back at the house I instructed everyone to make a Christmas list. One woman looked at me, puzzled. A list? It was her first Christmas in twenty years.

"Write down things that you wish for, but also that are practical," I explained. So many of the women had never before been asked what they wanted, and they were filled with joy at the simple act of writing to the Women of Vision about things they loved, their favorite colors, and what they needed. I sent the lists to Nancy, and she paired one of her women to shop for each one of ours.

Two weeks before Christmas, fancy SUVs pulled up to the house, and out hopped a couple dozen white women and a handful of children. But the Women of Vision hadn't shown up with just one gift for each woman: they had carloads of gift-wrapped presents.

The amount of gifts—and the quality—was remarkable. No expense had been spared: ten computer tablets for the women's schooling, a TV, a printer. But more than that, each gift included a card with a woman or child's name on it. Most of the residents were accustomed to hand-me-downs, if anything at all, so to hold a beautifully wrapped gift with your name on it, a gift that was purchased especially *for you*—that really meant something.

"Thank you for allowing us to come into your lives," Nancy announced as we gathered together. "We pray over your names and your gifts, and we want the best for you." Song sheets were passed around, and everyone clasped hands, women and children, black and white, South L.A. and Orange County. Together we sang "Silent Night" and "Jingle Bells."

This marked the beginning of a wonderful tradition. For fourteen Christmases now, the Women of Vision have come with their arms and hearts full, wanting nothing in return. Each year, as we gather together, I ask if any of the women would like to say thank you and tell a little about themselves.

One year, Rachel, who was the sweetest woman and relatively new to A New Way of Life, stood up before the group. Ready to go to her job at a nearby sandwich shop, she was outfitted in a matching cap and apron. "I got caught up in gangbanging and trying to be part of something I wasn't," she said. Then she paused, as the tears came. The Women of Vision gathered around her, grabbing hold of her hands, rubbing her back. Rachel took a deep breath and continued, "They told me we were loyal and a family, but I witnessed awful crimes where women were taken advantage of. And I stayed silent." When Rachel had first arrived she told me how a gun was put to her head and she was ordered to go get another girl. She did, and the girl was gang-raped. In court, Rachel had been too scared to talk about what had really happened, terrified the gang would seek revenge against her family. She was also shamed to the core that she'd played a part in this crime, even though she, too, had been a victim.

She continued, her lip quivering. "Now I am a registered sex offender." She cringed at the words. "I have a curfew, and have to wear this ankle monitor. I am so ashamed. I always wear flare legs to cover it. I encourage the kids here, stick with your families. Listen to your mom, and know that you always have your family. I thought I had nobody, but that wasn't true. I am so bitter I stayed silent when I saw awful things happening."

"There's a difference between hurt and bitter," I offered up. "And I don't see bitter in you, Rachel, I see hurt. But you will heal."

Another woman who was new to the house, Tara, was next to tell her story. "I found out about A New Way of Life in the prison yard," she said, then her face turned steely. Tara's guard was raised high, because that's how she had survived a life of people taking from her and preying off her.

"What are you grateful for, Tara?" I asked.

She crossed her arms. She started sentences but kept stopping.

I knew what was going on, because Tara reminded me of how I'd once been. Gratitude was buried so far under a heaping pile of hurt and pain and disappointment, it wasn't even an emotion you could access. Miraculous growth was possible, though, and, some months later, Tara would come to me after her tennis bracelet, a cherished gift from her mother, who'd died while she was in prison, went missing. She told me it was so hard not to react with violence. "But how you've been talking with me, Ms. Burton, that was teaching me how to respond." This, to me, was a major marker: having the maturity to handle what life throws at you.

Next, a soft-spoken woman, her hands resting on the shoulders of a teenage boy, stood before the Women of Vision. "This is my son," she began. "This is the first time I've told my story in front of my children, but I've written them about it. I am ashamed of what I've done, but not of who I am. I abused my stepdaughter. I had become a product of my rage and hurt. I was being abused, and then I hurt someone I had power over. By the grace of God, she forgave me, she's twenty today. I'm not my past, my past doesn't define me."

Though we were supposed to wait for Christmas Day to open the gifts, some of the Women of Vision snuck upstairs, where Sonya, a young woman who'd done well at A New Way of Life, was packing a suitcase to move to Oregon, where relatives and a fresh start awaited. "Open them now," the Women of Vision urged. Sonya unwrapped a pair of Ugg boots and a colorful fleece. "Ooo, I need warm things for where I'm going," she said, beaming.

"I know you wanted a Bible," one of the Women of Vision said as Sonya unwrapped her final gift. "So we got you a pink one. Whenever you pick it up, know we are thinking about you."

31

BEING BEHOLDEN

The California Department of Corrections and Rehabilitation has one of the highest recidivism rates in the country, with nearly half of women with a felony conviction returning to prison—and a 61 percent recidivism rate overall. The majority of people returned to prison within the first year of release.

The first time I met the Little Hoover Commission was during a 2003 hearing, when the independent state oversight agency was investigating the broken parole system for a report to be presented to the California state legislature. I didn't know what to expect when I went to Sacramento to watch the hearing, but I prepared myself for a bunch of typical bureaucracy, empty words that made it look as though people were doing something while everyone knew that absolutely nothing was likely to happen.

Instead, I was blown away. The Little Hoover Commission began by saying, "California's parole system is a billion-dollar failure." You couldn't get more direct than that. They didn't shy away or limit themselves to a wish list of fixes. Witnesses testified to the antiquated system and to the absurdly large recidivism rate for parole violations, many as minor as missing an appointment because a letter with the appointment date went to the wrong address. The goal of the correctional system, they stressed, should and must be that people who serve time go on to be law-abiding, contributing citizens.

They offered doable and cost-saving fixes, such as: preparing inmates for release with educational, vocational, and drug treatment programs, all of which have been proven to reduce recidivism; linking the success of wardens with the success of exiting inmates; assisting parolees at the community level to find jobs and to stay sober; not automatically re-incarcerating someone for low-level parole violations; and looking to drug treatment programs as effective—and cost-effective—alternatives to re-incarceration.

As I listened, I once again thought of all the years I pointed a finger at my own weakness, believing I had innate flaws and couldn't get my life together. Hearing all this, I wanted to cry. The system was broken, and it had set me up to fail. I just went down the path I was expected to follow.

I left Sacramento with hope that the Little Hoover Commission's report, "Back to the Community: Safe and Sound Parole Policies," would inspire a revamping of the parole system. The following year, the commission released a subsequent report, "Breaking the Barriers for Women on Parole," with a photo of me at graduation on the cover.

But, despite the hearings and two reports filled with compelling and sound arguments and realistic solutions, parole continued operating in the same, broken way; business as usual. Eight years went by, and not only was there no progress, but California's criminal justice system had worsened to the point the entire country took notice. In 2011, the U.S. Supreme Court ruled that overcrowding in California's thirty-three prisons created conditions horrendous enough to violate the Eighth Amendment's ban on cruel and unusual punishment. Ordered to reduce the state prison population by more than thirty thousand inmates, California began a reshuffling act.

As part of this, the California legislature and Governor Jerry Brown passed what they called public safety legislation—Assembly Bill 109—to shift responsibility of nonviolent offenders from the state to counties. New offenders would be sentenced to county jails instead of state prisons, and people being released were to report to local county probation officers instead of state parole officers. Though the parole system was finally being dismantled, this was hardly the way the Little Hoover Commission had recommended. The changes being implemented weren't long-term fixes that focused on rehabilitation and community support—these were work-arounds, duct-taping the whole, damn broken machine.

Along with the passage of AB 109 came a lot of government money into L.A. County. The sheriff got money, the Probation Department got money, and, eventually, the LAPD wanted to get in on some of the money too. None of this should have affected A New Way of Life, but it did, in dire ways.

For nearly a decade, A New Way of Life held a prison-aftercare contract from Walden House, which had since changed its name to Healthright 360. The contract now allotted us $42 a day per woman for housing, food, and transportation. For all this time, the contract had worked smoothly. But now, under AB 109, Healthright 360 was to report to the County Probation Department. They were now beholden to the government, and that, in turn, made A New Way of Life beholden too.

Suddenly, it was as if the intent of the entire aftercare contract changed. The Probation Department instituted rules to limit the women's freedom. If a woman wanted to leave the house to visit her children or relatives overnight, she no longer sought approval from me, she now had to have a pass approved by the Probation Department. This meant that I had to request passes in advance—but the Probation Department was often slow in processing, so if a pass didn't come back in time, I had to break the news to a woman, "Sorry, you have to tell your children you can't see them." The whole thing was damaging to relationships, tearing down the trust we were trying to build—trust between women and their families, and trust between the women and me.

Someone from the Probation Department routinely came by the house, and when I saw them nosing around, looking in closets and opening the refrigerator, my mind jumped right back to when I was a little girl, helplessly watching someone from welfare snooping around our rat-infested house. It got me in the pit of my stomach.

Things grew worse when the LAPD became involved. Wanting a slice of the AB 109 funds, the LAPD needed to figure out a way to insert themselves into the picture, so they kicked into action a small part of the legislation that allowed for compliance checks.

We found this out one day when the front door of A New Way of Life burst open and eight corn-fed police officers stampeded into the living room with guns drawn. One of the women, who was coming around the corner with her baby in her arms, was met with a 9mm pistol in her face. The police lined the women against the wall, handcuffed them, and searched the entire house, lifting up mattresses, going through drawers, claiming they were looking for drugs and guns, though there was no reason for the search, no tips or suspicion, no past issues with noncompliance in our home. But, under the rules of the contract, if they didn't come hunting, they didn't get paid.

I was stark-raving mad. I called a meeting with the watch commander, the sergeant, and the lieutenants. I explained why it was important for the women to feel safe, that raiding the house was uncalled for, we were law-abiding citizens, and these were women who were there seeking help and a safe place to live. "When we see cops, we don't see protection served," I said. "We see trauma, we see harassment. When these women are automatically viewed as guilty and treated like criminals in their home, I'm violating my promise to keep the home safe." As a solution, I asked if we could make appointments for the police to visit—not raid—the house, and to interview—not handcuff—the women.

"No," I was informed. The police mandate was to enter unannounced. The protocol was to handcuff and search the house. I left the meeting saying I wasn't going to allow the police in.

"If you don't want to play," they replied, "don't take the money."

Not long after, four police cars cruised up to the house. Out stepped eight officers, handcuffs clanging. The women did as I had instructed: they locked the doors and politely said they couldn't allow anyone inside.

The police were bewildered about what to do next, so they sat outside. As soon as I got the call from the women, I hurried over from the office. On the front lawn, the police and I got into it. "There's $164 million that is supposed to be spent on community-based organizations and housing," I said. "These raids are a complete waste of AB 109 money."

To my surprise, one of the officers agreed with me. Still, there was no resolution. They were trying to do their job; I was trying to do mine.

I went to the board of supervisors, I went to the city council, I went to State Senator Holly Mitchell, I went to the *Los Angeles Times*. And then, by chance, something happened. L.A. County Supervisor Mark Ridley-Thomas and I had been working closely together for many years but he'd never been to the house, so I invited him over. He showed up with the CEO of L.A. County, William Fujioka. We sat in the living room, drinking coffee and talking with the women. Suddenly, there was commotion from our second house a couple doors down. The police had burst in for a surprise AB 109 check and were handcuffing women. I hurried over, along with the county supervisor and the county CEO. I'd been spouting off about these raids, but that was nothing compared to the top brass witnessing the fierce intrusion with their own eyes.

After this, Mark Ridley-Thomas was compelled to visit the chief of police, who point-blank admitted that the police were being asked to carry out these compliance checks but were never given proper training. Mr. Ridley-Thomas then visited the county mental health director and described the harrowing events. The director said that was a recipe for re-traumatization, and likely to cause setbacks.

Word of Supervisor Ridley-Thomas's inquiries must have gotten around, because the next time the police showed up to the house, they knocked on the door, no guns drawn, no handcuffs at the ready.

Still, there were six officers, looking to do a compliance check on one woman who'd been at the house for six months. I watched helplessly as they rifled through her belongings and patted her down.

We weren't the only nonprofit dealing with these issues, but when I talked with other providers, they turned up their hands: what could they do, it was part of the contract now. I didn't feel that way. I could no longer keep standing for it. Something my mother once said kept echoing in my head, *All money ain't good money.* If experience had taught me anything, I needed to honor what she, long ago, hadn't.

But to terminate the Healthright 360 contract meant the loss of a guaranteed $200,000 a year for A New Way of Life. In addition to covering the cost of living, those resources helped fund our staff attorneys. If I temporarily forwent my salary, I calculated we'd have four months of reserves. It was, I prayed, enough time for us to figure out something else.

The director of Healthright 360 was a longtime associate and friend. But he was caught in the demands of the Probation Department. I told him I could no longer allow A New Way of Life to be caught up in what had become the "re-entry-industrial complex," and I didn't want to be profiting off people's misery and suffering. I cared more about my mission than the funding. I cared more about people than money.

I remembered the long-ago advice of Dorsey Nunn, who'd made the decision that his organization would not take government money. When I told him I'd terminated my contract, he said, "Susan, that's some bold-ass shit."

Throughout the years Dorsey and I had confided in each other about the struggle to serve our mission, and how funding requirements can sometimes be counterproductive to helping people. "There's a marked difference between recovery and the politics and business of recovery," he told me.

"I know," I replied. "But I don't just sign the back of the check, I sign the front of the check, too." I had an organization to run, women and children to house, salaries to pay. I needed another chicken to fall from the sky.

A month after I terminated the contract, I was invited to the Battery, a private social club in San Francisco, whose members were interviewing charities. Before potential donors, I presented A New Way of Life and asked for $225,000 in funding. When they called to tell me I'd been selected, they presented me with $278,000 to support the re-entry homes, no strings attached.

I continued on the faith walk. And funding continued to come in, from the California Endowment, from Californians for Safety and Justice, from the Ford Foundation, from the Women's Foundation of California, from the California Wellness Foundation, the Fund for Nonviolence, Serving California, the California Community Foundation, the W.K. Kellogg Foundation, Drug Policy Alliance, and many individuals across the nation. No compliance checks, no guns, no handcuffs.

32

LIVING AN IMPOSSIBLE LIFE

*Approximately 90 percent of women imprisoned for
killing someone close to them had been abused by that
person.*

In 2010, Tiffany Johnson was the first lifer to be released to A New
Way of Life. It used to be that lifers had little to no hope of being
released, but with the scaling back of the Three Strikes law and the
federal mandate for California to address prison overcrowding, lifers
were starting to come home. Of the many restrictions that followed
them out of the prison gates, lifers were assigned to a recovery home
for a minimum of six months. Despite a decade of trying, A New Way
of Life was never designated as that recovery home—no explanation
given. Just like there was no explanation when, one day, a call came
to expect Tiffany.

Tiffany arrived, quiet and controlled. She had coffee-colored skin,
short hair, and a beautiful smile. Her eyes were wide as she took
everything in, and she moved and chose her words carefully. But the
next morning, I opened the front door and found Tiffany in a chair,
rocking and hugging a Bible, tears streaming down her cheeks.

"I don't think I'm able to do this, Ms. Burton," she said. "I was trying to take a shower, and I didn't know how to operate it. For so long,
I've only known the prison showers. It's degrading. When I came

downstairs to ask for help, everyone was gone." She was in the house alone, after not having been alone in sixteen years. "I have to go to my parole agent," she continued. "I'm scared. I don't even have a coat. I thought I was prepared to be free, but I don't know how I'm gonna make it."

"I'm here to help you make it," I reassured her. "This is the process of detoxing from prison. You've got to relearn what it means to be treated with dignity and respect. It's okay to ask for help, and people are going to be there to help." I showed her how to use the shower—it wasn't the typical lever, instead you pulled down on the spigot—and then I went back to my house and got her one of my coats. I drove her to the parole office and, after that, we went to the grocery store.

"There's a lot of choices, a lot of colors, don't be overwhelmed," I cautioned, knowing how jolting it could be to go from years of no choices and not being able to make a single decision to navigating a world very different from the one you left.

We needed to find Tiffany a job. In prison, she'd held a unique job status within the Joint Venture Program, where private businesses set up operations inside California prisons and hired inmates for minimum wages. These were coveted positions because they paid dollars an hour, instead of the cents most other prison jobs paid. Tiffany was a good worker, and when a major contract came in from Xtreme, a company that manufactured chassis harnesses, she was quickly recruited to their team. A year and a half later, she was promoted to lead supervisor, though she didn't want the higher job. She had plenty of work, and it wasn't worth the 50-cents-an-hour raise, but she was forced to take the promotion. She oversaw twenty-five women on a line, and she became a master solderer.

From her salary, 40 percent was taken off the top—with half of that going to restitution or victim's services, and the other half to pay for room and board in prison. Federal and state taxes were also deducted, though she didn't have the right to vote. This seemed a violation—wasn't one of the founding principles of this country no taxation *without representation*?

When Tiffany was finally granted release from prison, the Joint Venture Program was sad to lose her. They offered her a job pitching the program to prospective California companies. But it was a pie-in-the-sky offer: you had to have a car, which she didn't, and they wouldn't provide one; plus, under regulations of her release, she wasn't allowed to travel more than fifty miles outside of Los Angeles, which wouldn't fit the job description anyway.

More practical was to get a job on the outside with Xtreme. Of her eleven years in the Joint Venture Program, she worked nine for Xtreme, implementing many of the systems and processes the company now considered standard. She sent the company a letter along with her résumé and portfolio. But she never got an interview—not even a return call.

I referred Tiffany to the California Department of Rehabilitation, and they found a job posting for a solderer at a family-owned company that made parts for refrigerated trucks. Tiffany set up an interview, though, unbeknownst to her, the human resources person was on vacation, so the company's typical background check was overlooked. Impressing everyone with a soldering test, Tiffany was offered the job on the spot. By the time the HR person returned and ran a background check, Tiffany had been on the job for two weeks and was proving to be an outstanding employee.

When the boss brought her in to discuss what her background check turned up, she had an opportunity to explain her circumstances. Despite company policy, she was allowed to stay on. Of course, we all knew that if that background check had been run first, it wouldn't have mattered how good a solderer Tiffany was. What should have been the normal way people were treated, was a rare lucky break.

Tiffany wasn't used to lucky breaks. When she began telling me about her life, I learned that as a child, she, too, had been sacrificed. Growing up in Oakland, she was the middle child of a single mom. Her fifth birthday is emblazoned on her memory: her mom hadn't bought her a present. That night, her mom left the house, returning later with presents and also with a new friend, an older white man, who was wealthy. Tiffany's mom became his secret girlfriend, hidden from his wife and family. Tiffany became his "special" little girl. For five years, he sexually abused Tiffany. The abuse from him stopped when she got her period—but continued from others. "It was like I had a target on my back," Tiffany said. "Anybody who likes to mess with little girls, come mess with me!" There would be six others during her childhood. And her mother's boyfriend would remain in their lives for another decade.

The older Tiffany grew, the more she blocked her childhood memories. All she knew was she didn't like to be around her mother's boyfriend, but she couldn't articulate why. Life went on; she became a certified nurse's assistant, she had children. One evening, she returned from Christmas shopping to all the lights out in her mother's house, though the kids were there with her mother's boyfriend babysitting. Tiffany's young son ran up to her. "Pawpaw said I had to stay in my room." Her son pointed to a young child who was staying with the family. "And that she had to sleep with him."

A lock in Tiffany's mind turned. Images came rushing back. She scooped up the little girl and said they needed to take her to the hospital. For hours they sat in the ER, but everyone else grew tired of waiting, saying the child was fine, Pawpaw wouldn't do anything. They convinced Tiffany to leave.

But once the memories had started, Tiffany couldn't make them stop. She felt all alone, swirling in thoughts and confusion. "You know how it is," Tiffany told me, "you don't talk to anyone about what happens at home." Yes, I knew how it was. She turned to drinking and drugs to blur the images from her mind.

Eventually, she mustered up the courage to tell her mother. Heads reeling, they walked to a nearby bar. After a night of heavy drinking, Tiffany grew flirtatious with a man at the bar. Her mother looked at her and said, "No wonder he did what he did with you."

Tiffany recoiled. "You're telling me I seduced a man when I was the age of five?" She stormed out. Her mother didn't go after her. It was her boyfriend who provided for her and the family; she didn't want Tiffany's allegations to be true.

Time passed. One night, after some more heavy drinking, Tiffany, her mom, and the boyfriend got to fighting. Tiffany's grandmother had recently died and among her belongings was an old gun. Her mom picked up the gun, aimed it at her boyfriend. She pulled the trigger. A bullet missed him and whooshed right by Tiffany's face. Shaken to the core, Tiffany waited until everyone left, then she slit her wrists. It was the first time she'd ever harmed herself. Her neighbor found her in time.

Some years went by and Tiffany became pregnant, with twins. Unable to afford the babies, she had an abortion. But it wasn't effective, and she was sent to San Francisco for a more advanced procedure. There, she began hemorrhaging, and wound up hospitalized for a few days. She returned to her mother's while she recovered, but that night she overheard her mom's boyfriend make a sexual comment about her youngest sister, who knew him like a dad.

When Tiffany spoke up, he denied having said anything. They began arguing and he kept denying it. Her mom claimed she was finally through with him, and she left the house, leaving him and Tiffany alone.

"Tiffany, nothing I did to you hurt you," he argued. "So why don't you just move on with your life? I'll give you money, get you a car, just move on with your life."

"You think a bribe can just erase everything?" Tiffany cried.

"Move on," he shouted. He kept saying it. "Move on, move on, move on." She was dizzy and weak from the surgery, from the lost blood, but something was happening. She remembered it as if she were watching herself on TV, not as if it were reality. Then, she blacked out.

When her mom came home, she had to slap Tiffany into consciousness. Tiffany woke to her mom screaming, "What have you done?"

Tiffany knew, but didn't. She was in shock. They took her children to her brother's, and planned to run. They'd drive to Texas, then figure out what to do next. Highway 5, a blank road, nothing out there. Tiffany sat in the backseat, staring out the window, thinking how she'd just left her children. What was she going to do now, live on the run? They were halfway to Los Angeles when Tiffany said, "Go back, I'll turn myself in. If I tell the truth, I'll get punished, but the truth will set me free."

The truth didn't set her free. The justice system didn't work that way. Justice didn't see her as a victim. She couldn't afford a lawyer, so she had a public defender. "I thought I could trust him," she told me. "But he didn't work for me. He did the same thing everyone else had done in my life: he abused my trust."

The day of jury selection, Tiffany was offered a plea bargain of fifteen to life. "Don't worry about it," the public defender told her. "It's just a title, you'll only do seven, seven and a half years, and you'll get out and your kids will be young enough, and you can start your life again." She took it.

When she arrived at prison and started talking to the other inmates, they laughed in her face. "Seven years? You have an 'L' behind your number. They don't let lifers out."

Desperate, Tiffany went to the main yard to find some lifers. The advice she was after was how to get out, but the advice they gave her was how to live within: "You're in a whole new world now, and you can't live in this world and still try to live in your old life too. Whoever you have as caretaker for your kids, you need to let them raise your kids, and you need to become friends to your children instead of trying to parent them from in here." This turned out to be sage advice, and Tiffany managed to at least create a bond with her kids.

In prison, Tiffany saw a flyer for A New Way of Life. She wrote me, saying she was a lifer and if or when she could go before the Board of Prison Terms, could she get a letter saying we'd accept her to live there? I wrote back saying we'd have a bed waiting.

Two years later, she was allowed to go before the board, but was denied. Six years later, she was allowed to go again. This time, with the money she'd earned from the Joint Venture Program, she hired an attorney to instruct her how to prepare. I wrote her an updated letter, saying a bed was waiting. She was found suitable, and the board's recommendation went before the governor.

For four months she waited. Finally, Governor Schwarzenegger approved her release.

By now, Tiffany's children were grown and all living in the Bay Area. Not that it mattered: lifers weren't allowed to have family or friends pick them up, and the board had mandated she not be near her mother. Her parole agent picked her up from the prison gates and drove her straight to A New Way of Life. She hadn't been in a moving vehicle in well over a decade and got car sick several times along the long drive. But it gave her time to process that she was outside of those prison walls. "I was scared, excited, confused, anxious, terrified," she described. "Still in disbelief that I'm walking into a house. I hadn't walked up stairs in sixteen years. I couldn't wait to sleep in a bed that didn't have a metal frame, but a real mattress and box spring. I was so excited to shut the bathroom door."

Tiffany had been living with us for a couple of months when I brought her up to A New Way of Life's board of directors. It was important to me to have a resident sit on our board, something I'd started after I moved out of the house, since no policy decisions should be made without the input of those directly affected. The board approved Tiffany to be our resident member.

At Tiffany's first board meeting, she sat quietly, taking it all in. Later, when the board wrote checks to the organization, Tiffany took out a checkbook too. She wrote a check for $40. I knew she had a $15-an-hour job, so this wasn't chump change. At the next board meeting, two months later, Tiffany again took out her checkbook. I said she should only give what she could afford. She replied that she took seriously the responsibility of being a board member, and she wrote another check for $40.

Tiffany became active in many facets of A New Way of Life and, when she complained to me that she didn't see much chance of ever advancing above a line solderer at the small, family-run company where she worked, I offered her a community organizer position with us.

In addition to her role, Tiffany was quick to spot where else I needed help. She did whatever was necessary for the organization, and I came to rely on her as my right-hand woman. I was now in my early sixties, and for the past fifteen years I had morphed so fully into my work I could no longer tell what was me or what was A New Way of Life. The organization dictated to me what it needed, and I heeded its every call, seven days a week, all hours. For the first time, I began to look up and realize I was exhausted. Though I wasn't yet ready to retire, I needed to think seriously about what would happen when that day came.

I looked over at Tiffany, working away at her desk. Front and center she had an engraved plaque that said, "Imagine Life's Possibilities." I knew A New Way of Life would be in good hands.

33

THE HOUSE THAT
DISCRIMINATION BUILT

*Nearly 80 percent of formerly incarcerated women are
unable to afford housing after release.*

*Most public housing authorities automatically deny eligi-
bility to anyone with a criminal record. No other country
deprives people of the right to housing because of their
criminal histories.*

When Los Angeles's Department of Housing organized a working group to look at the significant barriers to public housing, I was invited along with housing providers and other nonprofit
leaders from groups for the homeless, the mentally ill, and the HIV
community. But when I looked around the room and saw I was the
sole representative from the formerly incarcerated community, this
seemed ridiculous—those with a criminal record were the only
demographic *banned* from public housing.

Once again, I was the thorn in the conversation, pointing out what
everyone was happy to skirt around: that the Department of Housing
excluded people with criminal records because it was easier to dis-
qualify than it was to do the work of meeting with people and coming
to a conclusion based on an individual in the here and now, not on
something that happened a long time ago.

"Housing policies continue to punish people who've paid their debt to society," I began, of course, having jumped to my feet. "But it goes beyond that. If a mother and children are living in subsidized housing, and it's the father who has the criminal record, he isn't allowed to live with his family. It's heartbreaking when people getting out of prison can't be reunited with their spouse and kids. These policies tear families apart."

When I was done, everyone looked at me like I had egg on my face. Only Peter Lynn, the housing authority's director of Section 8, perked up. He got it, and from that day forward, he would be my ally. This was in 2011, and for two years, our working group met. Finally, we nailed down a proposal, the Re-entry Family Reunification Pilot Program, under which formerly incarcerated people would be, for the first time, allowed to move in with their families who lived in Section 8 housing. Support services would be provided, and the University of Southern California would follow families to track mental and physical health, education, and income. If these indicators improved, as we suspected they would, we could make a solid argument to change the policy that banned people with records from residing with their families in subsidized housing.

But the pilot was the opposite of smooth sailing: the housing authority wanted to roll out the program under law enforcement, rather than through a community-based group, and they brought in the sheriff's department, the corrections department, and the probation and parole departments. It seemed impractical to me, and apparently to law enforcement, too, because before long, they stopped showing up to meetings. Disturbingly, their absence didn't seem to matter to the housing authority, which continued on with its original plan.

I took the program proposal to County Supervisor Mark Ridley-Thomas, and he committed funding. We were set to go—except, we went nowhere. Even though it wouldn't be costing the housing authority a dime, there were delays and resistance. Their administrative culture had been the same for a long, long time, and here we were, trying to change things. Bureaucracy, I had learned, was allergic to change.

Finally, we were granted the go-ahead and my job was to find twenty-five qualified people about to be released to reunite with their families in Section 8 housing. I applied for clearance to enter the jails to conduct my interviews. At this point, it was ridiculous that I even had to apply, especially since the program was under the umbrella of the sheriff's department, but I jumped through the paperwork hoops, again. And then, yet again, when, absurdly, my clearance came back denied.

Once my clearance was finally sorted out, I began interviewing prospective inmates. But there were so many stipulations in the program guidelines, I was having trouble finding candidates. The person with the criminal record had to have a family who was already living in Section 8 housing in the city of Los Angeles. If the family was in a housing project, they didn't qualify. If the family didn't live in L.A. proper but in a neighboring city in L.A. County, such as Compton or Inglewood, they didn't qualify. If there was any record of domestic abuse, they didn't qualify.

After screening hundreds, we finally were able to sign up a handful of families. We hired a therapist to work with the families, we purchased new stoves and refrigerators for the Section 8 homes that needed them, we even bought Christmas gifts for the children. And then, we found ourselves shocked: families were backing out.

I ran around asking the families what was going on. An all-too-familiar picture began to form: they were scared. This was their home on the line, and when they'd signed their lease, they were told they'd be evicted if anyone with a criminal record was living there.

"I guarantee you will not lose your housing," I said. "Even in the worst-case scenario of their spouse reoffending."

"It just sounds too good to be true," one woman told me. Others echoed the same sentiment, thinking it must be some sort of government trick, that there had to be a catch. How could I blame them for thinking this way? Historically, housing policies always discriminated. Their reactions were rooted in a dark history of housing covenants, redlining, and all the other hush-hush ways that black people were kept out. Banks continued their secret discriminatory practices all the way up until 1975, when the unlikely pair of a black Methodist minister/community organizer joined with a white housewife/mother of six in Chicago to expose what was going on and demand passage of the Community Reinvestment Act, making it illegal for banks to discriminate. This was recent memory for many of us. Sadly, the thinking around housing that had become ingrained in the black community was: *No way could someone be looking out for our best interests.* That was how beaten down people had become. Even in the face of us trying to make historic change.

A couple more years passed, and we only had fifteen families enrolled in the pilot program. The level of patience and tenacity just to take these incremental steps was exhausting. But there I was, trying to make progress, all the while knowing that working within the confines of government administration meant real change wasn't likely to happen anytime soon.

I funneled my frustration back into building a movement. Real progress was only going to happen outside of government. The problem was not going to become the solution.

34

WOMEN ORGANIZING FOR JUSTICE AND OPPORTUNITY

Black women represent 30 percent of all incarcerated
women in the United States, although they represent less
than 7 percent of the country's population.

By 2012, A New Way of Life had leased two more houses in South Los Angeles, bringing our total to five homes, where some seventy-five women and more than twenty children lived. Even though we'd expanded, I wanted to maintain a strong, personal presence in all the houses. "This is not a rest home," I instructed the women. "Each day, you need to be moving your life forward." The women never hesitated to comment that I ran a tight ship.

More than being responsible for just themselves, each woman was encouraged to participate in whatever was going on in the homes and with the organization, whether that was rallying for policy changes or helping to promote our first annual film festival of criminal justice–related documentaries. My goal was for the women to be engaged—for the betterment of themselves and their community. Most of these women, like myself, had been talked into a plea deal and into giving up their constitutional rights. They then spent years with all rights legally stripped from them. But going back, long before they ever went before a judge, most had little power over their lives;

most were victims. It was time for them to understand that they had a voice, and the importance of using it.

But when I harped about what was possible to achieve, the women often said things like, "But that's for people like you, Ms. Burton."

"People like *you*," I corrected. "I'm just like you."

Many of our women had post-incarceration syndrome. I'd experienced it, where I'd been so conditioned to feel shame and to believe I was a bad person who didn't deserve a better life. For a long, long time, I believed I was insignificant. Now, I marched around the houses telling the women, over and over, *Your life matters.*

I tried to get them to see it wasn't just about landing in prison, it was a long road that had led them there. "Did you grow up having adequate shelter and enough food?" I asked. "Did you always feel safe? Did you have a sense of security in your family? In your life? As you got older, did you have access to therapy? To a drug treatment program?" Rarely did I hear anyone answer yes. "When you were a little girl, did you have swimming lessons or ballet class? Were you exposed to the arts, encouraged to be a part of team sports? Did you have access to a tutor if you needed help in school?" Again, all no.

Without exposure to things, how was someone supposed to realize her talents, strengths, and what was possible to achieve? These shouldn't be activities reserved for people of privilege, schools should provide these too. But in so many urban communities, classrooms were overcrowded, with inadequate teaching tools and shabby materials. These schools tended to operate from a place of punishment—just like the criminal justice system.

"We don't come into the world lying and cheating and stealing," I reminded the women. "No child says she wants to grow up to be an addict. So, what happened? When did you learn destructive methods of escape? That's the root I want to yank at. What happened to shape you, to compel you to make the decisions you did, to make you feel powerless, to make you feel desperate, to make you feel hopeless? We have to acknowledge there's a difference between who you are and the environment you were in. And that, now, you can be the designer of your own destiny. You can create your own community of support and love and hope."

As I worked to empower the women, I felt a familiar desperation envelop me—this was extremely important work, but it was, still, one by one. Just like Saúl had taught me with advocacy and movement building, I needed to bring this to the next level and onto a bigger stage.

After I happened upon an introduction to Susan Tucker, the program director for Open Society Foundation's Soros Justice Fellowship, she traveled from New York to see A New Way of Life and encouraged me to apply for the fellowship. As I wrote my proposal, I set about designing a six-month intensive program called Women Organizing for Justice, which would be the culmination of everything I'd learned and experienced, and a way of formalizing all the lessons I'd been individually imparting to the women. The proposed program would cover six areas:

- Prison systems and conditioning: learning about power structure, exploitation of prison labor, "a return to slavery," and the relationship between private industry and prison-related unions
- Community organizing and civic engagement: identifying issues, developing engagement campaigns, organizing conferences and training, doing voter registration, learning how to work with the media
- Studying movements: women's suffrage, civil rights, LGBT, farmworker and labor rights
- Teaching women how to tell their story: training in public speaking, marketing yourself and your ideas, how to facilitate meetings
- Government and political structure: how government operates, bureaucracy and obstacles to creating change, how to push legislation through

- Health and wellness: nutrition and self-care on a budget

I received a Soros Justice Fellowship in 2006, and the first annual Women Organizing for Justice program was launched. Women filled out applications to participate—the exact opposite of any other application, the only requirements were the ability to attend biweekly meetings *and* having been formerly incarcerated. Our inaugural class was twenty-five women, and every year since, we've inducted another couple dozen women into the fold.

Together, we attended L.A. County Board of Supervisors meetings, and we even provided testimony when the AB 109 legislation was introduced. We traveled to Sacramento for the Formerly Incarcerated People's Quest for Democracy, and lobbied for legislation to end the disparity in sentencing for possession of crack versus powered cocaine. We also took an annual retreat, somewhere outside of L.A.

For the class of 2015, we gathered at a resort in Palm Desert. But we weren't there to vacation; we had a weekend of learning.

We started off with a video walking the class through the history of systematic discrimination in the United States: from slave laws, to Jim Crow, to real estate redlines that kept neighborhoods white, to opium drug laws that targeted Chinese immigrants, to how Mexicans were unfairly affected by marijuana laws, and how laws around crack cocaine disproportionately punished African Americans.

"How do you feel after watching this?" I asked.

"Keep minorities in oppression," someone called out.

"You've been in a broken world," I said. "But you think it's you. Now, you're willing to show up here and face this. That, alone, is courageous."

"My parents came from Alabama to California to make it better for me," Charsleen, a woman with dark skin and a head full of curls offered up. "But we lived in the projects, infested by gangs. We had food stamps, and I wouldn't want to go to the store, it was humiliating. Where I live now is just one notch above where I came from. Me and my dog walk every morning, and when I see graffiti, I get my neighbors together and we paint over it. We got a speed bump put on our street. But, my neighbors, the mom, dad, *and* the oldest child, got to go to work. Even the college I go to now in my neighborhood has a retention rate of 12 percent."

"I went through the foster system," another woman said. "When I was eighteen, I went into transitional housing. A social worker told me, 'Don't get too comfortable here.' I didn't get what she was saying. My housing was only a couple hundred a month, and I thought, why would I ever leave? But then, I felt like I got trapped there."

I knew what she meant. I'd seen so many people strung along by welfare or Social Security checks, caught between fear and trying to change their lives. "Be thoughtful about what you're doing," I said. "Don't be frivolous with your resources, but be creative, be responsive. Recognize that whatever happened in your life, that was your *experience*, but it's not who you are. You can separate from that experience and understand your importance and what you have to give to the world. Hey, we're stronger and better because of our problems."

"How do you stay encouraged, Ms. Burton?" someone asked.

"Call a friend," I said. "Speak out."

We discussed the Black Lives Matter movement and activist and professor Angela Davis, regarded as one of the most outspoken advocates of prison reform and prisoner's rights. After spending sixteen months in prison before being acquitted on wrongful charges, she popularized the term *prison-industrial complex* to describe the explosion of the prison population and the profit-driven—and extremely lucrative—industry that sprang up around building and supplying prisons with goods and services. The term also came to stand for the misguided belief that locking up people who were drug addicted, mentally ill, or homeless would solve all our problems.

We did an exercise where I placed signs around the room with four roles: Helper, Advocate, Organizer, and Rebel. "I can see points in my life when I've played all these roles," I explained. "I started A New Way of Life as a helper, thinking if women just have a place to go, everything will be all right. Then I realized there needed to be more, and I started advocating. Then I thought, it's gonna take more of us to make some real change, so I became an organizer. And at my core, I'm a rebel."

Sticky dots were passed around, and I instructed the women to place dots next to how they saw themselves. After everyone had stuck their dots, the vast majority were congregated on Helper.

"I had to step up at a young age and help my mother and my grand-mother," one woman explained.

"I remember my aunt getting so high and knocked out in the bath-room, and I'd have to clean her up before my cousins saw," another said.

"At two years old, I saw my father beating my mother, and I grabbed a knife and pointed it at his dick," a woman described. "I had to protect my younger sister. I was protecting her from the time my mother was pregnant. Helping was necessary in order to keep peace in the house."

"Admire your distinct attributes and characteristics," I said. "And grow toward who you're going to become. Know how beautiful, won-derful, smart, strong, and courageous you are, in and of yourself. Each one of us, right now."

I brought Saúl Sarabia before the group to give his Organizing 101 talk, what had first inspired me all those years ago. "What can we use to get people in the door? To make them interested in activ-ism and realize it's important to have a collective voice?" he began. "Our job is to be effective at communicating that we have something deeper to offer. Sometimes, this means we must alter our language, and that's tough. But you have to be able to articulate your point. In certain neighborhoods, for me to talk like I went to law school can push people away. But when I go to city hall, talking like a lawyer certainly helps.

"Take, for example, some of the best recruiters: gangs. I remem-ber when gangs came into my neighborhood to move cocaine, they were recruiting thirteen- and fourteen-year-olds, saying, 'I can get you those tennis shoes you want.' They knew what mattered to the people they were trying to recruit." The women nodded, some, all too knowingly, having been gang members themselves.

"Let's look at A New Way of Life's legal clinic, where we do nine hundred expungements a year," Saúl continued. "If we ask people there if they're interested in joining our movement, nine out of ten are going to say, 'No thanks, I just came here to get my record clean.' That's okay, we don't need all nine hundred people, we need ninety. With each group, it's about finding that one person who really wants to be involved. When we do find someone who seems interested, we always end with, 'Can I count on you to be there?' A lot of organizations, when they're trying to recruit, they just want the bodies but have no intention of handing over the microphone. They see themselves as the experts, not you. We, on the other hand, believe that the people most directly affected by a problem will have the best solutions, because they lived it. This isn't just about A New Way of Life, it's about all of us. It's about building a national movement. There's around 100 million people in America with criminal histories. If we had just a tenth of those people in our movement, this would be a completely different country."

The Women Organizing for Justice program spanned six months and, at the end, we held a graduation ceremony. "But we don't graduate from leading," I said, standing before the women in a conference room at the administrative office of Supervisor Mark Ridley-Thomas. "We just lead deeper, with skill, knowledge, and confidence. Over the past year, we have come together to learn, to cry with each other, to laugh with each other, to share intimate moments, and to support one another. I know you all are going on with your lives. You're working. Some of you are in school. You're moms. We give what we can give. It's all appreciated, and it all counts. Thank you for your dedication."

I introduced Vonya Quarles, who'd been in the Women Organizing for Justice class of 2011. "I'm a third-generation convicted felon," Vonya began as she stood before the group. "I spent years in my addiction, and blamed a lot of things for it. I was paroled in 1990, got a job, and thought I could distance myself from my past. I was able to hide out, but I lived in fear that my job would find out about my record and boot me. For so long I thought I was supposed to be sent to prison because I had a behavioral problem. It was through this program that I realized the answer wasn't to feel shame, but to look at the bigger issues."

I'd witnessed Vonya being awakened to a part of herself she didn't know existed. She founded a nonprofit, called Starting Over, in Riverside, California, to help people with transitional housing. And then she enrolled in law school, even though she was told she'd probably never be able to practice law. She even managed, during this time, to found the Riverside chapter of All of Us or None.

One of the chapter's first endeavors was to deliver voter registration forms to Riverside's five county jails. But when Vonya went to collect the completed forms, there were only five, and they were all marked Republican. Out of four thousand inmates in a largely Latino city, this seemed odd. She requested that All of Us or None be allowed to enter the jails to conduct voter registration, but the sheriff's office delayed responding until near the voter registration deadline, and then rejected the request. Vonya called me. "I think we have a legal issue here."

She was still a law student, so I connected her with Josh and another staff attorney, CT Turney, who'd also got her start with us as a UCLA Law intern, and they got to work. In 2012, a victorious ruling came down in *Riverside All of Us or None v. Riverside County Sheriffs*. The sheriffs were ordered to comply with providing voter registration forms to everyone in jail, to change the jails' requirements for voter registration, and to include the updated voter procedure in each jail guide.

Vonya completed law school after four years of night classes. But, to be allowed to take the bar exam, she had to meet the "good moral character" requirement, which her conviction record threatened. She labored over her application before deciding to reveal everything, explaining how, in the two decades since she'd been incarcerated, she had become a different person. Months passed and, hearing nothing from the California state bar, she feared the worst. At last, she received a notice that she was approved to sit for the bar. In 2013, she passed.

"I challenge you to not let your activism end here," Vonya concluded to the graduating class. "Take what you've learned, partner with other people. Walk out into the community and say, 'I'm a part of this too.'"

Vonya wasn't the only woman from the program who'd been inspired to create her own nonprofit. Lisa James first came to A New Way of Life as a resident. She had a soft, tender presence, though I saw a hint of restlessness that she knew greater things awaited. But she hadn't always been that way and had spent several years on the streets before winding up in prison over a gun charge. While Lisa was incarcerated, her mom stepped in to care for Lisa's three sons, aged seventeen, five, and three. After her release, Lisa regained custody of her boys—but was served by the county with a bill for back payment of child support for $32,000. The minute she managed to find a job, her wages were garnished, with 25 percent automatically going to the county. And she was in for another surprise: because her debt was in arrears, the total amount she owed ballooned to an unbelievable $40,000. She felt like she was being pushed underwater. A single mom providing for three sons was virtually impossible with a minimum-wage job in the first place—let alone with a quarter taken off the top and no end to debt in sight.

The debt followed her every step: there it was when she tried to rent an apartment and renew her driver's license and apply for a higher-paying job that required a background check. She tried to seek help, and went through the process of declaring hardship, at which point her monthly payments were adjusted to what the county called "affordable," though it was hardly affordable and did nothing to stop the arrears from mounting. She applied for a compromise of arrears, but was denied. In the periods when she couldn't find work, even her unemployment benefits were garnished. It made no sense: she desperately needed to support her children in the present but couldn't get out from under inflated past child support. For nine years, she paid toward the debt. After a stretch of having consistent employment at Walmart, she again applied for a compromise of arrears. This time, she was approved. At last, with her balance adjusted, she could make her final payments and be rid of the biggest burden of her life.

In the midst of all this, Lisa volunteered at All of Us or None and, when we had the budget, I hired her to work on the Ban the Box campaign. She also attended L.A. City College and earned a certificate in drug and alcohol counseling. She eventually was inspired to start her own nonprofit, Women in Transition, in Long Beach, California, to provide life skills education, help with navigating and getting off welfare, and assistance with housing for homeless women. Her sons, too, were doing well. Her oldest had graduated from Southwest College and was a barber, her middle son was going into the navy, and her youngest was in high school.

To conclude our graduation ceremony, I called the women up to receive certificates from the State of California Senate and the County of Los Angeles, each inscribed with their names. When Charsleen, who'd since become our volunteer legal clinic coordinator, received her certificates, she stood in front of the class, beaming. "I had no idea what leadership actually was or what it could do for a person," she announced. "I was an ex-con. I know Ms. Burton doesn't like that word, but *ex* means something—that you no longer exist. Everybody expected me to fail. I was a chronic drug addict." Her hands fluttered to her face. "I lost my teeth, lost my complexion. But, with leadership training, I began to listen, and I began to say, teach me what you know, let me learn the meaning of those words. I learned how to stand up for myself and speak for myself, which I'd never done before."

35

WHAT WOULD MS. SYBIL BRAND THINK?

Over the course of more than two decades, extreme overcrowding in California prisons led to horrendous conditions coupled with a shortage of medical specialists, resulting in a likely preventable death at least every week.

In 2013, Mark Ridley-Thomas appointed me to be one of ten members of the Sybil Brand Commission, a group of citizens designated to inspect Los Angeles County institutions, from prisons to county lockups to children's group homes. While the commission was diverse, I was the only formerly incarcerated person on it, and I hoped to bring a critical eye to issues affecting inmates and children. I was honored to participate, but our responsibilities were daunting. Every Wednesday, the entire commission met. Each commissioner was responsible for two weekly inspections, and we rotated among the hundreds of county courts, camps, jails, and group homes.

In order to fulfill my role, I had to, once again, apply for clearance. Though I'd been approved several times in the past for sponsored programs, I had more recently been trying to gain personal clearance to visit my nephew in prison. But just like most every civilian with a criminal record, I was denied. The state policy was forced estrangement: spouses prohibited from seeing each other, or from bringing children to visit the incarcerated parent; adult kids cut off from reconnecting with an incarcerated parent; an auntie, such as myself, trying to be a supportive presence and positive role model in her nephew's life.

So here I was, once again filling out all the paperwork, though I assumed that with the L.A. County Supervisor's office behind me, my approval would go smoothly. How wrong I was. Different clearance protocols existed for county, state, and federal agencies—and guidelines were used selectively. I had to wait and wait, holding up my role on the commission, until, finally, my approval came through. But even though you had clearance one day, it was subject to change if anything in the system changed. A warden or chief retiring or being replaced, or an arbitrary change in policy, could render any current clearance invalid—and you'd be required to start all over again.

As part of the Sybil Brand Commission, I believed I'd be walking into prisons with some influence. The first thing I wanted to address was that I'd been noticing an alarming trend that antidepressants were being pushed aside in favor of new and stronger antipsychotics, which could double as sedatives. I heard many women complain that their dosage was too high and they felt cloudy. But in prison, complaining basically meant your dosage wasn't high enough. The correct dose, it seemed, should subdue you, should shut you up. *The Seroquel Shuffle*, it would later be called, coined for an antipsychotic drug so powerful, prisoners could barely lift their feet when they walked. In prison, the zombie apocalypse was real. But when I brought up what I was seeing, the commissioners felt it was beyond our expertise to be commenting on medical aspects.

I was shocked to learn that when other commissioners toured a facility, they didn't speak with inmates. They only spoke with administrators. To me, this seemed a gaping and absurd hole in the oversight process. How do you do an institution-wide inspection and not talk to the people who live there?

When we visited a group home, I introduced myself to the kids and asked, "Do you have activities? Are you forced to go anyplace? Are you forced to go to church? Are you kept from going to church?"

When I reviewed children's case files, I was astounded at the levels of psychotropic drugs they, too, were receiving. "There's no indication of anything to address behavior, they're just drugging them," I said to the commission. "There's evidence these medications can have all sorts of side effects, including reproductive damage." But the chairwoman told me I was overstepping my bounds.

When I inspected jails, I talked with the inmates. "They're withholding my anxiety medication," one woman told me. "They said they don't have enough doctors right now, so I can't see anyone." She looked at me desperately. "I'm at the point, I want to take my life."

When I recounted the interaction, some of the commissioners responded that people fabricate things.

But what about all the unacceptable conditions we could see with our own eyes? In a men's jail: what looked like a cow's watering bin, but was a stopped-up and overflowing urinal. In a women's jail: white specks blowing out of the vents; brown water coming out of the faucets; moldy and rusted showers, the water temperature going from cold to scalding, blistering women's skin. In the halls, I watched inmates cast their heads down when guards passed, as though we were back in the Jim Crow South, when blacks weren't allowed to look whites in the eye.

Still, within the commission, I was put off, treated as though I didn't have any expertise or knowledge. Finally, I couldn't take it anymore. I threw up my arms. "Well, hell, if we're not going to actually do anything, why am I here?" I thought back to Sybil Brand herself. Her namesake county jail, where twice I'd been an inmate, had become so run down it was shuttered in 1997 and was now used for storage and the occasional bleak setting for a film or TV crime show. Now, here I was, trying to honor Ms. Brand's legacy, but her namesake commission was turning out to be an exercise in futility. Our mandate was hugely important, but there was little if any room for meaningful action.

I went to Mark Ridley-Thomas with my concerns that the commission could be more effective. After further review, he put forward a board motion to limit the term of the chairperson. It took over a year, but, eventually, a new chairwoman came aboard.

At last, we could start making some progress. Word got out to the institutions that the Sybil Brand Commission would no longer be politely peeking around and leaving quietly. Now, as we inspected a facility, the top brass joined us. When we pointed out something that needed to be corrected, the correction was made. Plumbing was fixed; women were sent to the proper medical specialists; inmates who were eligible to vote were registered.

In a juvenile detention center, I spoke with a thirteen-year-old boy. "Why are you here?" I asked.

"Because I had bad attendance in school," he replied.

"Why weren't you going to school?"

"I couldn't go by myself because of the gangs."

I felt a stone in the pit of my stomach. Here was a kid being punished because his neighborhood was too dangerous for him to walk to school? How was I supposed to write this up in a report, that the entire situation was foul? Sure, we were making changes, but mostly spot corrections. As for systemic overhauls that could lead to a truly lasting impact, we weren't making a dent. Not a single change the commission engaged in was going to stack the odds against this kid winding up in prison one day. Sadly, through no fault of his own, he was already halfway there.

One day, I received a call from Congresswoman Karen Bass. She was working on federal legislation to address family reunification for those with criminal records, and asked if she could accompany me on an inspection.

Together, the congresswoman, Commissioner Cheryl Grills, and I walked through the Los Angeles County Jail for Women in Lynwood, asking inmates if they'd speak to us about their children. Women's eyes welled with tears as they talked about being separated from their kids. Some women had already lost their children to the Department of Children and Family Services, others were somewhere in the process, knowing that, but for a miracle, the loss was inevitable.

We stopped to talk with four women who were concocting something on paper plates. "It's Chinese food night," they told us. They explained how, the day before, they'd had cabbage on their dinner plates, and had scraped it off into plastic bags. They were adding the cabbage to ramen noodles they'd bought from the canteen, along with slices of summer sausage. To make sweet-and-sour sauce, they mixed packets of hot sauce with apple jelly that they'd collected at breakfast. When the meal was prepared, they sat down together for their version of a family dinner. It was endearing to watch these women making the best of things with their jailhouse feast.

But I had my commission hat on. "How much did you pay for the noodles at the canteen?" I asked. Each single package was $1.18. On the outside, you could get a 12-pack for under $1.50. "And the summer sausage?" A mini-size was $3.75.

Later, I talked with the sheriff about the exorbitant prices in the canteen, and about the lack of practical choices; for example, they carried only mini-bottles of shampoo and conditioner. The following week, when I arrived for our inspection, the sheriff proudly told me they'd procured 12-ounce bottles of Pantene shampoo.

"Great," I said. "How much are you charging?"

"Ten dollars."

My jaw hung open. "I can get a 12-ounce bottle of Pantene at the drugstore for 3 or 4 bucks."

He shrugged. "That's the price."

I crossed my arms. "That's exploitation."

The Sybil Brand Commission requested to talk with the prison commission that approves the vendor contracts. But we were told they didn't have to comply, that these matters were not subject to the Brown Act, which protected the public's right to participate in local legislative meetings. In other words, I could rant and rave all I wanted, but nothing was going to happen.

36

WITHOUT REPRESENTATION

In most states in America, anyone convicted of a felony loses the right to vote until their sentence plus parole or probation is complete. Voting rights may be permanently revoked in ten states (Alabama, Arizona, Delaware, Florida, Iowa, Kentucky, Mississippi, Nevada, Tennessee, and Wyoming), even after someone has been released from prison and completed parole and probation—and while still requiring payment of taxes.

Eight states (Idaho, Illinois, Indiana, Kentucky, Michigan, Missouri, South Carolina, and South Dakota) restrict voting for anyone convicted of a misdemeanor.

Only two states, Maine and Vermont, allow voting from prison.

When Attorney General Eric Holder established the Federal Interagency Reentry Council in 2011, it seemed to signal that something big was happening. Representing twenty federal agencies, the re-entry council's bullet-pointed mission was to "make communities safer by reducing recidivism and victimization, assist those who return from prison and jail in becoming productive citizens, and save taxpayer dollars by lowering the direct and collateral costs of incarceration." Everything about this was what I, what all of us, had been waiting for—a clear direction to the agencies making policy and, we hoped, an opening of the door to change policy. The Obama administration was going to get it right, finally affecting mass incarceration in a major way.

But a year passed, and then another. I had dared to, once again, get all hopeful. I had, once again, underestimated the bureaucracy of government, all its traps and tricks.

At a Drug Policy Alliance conference, I met Daryl Atkinson, an attorney at the Southern Coalition for Social Justice and one of the nation's leading advocates for restoring rights to those with a criminal record. As we got to talking, I expressed my disappointment with the federal re-entry council. Not long after our conversation, Daryl was honored by the White House as a prestigious Champion of Change. But rather than simply accepting the award and heading home to North Carolina, Daryl used the spotlight, conveying, *Hey, this recognition is great, but one thing that would be impactful is for y'all to hear from a group of formerly incarcerated people on what things can be done to create real change.* Remarkably, the Department of Justice listened.

Daryl assembled seven others from across the nation, people he said were strong thinkers and leaders: from northern California, Dorsey Nunn and his Legal Services for Prisoners with Children colleague Manuel La Fontaine; Reverend Kenneth Glasgow of the Ordinary People Society in Alabama; Glenn E. Martin of JustLeadership-USA in New York; Norris Henderson of Voice for the Ex-Offender from Louisiana; Reverend Vivian Nixon of College and Community Fellowship in New York; and me. I flew to Washington, D.C.—on my own dime. Once again, with hope.

Together, the eight of us walked into the Department of Justice with four demands: a federal Ban the Box, changes to public housing laws to not exclude those with criminal records, Pell Grants for prisoners wanting to pursue a college education, and use of the bully pulpit to express the evils of disenfranchisement.

As we spoke, the Department of Justice folks nodded and took notes, but I left Washington wondering if it was really a call to action or merely a meet-and-greet.

I was encouraged when Daryl let us know the DOJ requested that the eight of us return. We all dug into our own pockets for air and hotel fare for another two-hour meeting, where the DOJ referred to us as Subject Matter Experts. Reverend Glasgow dubbed us the "Super 8."

We were asked to return a third time. But between our meetings, I wasn't hearing about much that was actually happening, and I soon grew impatient. I felt like I was operating in dog years—there was so much to be done that I needed to achieve seven years of progress packed into every 365 days. But the government was operating at a sloth's pace, especially to take commonsense action. Though it was a boon that the Federal Interagency Reentry Council existed, it needed to move beyond writing papers to implementing real changes.

We in the Super 8 took things to the next level and organized conferences in Atlanta, Oakland, and New York to get the DOJ staffers outside the Beltway and into highly affected communities. There, they spoke directly with those impacted by mass criminalization and saw firsthand how desperately change was needed. After a year, we noted a bit of movement in a couple of the areas where we'd demanded change. HUD publicly stated the importance of second chances—sure sounded good, but where was some actual policy change in housing? President Obama banned the box for job applications for federal agencies—a start, but what did this do for my community, for most communities, where there were few to no opportunities to work at a federal agency?

Perhaps the most notable thing that came from our Super 8 meetings was adherence to our recommendation that the Federal Interagency Reentry Council hire a formerly incarcerated person. Glenn Martin said it best: "Those closest to the problem are closest to the solution—but furthest from resources and power." The time had come; we wanted a seat at the table. In 2015, Daryl Atkinson was named the first ever Department of Justice Second-Chance Fellow.

"I've been an insurgent my whole career," he said when I called to congratulate him. "So this will be like putting on a new skin." I knew Daryl was the perfect person to walk in there. If anyone could bring about some change, he could.

Daryl himself was formerly incarcerated, having pled guilty in 1996 to a first-time, nonviolent drug offense, for which he served forty months in prison. After his release, he completed college and then took a faith walk, enrolling in law school. He hadn't known a single attorney with a criminal record, but he fought the system and, like Vonya, eventually earned the right to practice. "Make them tell you no," Daryl went on to advise others with a criminal record who dared to have big dreams. "We have to be willing to press up against these artificial barriers, otherwise you never make a demand on the system."

Now it was his turn to do just that, on the country's highest platform. After several months of his fellowship, I asked him about the progress he was seeing. He took a breath. "There's a competing tension," he described. "On one hand, you're close to the levels of power, the levels that can have the most and broadest impact. But, at the same time, it's at this level where the imagination of what's possible seems the smallest."

37

PROP 47

One in five inmates in California is behind bars for a low-level crime, such as simple drug possession or petty theft. Annually, this is forty thousand offenders punished in the same way the state punishes those who commit violent and heinous crimes.

In 2013, I began hearing rumblings of a new state ballot measure, California Proposition 47, to reduce certain nonviolent felonies to misdemeanors. In theory, this would be life-changing for so many people, but I was skeptical. I knew how diluted California props tended to become. Sure, it all sounded great now, but what would Prop 47 really end up doing?

Then I received a call from Robert Rooks, the state director of the NAACP, telling me he was leaving to go work with Californians for Safety and Justice, the new nonprofit initiating Prop 47. The more I learned about the initiative, the more my skepticism faded, and I realized the truly profound impact this could have on people like me and communities like mine.

Under Prop 47, an estimated 1 million people in California could be eligible to reduce their sentences, clean up their records, and change their lives. Prop 47 called for downgrading six low-level felonies to misdemeanors: simple drug possession, and petty theft, shoplifting, receiving stolen property, forgery, and writing a bad check, so long as the value was under $950.

The act would also go further, retroactively affecting those who already were sentenced by reducing their time and sending them home. This measure would ease overcrowding in prisons and jails and save taxpayer money—an estimated $100 million dollars annually—with the savings to be allocated to community-based drug and mental health treatment programs, school programs for at-risk kids, and crime victim services.

For those like me, who'd already served time, Prop 47 would allow us to clean up our records by reducing applicable felonies to misdemeanors. This would forever lift the burden and stigma of having to check that felony box.

But we had a battle before us, with formidable opponents. Prop 47 threatened to take the wind out of law enforcement. It would take the wind out of judges. And it would take the wind out of the lucrative prison-industrial complex.

Then again, we did have reason to be optimistic. In 2012, Proposition 36, the Three Strikes Reform Act, had overwhelmingly passed, removing the mandatory twenty-five-years-to-life sentence for a third nonviolent offense (though it still fell disappointingly short by not touching the mandatory double sentence for a nonviolent second offense). In the first two years of the act, over nineteen hundred prisoners who were serving life sentences were scheduled for release, saving the state an estimated $20 million. Opponents of the reform had growled that crime rates would spike. But, as the former lifers were freed and tracked, recidivism rates were a mere 3 percent—a tenth of the state average.

I was front and center when Californians for Safety and Justice organized a meeting in L.A. to discuss their strategy to mobilize voters around Prop 47. As they described the TV ads and paid media they had planned, I started waving my arms. "Hey, you left out my community. I didn't hear anyone mention knocking on doors in South L.A. That's the community that's most directly affected by this."

Heads shook. "It's the rare campaign that does direct voter contact where the voter turnout is low," I was told.

I was all too used to hearing that my community had low voter turnout, which was why no campaigns put money or resources there. But to me this was the dog chasing its tail: if no one engages the voters in low-income communities like South L.A., why would they be inspired to go to the polls? I saw this as the perfect opportunity—Prop 47 was a powerful organizing tool since it directly affected people in my community. Fortunately, the executive director of Californians for Safety and Justice, Lenore Anderson, agreed. "Political advice be damned," she said. "We're trying to build a movement, not just win a campaign."

Lenore allocated a grant for A New Way of Life to begin training in direct voter contact, community education, and outreach. I employed the women at A New Way of Life and some members of All of Us or None to travel throughout South L.A., Long Beach, and Compton, knocking on the doors no one else wanted to knock on. We held community forums; we stood outside grocery stores; we walked and we talked, in all the places that for so long had been ignored.

No surprise, people were interested. Most every person we spoke with had been impacted in some way by the War on Drugs. These were citizens and voters who knew that tough-on-crime policies hadn't worked, and that no one was safer as a result. These were voters who lived the devastation created by the government's and the media's dogma that drug crimes deserved little leniency. They knew harsh drug sentences didn't ultimately curb addiction or help young people "just say no." And, they knew the difference the Three Strikes Reform Act had made on their families. They vowed to get out to vote.

Working with the County Register-Recorder and the L.A. Sheriff's Department, we went into the men's and women's county jails and registered people to vote. The rules about voting rights weren't widely known. Though incarcerated, many of the inmates were not yet convicted and still had the right to vote. Plus, anyone serving time for a misdemeanor conviction maintained the right to vote in Cali-

fornia. I was astounded to discover that, of the approximately sixteen thousand inmates in L.A. County jails, an estimated half were
eligible to vote—but, outside of independent efforts like mine, these
inmates wouldn't have been engaged in the voting process. Another
way that our justice system's mantra of "innocent until proven guilty"
had fallen short.

Some of the sheriffs were happy to comply with our registration
efforts, but you could look in the eyes of others, the "old guard," and
see their disdain for what we were trying to do. No matter, they had
no choice; it was the law.

As election day grew near, we staffed a Tele-Town Hall, calling
thousands of people in L.A. County. When I looked around the room
at the women of A New Way of Life on those phones, I counted the
many who were still on parole and did not, themselves, have the right
to vote. This, I realized, was a new type of underground railroad.

Going into the vote, Prop 47 was endorsed by the *Los Angeles
Times* and the *New York Times*. We felt hopeful we had it. Then again,
I'd felt that way with the Ban the Box vote, and it had flipped against
us. I went on the radio with Mark Ridley-Thomas, reminding people,
Get up, get out to vote!

On election day, I was with the Sybil Brand Commission doing a
jail inspection and saw the room designated for voting. A prisoner
could take a seat at a desk, fill out a ballot, and drop it in a box; the
only difference was that there was no curtain. I stood for a while and
quietly watched people in prison uniforms casting their vote. An
amazing sight.

All the effort paid off. Prop 47 passed with nearly 60 percent of the
vote—and, in L.A. County the numbers were an even more impressive 64 percent. My community had mobilized and showed up. It was
as though voters were saying, "The laws were too harsh, the system
was unjust. We're sorry for what happened, and here's how we're
making up for it."

All of us who had organized the campaign celebrated with a huge
party downtown at L.A. Live. Making for an odd juxtaposition, in

the party room next door another celebration was taking place for the reelection of Sheriff Lee Baca, who was regarded, especially in my neighborhood, as overseeing a department rife with corruption and abuse. Baca had been with the L.A. County Sheriff's Department since 1965, and was now entering his fifteenth year as head of it. Though California sheriffs were elected every four years, the job held no term limits, and rarely had an incumbent been unseated. They were all cronies, indoctrinated in the same old-boys'-club ways. In L.A. County—the largest sheriff's department in the world—the average sheriff stuck around for two decades. Which was why there'd been only four sheriffs since 1932—fewer sheriffs than there'd been popes at the Vatican during the same timeframe.

So, there was Baca, celebrating another victory—even though, just two years earlier, the ACLU had filed suit to remove him after documenting an unprecedented amount of severe inmate abuse. The ACLU's title of their report said it all: "Cruel and Unusual Punishment: How a Savage Gang of Deputies Controls L.A. County Jails."

Of course, in my community, we'd long since known how it was when law enforcement was given exclusive power over a vulnerable population. In 2007, we invited Sheriff Baca to attend All of Us or None's Peace and Justice Community in Compton to discuss conditions of confinement and his policies around use of force. Though he did show up, instead of engaging in a productive discussion he made a simple announcement: "You all need to pray," he said. *We need to pray?*

It would take until 2016 before Baca would be charged with lying to federal investigators during an FBI probe into civil rights abuses and corruption in the county jail system. It didn't surprise me when he pled guilty—or when he withdrew his guilty plea after the presiding federal judge rejected the proposed six-month prison sentence as too lenient—but what did surprise me was that Baca got to keep his nearly $330,000 annual pension, courtesy of the taxpayer.

On that triumphant night, seeing the sheriffs partying it up next to us cast a shadow over our Prop 47 victory. It spurred in me that nagging urgency, that perpetual reminder that although this was a major step in the right direction, we still had far to go. The following day, before a single person was even released under Prop 47, there was already grumbling about a spike in crime rates.

When Saúl and I spoke about the passage of Prop 47, he shared my guarded outlook. "It's a good law on paper, though not perfect," he said. "But we know from the civil rights movement that having laws by themselves is not enough. The legislation is not the victory, the successful implementation is the victory."

He was right, and we got to work restructuring our legal clinic to include processing of Prop 47 petitions so that people could reduce applicable felonies to misdemeanors.

With the help of our staff attorney, CT Turney, I filled out a Prop 47 petition for myself. As I did, something came over me, blotting out my mixed emotions and momentarily silencing the voice in my head that nothing I was doing was really enough. With the approval of my petition, I would, for the first time in my adult life, have no felonies to my name. Just think, to erase the felon branding I'd been wearing for four decades, to no longer be identified and judged by crimes I'd committed when I was a person so different from the woman I was today, and to—hallelujah—be able to visit my nephew and others in prison without having to declare I was a convicted felon.

As I delivered my petition downtown to the clerk's office, a camera crew from Californians for Safety and Justice followed me, along with Supervisor Mark Ridley-Thomas's justice deputy Derric Johnson, to witness the momentous event. While the actual act of filing was mundane, the significance engulfed me. This was the embodiment of hope, for myself and for a million others. The maddening and disheartening cycle of qualified people ready and wanting to work but getting knocked down by the stigma and restrictions of their records, Prop 47 could bulldoze through that wall of No. At last, I could feel the sun shining through.

Some sixty days later, a judge granted my petition. The attorneys and I then decided to push the boundaries of the law further, by following up the Prop 47 success with a petition for expungement. A legal one-two punch: Prop 47 had reduced my old felonies to misdemeanors, which then, technically, made me eligible to expunge the misdemeanors. It seemed logical, but it hadn't been done before, and we didn't know if the judges would go for the extra measure. Especially since many judges weren't terribly happy about Prop 47 because they felt it diminished their power—and it had.

We filed for expungement, and waited. Some months later, CT hurried into my office, waving a piece of paper.

"We got it!" she exclaimed.

"We did?" I had to see the approval for myself. Wow, did that feel victorious.

The first wave of implementation saw over 4,400 people who met Prop 47 criteria released from state prisons. Thousands more from county jails were re-sentenced and eligible for early release. The impact was greatest for women prisoners, the majority of whom were incarcerated for low-level crimes.

Stanford Law School later released a Proposition 47 Progress Report, citing the exceptionally low recidivism rate of prisoners whose sentences were reduced under Proposition 47: 5 percent.

Ingrid Archie, who'd been arrested after leaving her baby in the car while she ran into the Dollar General store, was in county jail awaiting sentencing when Prop 47 passed. Before going in front of the judge, she asked her public defender if she qualified for Prop 47. No, her lawyer told her, and advised that Ingrid take the plea deal of three years; otherwise, she'd be looking at seven.

After a couple of months in prison, Ingrid saw a flyer about Prop 47. As she read the details, it seemed she *did* qualify. Her original felony charge a couple of years earlier for petty theft—she'd stolen two items of baby clothes—was far under the $950 threshold. Because she'd been on probation for the petty theft when she was arrested at the Dollar General store, she automatically received a prison sentence—but Prop 47, it seemed, would override that. She wrote to the court, asking to have paperwork sent to her if she was eligible. A Prop 47 petition arrived, along with mailing instructions.

Five months later, she was approved and her charges were reclassified as misdemeanors. After another four months, she was granted a release date. She called me to pick her up.

During the eight months Ingrid had been incarcerated, she lost custody of her three daughters. The youngest, who'd been four months old when Ingrid was arrested, was placed by the Department of Children and Family Services with Ingrid's sister. Ingrid's two-year-old was with her father. And her teenager, Simone, was placed by DCFS with her stepmom, in a house with three teenaged stepbrothers. Ingrid had, at least, felt relieved that all her daughters were with family.

Because Ingrid had completed parenting classes in prison, she was allowed monitored visits with her kids. The day after she was released was Simone's fourteenth birthday, and her stepmom brought her to A New Way of Life for a surprise birthday gift of seeing her mom. Only, Ingrid was more surprised.

"Simone, are you pregnant?" she asked as soon as she saw her.

Everyone denied it. "She took a pregnancy test," her stepmom insisted.

A month later, Ingrid got a call that Simone was in the hospital. She raced there. Simone's blood pressure was spiking, she was threatening to seize, her kidneys were failing. It was preeclampsia, the doctor told Ingrid, and they needed to perform an emergency C-section.

Ingrid stumbled outside for some air and fell down crying in the parking lot. Her thoughts raced to who might be responsible.

She called me. "I am going over there, and—"

"Ingrid," I said. "Don't."

"I don't care if I go back to prison. If I had known about this when I was in there, I never would've made it out."

I told her to call the DCFS social worker, which she did. Once she calmed down, she went back inside the hospital. She was a thirty-four-year-old single mom of three, and now a grandmother.

Ingrid had never known a point in her life when she wasn't faced with desperation. Here was a person who'd grown up in chaos and was trying so hard to move herself and her family forward. The first time Ingrid had been incarcerated, she earned her GED, determined to leave prison with something. When a substance abuse program was offered, she jumped at that, too, and was able to work one on one with a counselor. "It made me understand why my mom chose drugs over her children," Ingrid had told me. "It didn't make the situation better, didn't make me feel better, but I understood."

Ingrid had always been eager to work, and when she first came to A New Way of Life, I connected her with Bed, Bath and Beyond. Because of her record, she could only be hired for seasonal work, and when that job ended, she found a job at a Verizon call center, until her background check came in and she was let go. Upon her release this time, we found her a temporary job at the nonprofit First to Serve, as the house manager of a winter shelter, doing intake, making sure people got a shower and a bed, and deescalating any situations.

Ingrid's granddaughter was doing well, but Simone needed to be stabilized. For two weeks, Ingrid slept in the hospital. But when Simone was at last released, Ingrid wasn't allowed to care for her. Simone and the baby were sent to a group home.

It would take a year of paperwork and calls and hearings before Ingrid could bring her children home. Eventually, we secured her housing, and she and the girls moved into a two-bedroom duplex in South Central. Throughout everything, Ingrid was always quick with a hug, maintaining a steadfast warmth and optimism. She joined A New Way of Life in promoting our legal clinic by canvassing the area and letting people know about their rights. When she held voter registration drives in South L.A. neighborhoods, she stayed in touch with the people she registered, keeping them abreast of community and policy issues that might be important to them, and reminding them to get out to vote. I admired her so much, I hired her full time. Her job title: Prop 47 specialist.

38

THE MOVEMENT

Unarmed blacks are killed by the police at five times the rate of unarmed whites. At least one in three blacks killed by police were identified as unarmed.

In 2015, police killed at least 102 unarmed black people, nearly two each week. Of these cases, only ten resulted in police being charged, and only two cases saw convictions of the officers involved. One officer received a four-year prison sentence. The other officer was sentenced to jail for one year, though he was allowed to serve his time exclusively on weekends.

Fifty years ago, they were six hundred brave and strong. On March 8, 2015, I stood where they stood, above the Alabama River, feet planted on the Edmund Pettus Bridge, named for the Confederate general and grand dragon of the Alabama Ku Klux Klan. I could almost taste the blood spilled on that Sunday, March 7, 1965. Blood of the peaceful protestors on the "Walk for Freedom," from Selma to the state capital of Montgomery in support of voting rights—even though the Fifteenth Amendment to the United States Constitution, ratified nearly one hundred years earlier, granted citizens the right to vote, regardless of race, color, or previous servitude. But, as it turned out, only on paper.

In 1965, in Dallas County, Alabama, more than half the population was black, but 98 percent of registered voters were white, despite many months of thwarted voter registration efforts. On the bridge that day, unarmed men, women, and children, lined up two by two, were met with a wall of state troopers in helmets and gas masks, some on horseback, flanked by a posse of Confederate flag–waving men who'd heeded the sheriff's call that morning to report to the courthouse to become deputized.

The civil rights marchers voiced their desire to talk. But talking wasn't on the other side's agenda—Alabama governor George Wallace had ordered the use of "whatever measures" necessary. Clubs beat, horses charged, dogs bit, tear gas fired. Screams arose from one side, cheers from the other. Heads were bashed unconscious, eyes blinded, people trampled.

It was another horrific day in Alabama, what would become known as Bloody Sunday. A couple weeks earlier, during a peaceful civil rights demonstration in a nearby town, a twenty-six-year-old black man, Jimmie Lee Jackson, his mother, and his eighty-two-year-old grandfather ran into a restaurant for cover from violent state troopers. Badly beaten, Jimmie—a hospital worker, army veteran, and church deacon—was trying to protect his mother from a policeman's club when he was fatally shot. The officer who shot him, identified to the public only as Fowler, was transferred to Birmingham, where he was promoted. A year later, Fowler would kill another unarmed black man inside a jail.

Holding a mirror to the present day, these events in 1965 were a heartbreaking reminder of how, the more things changed, the more they stayed the same. Here in Dallas County, now 80 percent black and the poorest county in Alabama, with nearly a third of the population living below the poverty line, I stood on the bridge that *still* bore the name of the Ku Klux Klan leader, and I stood with the Formerly Incarcerated and Convicted People's Movement. We'd lost the gains of the civil rights movement on the back of the criminal justice system.

Dorsey Nunn on my left, Daryl Atkinson on my right, we held a sign that said, "FROM THE BACK OF THE BUS TO THE FRONT OF THE PRISON." We were starting on the reverse side, in Montgomery and facing Selma, the destination the original protestors never made it to. Reverend Kenneth Glasgow declared, "We're marching in reverse because we got to go back and fix some things."

I could feel the spirit of Dr. Martin Luther King. I met an old man using a walker, who'd been there on Bloody Sunday and, every year since, had crossed the bridge. Same with a woman in a wheelchair being pushed across; fifty years earlier she'd been knocked unconscious and tossed like litter to the side of the bridge.

When we arrived to the top, I looked out to the Selma side. The sight sent chills over me. There awaited thousands upon thousands, a massive crowd squeezed so tightly together people could barely move. As a ribbon was pulled back, everyone else started across. In that moment, my persistent worries that I could never do enough, that I was barely making a dent, vanished. Moving toward me was a collective force. Moving toward me, shoulder to shoulder, inch by inch, was determination.

39

THE ARC BENDS
TOWARD JUSTICE

In the U.S., up to 100 million people have a criminal record—that's one in three Americans.

"Let us realize the arc of the moral universe is long, but it bends toward justice."
  —Rev. Dr. Martin Luther King Jr.

Sitting at LAX waiting on a plane, I made a call to my brother Melvin, but he didn't answer. The next morning, I got a call that an aneurysm had taken him with no warning. The time of his death had been the time of my call.

I'd made that vow to myself about grief, about not allowing the devastation to overtake me; nevertheless I was devastated. I'd again be devastated some time later, when I learned the truth. Melvin and Beverly's daughter, Michelle, then in her mid-twenties, came to me with his death certificate. "I thought you said my daddy died of an aneurysm."

Confused, I saw the cause of death was recorded as acute cocaine toxicity. My head spun.

My own brother.

Sobriety wasn't just about abstaining. It called for a certain level of humility and a change inside. Melvin could get there partially, but he couldn't get there and sustain it. Once I was able to get my hurt, anger, and disappointment in check, I was engulfed by a profound sadness. Melvin had been able to help me, but not himself. And here I was, helping all these other people, but in the end I couldn't save my good brother.

Drugs are insidious. A social ill for some folks, a criminal ill for others. Just like me, Melvin had served time, but what good had that done? Taxpayers pay up to $60,000 per year to incarcerate a person. For the same fee as tuition at an elite university, I sat behind bars with no hope of a long-term plan, and I came out, each time, angry, demoralized, and primed to reoffend. To think what a different world we'd live in if someone like me, someone like Melvin, could have been sent down a productive path instead of to the Department of Corrections.

In 2015, I stood before Yale Law students to speak about women and mass incarceration. Thinking of the exorbitant price tags that both prison and higher education carry, I asked, "Why couldn't I have gone to Yale instead of jail?" The crowd of future influencers roared. "Yale not jail!" sparked across social media.

Jail had done nothing to stop my addiction. Education, hard work, dedication, a support system, and knowing there were opportunities for me and that my life had value: these were what had made all the difference. For the past twenty years of my sobriety, I deployed each of these facets, every day. I kept up with my Alcoholics Anonymous meetings, every Wednesday in Watts was my women's Stag meeting, and every Sunday was my "Tired of Being Dogged Out" meeting. And from the crack of dawn until I couldn't keep my eyes open my life was pure knuckle and grit and nonstop work. Turning pain into power, turning despair into hope. But, just like dealing with addiction, if there's one thing I've learned without a doubt: a system doesn't work just because it's there. You have to make it work. And, when it comes to government systems, *we* have to make it work.

We have to call and write, and we have to show up. It can't just be a handful of big mouths like myself; it has to be a community. The community is the ears, eyes, and mouths required to keep the system functioning for the good of the people. We all must speak up, we all must step up.

I wanted to tell my story as a call for mobilization. Together, we can end discrimination. Together, we can push our government to remove barriers and open up doors for people who are qualified in the here and now. People who should not be held stagnant. People who should not forever be kept in the place when they were at their lowest. Together, we can make these changes. And we must.

It often seemed our government could gear up real quick to punish, but not so when it came to restoration. It took ages to address bad policy. Though these incremental changes made me cross-eyed with frustration, I still could look in most every direction and spot some positive movement. In 2010, Congress overwhelmingly passed legislation to reduce the gap in sentencing for possession of crack cocaine versus powered cocaine—where the disparity used to be 100 to 1, it's now 18 to 1. (A step in the right direction to reduce racial discrimination, but why was there any disparity for drugs that were pharmacologically the same? Even President Obama believed the gap should have been closed entirely.)

In 2014, Senate Bill 260, Justice for Juveniles with Adult Sentences, became law in California, offering a second chance to prisoners who were under the age of eighteen at the time of their crime, but who were tried and sentenced as adults. This was in response to a growing body of scientific research on brain development showing that the judgment and decision-making centers of the brain did not fully develop until one's twenties—and that the law didn't take into account an adolescent's ability for dramatic growth, maturity, and rehabilitation.

A New Way of Life had been a major advocate of the bill and, after it passed, we were deluged with letters from incarcerated women now eligible to go before the Board of Prison Terms, seeking release. We responded to every letter with proof of acceptance to A New Way of Life. But we knew that, despite SB260's existence, it was still a long road for these women. If they were found suitable by the prison board, they'd then get in line for approval from California's governor.

We have yet to receive a single woman released under SB260, but we continue to wait with open arms.

In 2015, buoyed by a RAND Corporation study estimating that for every dollar invested in education behind bars, four to five dollars would be saved on re-incarceration costs, the Obama administration's Department of Education launched the Second Chance Pell Pilot program. The following year, sixty-seven colleges and universities partnered with a hundred federal and state penal institutions to offer Pell Grants and education for inmates. Pell Grants were what we'd been fighting for, and now, 12,000 inmates were also students, pursuing degrees. It was a beautiful start—but still a small fraction of the hundreds of thousands of people released annually.

In 2016, the Department of Justice announced the end of funding for privately operated prisons, deeming the facilities unsafe, ineffective, and costly. Good riddance—but this only applied to thirteen prisons and affected a mere 11 percent of federal inmates. There was no change for the majority of inmates housed in state prisons—including privately funded state prisons.

Turning my sights closer to home, the picture was warmer. A New Way of Life was serving as a vital springboard for women, for advocates, for community organizations, and for public interest attorneys. Our re-entry legal clinic, held monthly in both Watts and Long Beach, annually filed over nine hundred expungement petitions and over three hundred Prop 47 petitions. We also added legal assistance to help reduce compounded fines on traffic citations, resulting in the reduction of hundreds of thousands of dollars in court-ordered debt. Continuing to screen clients, our attorneys litigated around a dozen employment rights cases annually.

With grant funding, we tracked the success rate of the women of A New Way of Life, noting improvement year after year. In 2015, we saw a mere 4 percent recidivism rate, which meant that 96 percent of the women of A New Way of Life stayed out of prison. Couple this with the fact that our services were provided for less than half the cost of incarceration.

In addition to the recidivism stats, I looked to other benchmarks that, to me, more broadly defined successful re-entry: maintenance of sobriety, securing safe and stable housing, compliance with probation or parole, accessing physical and mental health services, gaining employment, or enrolling in school. On average, eight out of every ten of our women met these annual benchmarks. Surrounding me was a growing community of women who were getting their lives together and staying healthy and productive.

In the office, a call came through from a counselor in the women's prison. Usually, when a counselor called me, it was regarding a hard-to-place woman, someone with severe medical or mental health issues.

"We have a sixty-five-year-old woman who wants to come to your home," the counselor began. I waited for a list of issues, but instead she said, "She's sitting here with me. Would you like to talk with her?"

I could hear the phone being shuffled to someone else.

"Sue?" a voice said. It was instantly familiar. My mind darted to the only other bit of information I had: a sixty-five-year-old woman. I knew for certain—we were the same age—that it was Beverly. It had been nearly a decade since we'd last talked, and I'd long ago stopped looking to her kids for updates, a prickly topic.

"Sue," Beverly said. "I'm tired. And I need help." I could hear tears in her voice.

To call me, of all people? I thought of the humility it must have taken for her to make this call, and I got choked up too. All our houses were completely full, but I said, "Beverly, I'll have a bed for you. But . . . are you sure? We have rules."

"I'm sure," she said. "I don't want to come back here."

I sat for a while after we hung up, staring into the distance. I thought of the people Beverly and I had been, together, and then how we diverged. I thought of our hopefulness as we founded A New Way of Life, and our disappointment and resentment when things fractured. But Beverly was family. Especially now that we no longer had Melvin. Despite our struggles, I felt an immense sadness for her. While I was beginning to set my sights on retirement, she would be starting over to create a life. I knew that to put aside her hurt feelings toward me and, more so, to put aside her pride, meant she fully respected that the community of A New Way of Life was her very best shot. And Beverly, like Melvin, always did like the best.

Never in my wildest dreams would I have thought she and I would come round this circle—never in my wildest dreams would I have thought I'd come round so many circles.

I smiled to myself, and then got to work to make sure Beverly had a bed waiting for her.

ACKNOWLEDGMENTS

There are so many people who deserve to be thanked; their names could fill another entire book. I am grateful to everyone who gave their time and bravely shared their stories within these pages, from activists, politicians, and scholars to the women and families of A New Way of Life.

My deepest thanks to Leslie M. and Diane P. for guiding me through the Twelve Steps and introducing me to so many wonderful friends of Bill W., who sustain me to this day. Special thanks are also due to Howard and Jan Oringer, who have spent time in the A New Way of Life living rooms and whose friendship and generosity have been deep and lasting, I am very grateful to Tessa Blake and Emma Hewitt, whose touching 2012 short film, *Susan*, illustrated the heart and soul of what A New Way of Life does and why our work is so important.

There are so many others: friends who stood with me in personal conscience and conviction, never seeking attention or glory. These are individuals who have volunteered and worked at A New Way of Life as well as private donors and charitable foundations; all have encouraged, supported, and nourished A New Way of Life's mission. They continue to join us in our efforts to address and end the mass incarceration of women. I thank them from the bottom of my heart.

Thank you to my early readers, Katie Davison, Gwen McKinney, and Adam Culbreth, and to my daughter, Antoinette Carter, and granddaughter, Ellesse Johnson. They listened and provided words of wisdom and encouragement to help me get to the finish line with this book. Cari Lynn, my co-author, made it possible for me to tell my story and I am most fortunate to have had her help. She did a lovely job capturing not only my story but also my voice. Ronda Trotter was very helpful to me at a crucial moment and helped me get to the finish line.

John Legend's support has been very meaningful to me and I stand with him in commitment to #FreeAmerica.

I am deeply grateful to have been a Soros Justice Fellow and to have had the chance to meet inspiring people from all over the country who are working to spur debate and bring reform to the criminal justice system—and to reduce the destructive impact current criminal justice policies have on women and children and families.

I want to thank Uber for their support of A New Way of Life and for standing at the front lines with us to give people equal opportunity for jobs.

This book would not have been possible without Michelle Alexander, who first introduced me to Ellen Adler at The New Press. Reading *The New Jim Crow* allowed me to achieve a level of self-forgiveness, not only for my benefit, but to help me promote the healing of other justice-involved individuals living in trauma from the effects of mass incarceration. From our very first conversation, Ellen Adler believed in the urgent need for this memoir so that I could lend my voice to the narrative describing the mass incarceration of women and help break down the ongoing systemic barriers that must be overcome. Thanks are also due to Tara Grove, Emily Albarillo, and everyone else at The New Press who has been so supportive.

Finally, I especially want to thank George Cameron, Gena Lew Gong, Dorsey Nunn, Saúl Sarabia, and Michelle Alexander. They selflessly offered faith and insight, and pointed me toward the concrete ideology that helped me make sense of my story while I was becoming Ms. Burton. —S.B.

To everyone who appears within these pages, thank you for bravely and patiently sharing your stories, some painful, all triumphant. In the process of writing, I have been fortunate to spend a couple of years in Susan's world, surrounded by bright minds, pure grit, and constant inspiration. Thank you to the women and families of A New Way of Life, and to Susan's colleagues, friends, and relatives who invited me into their homes and their lives.

Thank you to Tessa Blake, whose beautiful short film, *Susan*, planted the seed for this book. And to Cindy Chupack and Laura Brady Saade for bringing us all together. To Anita Ugent, Katie Davison, and Linda Fibich, who braved various—and lengthy—drafts of the manuscript. These women never failed to provide support and encouragement when I needed it most. And to David J. Cohen, who is always steadfastly there for me.

This book would not have been possible without the unwavering dedication and support of the outstanding team at The New Press. Ellen Adler, we knew The New Press was the absolute right home for this book; it's been an honor to have you as our champion and our guide. Tara Grove, your keen editorial insight made this book everything it was meant to be. And to Emily Albarillo, with the patience of a saint, and Liana Krissoff. Thank you to Katherine Porter and Sofie Syed, who guided us with the utmost care and generosity. And to Angela Baggetta of Goldberg-McDuffie Communications. From start to finish, it's been a joy working with you all.

Meeting Susan has changed my life, and I am grateful to have played a part in telling her important story. Thanks, Susan, for giving me the honor.—C.L.

FURTHER READING

Arrested Justice: Black Women, Violence, and America's Prison Nation, by Beth E. Richie

Burning Down the House: The End of Juvenile Prison, by Nell Bernstein

Freedom Is a Constant Struggle: Ferguson, Palestine, and the Foundations of a Movement, by Angela Y. Davis

Golden Gulag: Prisons, Surplus, Crisis, and Opposition in Globalizing California, by Ruth Wilson Gilmore

Hell Is a Very Small Place: Voices from Solitary Confinement, edited by Jean Casella, James Ridgeway, and Sarah Shourd

Just Mercy: A Story of Justice and Redemption, by Bryan Stevenson

Let's Get Free: A Hip-Hop Theory of Justice, by Paul Butler

Liberating Minds: The Case for College in Prison, by Ellen Lagemann

Mass Incarceration on Trial: A Remarkable Court Decision and the Future of Prisons in America, by Jonathan Simon

The New Jim Crow: Mass Incarceration in the Age of Colorblindness, by Michelle Alexander

Orange Is the New Black: My Year in a Women's Prison, by Piper Kerman

A Plague of Prisons: The Epidemiology of Mass Incarceration in America, by Ernest Drucker

Prison Profiteers: Who Makes Money from Mass Incarceration, edited by Tara Herival and Paul Wright

Pushout: The Criminalization of Black Girls in Schools, by Monique Morris

A Question of Freedom: A Memoir of Learning, Survival, and Coming of Age in Prison, by Dwayne Betts

Race to Incarcerate, by Marc Mauer (also available in a graphic edition with Sabrina Jones)

Understanding Mass Incarceration, by James Kilgore

Upper Bunkies Unite: And Other Thoughts on the Politics of Mass Incarceration, by Andrea James

Writing My Wrongs: Life, Death, and Redemption in an American Prison, by Shaka Senghor

SUGGESTED RESOURCES

Alcoholics Anonymous
www.aa.org

Books Through Bars
booksthroughbars.org

Californians for Safety and Justice
www.safeandjust.org

Cocaine Anonymous
ca.org

College and Community Fellowship
collegeandcommunity.org/ccf

Drug Policy Alliance
www.drugpolicy.org

Essie Justice Group
www.essiejusticegroup.org

Families Against Mandatory Minimums
famm.org

Families for Justice as Healing
justiceashealing.org

First to Serve
www.firsttoserve.org

The Innocence Project
www.innocenceproject.org

JustLeadershipUSA
www.justleadershipusa.org

Legal Services for Prisoners with Children
www.prisonerswithchildren.org

Narcotics Anonymous
www.na.org

Nation Inside
nationinside.org

The National Council for Incarcerated and Formerly Incarcerated Women
and Girls
thecouncil.us

National Directory of Programs for Women with Criminal Justice
Involvement
nicic.gov/wodp

The Osborne Association
www.osborneny.org

The Real Cost of Prisons Project
www.realcostofprisons.org

The Sentencing Project
www.sentencingproject.org

Vera Institute for Justice
www.vera.org

Women of Vision
www.womenofvision.org

The Women's Prison Association
www.wpaonline.org

NOTES

Dedication

v *Disproportionately, these women are black and poor.* Beth Richie, *Research on Violence Against Women and Family Violence: The Challenges and the Promise*, National Criminal Justice Reference Service (NCJRS), 2004, https://www.ncjrs.gov/pdffiles1/nij/199731.pdf.

Prologue

xx *Watts still struggled for redemption.* Kirk Siegler, "After Years of Violence, L.A.'s Watts Sees Crime Subside," NPR, July 25, 2013, http://www.npr.org/sections/codeswitch/2013/07/25/205198028/Once-Crime-Ridden-South-L-A-s-Watts-Sees-Violence-Drop.

xxi *nearly six times the rate of whites.* "Criminal Justice Fact Sheet," NAACP, http://www.naacp.org/pages/criminal-justice-fact-sheet.

xxi *a mere 4 percent recidivism rate.* California Department of Corrections and Rehabilitation, *2014 Outcome Evaluation Report*, CDC Office of Research, July 2015, http://www.cdcr.ca.gov/Adult_Research_Branch/Research_Documents/2014_Outcome_Evaluation_Report_7-6-2015.pdf.

xxii *annual cost of up to $60,000 to incarcerate a woman.* Center on Sentencing and Corrections, "The Price of Prisons: What Incarceration Costs Taxpayers," 2012, Vera Institute, http://archive.vera.org/sites/default/files/resources/downloads/price-of-prisons-updated-version-021914.pdf.

1: Now What?

3 *imprisons more people than any other country in the world.* "Correctional Populations in the United States, 2014," Bureau of Justice Statistics, January 21, 2016, https://www.bjs.gov/content/pub/pdf/cpus14.pdf.

3 *imprisoned for nonviolent offenses.* "Fact Sheet: Incarcerated Women and Girls," The Sentencing Project, November 2015, http://www.sentencingproject.org/wp-content/uploads/2016/02/Incarcerated-Women-and-Girls.pdf.

5 *the average time for someone to relapse.* Joshua Vaughn, "Roadblocks to Recovery: State Policy Causing Potential Problem for Substance Abuse Treatment," *The Sentinel,* December 26, 2015, http://cumberlink.com/news/local/closer_look/roadblocks-to-recovery-state-policy-causing-potential-problem-for-substance/article_dce32535-5f5a-5c2e-a63c-5ee26d40cc5b.html.

2: Land of Opportunity

Changed names first appearing in this chapter: Mr. Robinson, Ms. Robinson, Curly

8 *only 5 percent of the city's residential areas allowed blacks.* Dana Cuff, *The Provisional City: Los Angeles Stories of Architecture and Urbanism* (Cambridge, MA: MIT Press), p. 179.

11 *the most violent neighborhood in L.A.* Celeste Fremon, "Let No Child Be Left Behind: The Pico Gardens and Aliso Village Housing Projects Make Up the Most Violent Neighborhood in L.A. There, a Community of Mothers Fights for Peace, Facing Their Sorrow and Offering Friendship—and Grace," *Los Angeles Times,* October 15, 1995, http://articles.latimes.com/1995-10-15/magazine/tm-57243_1_housing-projects.

3: Daddy's Girl

14 *consistently twice as high as for whites.* "Labor Force Characteristics by Race and Ethnicity, 2014," U.S. Bureau of Labor and Statistics, https://www.bls.gov/opub/reports/race-and-ethnicity/archive/labor-force-characteristics-by-race-and-ethnicity-2014.pdf.

14 *nearly the same rate of unemployment.* Gillian White, "Education Gaps Don't Fully Explain Why Black Unemployment Is So High," *The Atlantic,* December 21, 2015, http://www.theatlantic.com/business/archive/2015/12/black-white-unemployment-gap/421497.

4: Hit the Road

19   *children under the age of six live in poverty.* "Quick Facts," State of Working America, Economic Policy Institute, 2013, http://stateofworkingamerica
.org/fact-sheets/poverty.

5: The Sacrifice

26   *sexually assaulted before the age of eighteen.* Diane Bloom, Diane Owen, and Stephanie Covington, *Gender-Responsive Strategies: Research, Practice, and Guiding Principles for Women Offenders,* National Institute of Corrections, June 2003, http://static.nicic.gov/Library/018017.pdf.

6: Things You Don't Talk About

Changed name first appearing in this chapter: Cupcake

34   *had at least one child as a teenager.* Bloom et al., *Gender-Responsive Strategies.*

35   *most densely populated neighborhood in the country.* Carey McWillians, "Watts: The Forgotten Slum," *The Nation,* April 2, 2009, https://www
.thenation.com/article/watts-forgotten-slum.

37   *tens of millions of dollars in property damage.* "Watts Riots of 1965," *Encyclopedia Britannica,* August 24, 2015, https://www.britannica.com
/event/Watts-Riots-of-1965.

7: The Life

Changed name first appearing in this chapter: James

46   *Only 1 percent reported having received counseling.* "Prostitution and Trafficking Chapter," *By the Numbers: Sexual Violence Statistics Manual,* Illinois Coalition Against Sexual Assault, 2007, http://www.icasa.org/forms
.aspx?PageID=475.

8: From the Skillet to the Frying Pan

54   *larger than the entire population of Wyoming or Vermont.* "Prisoners and Prisoner Re-Entry," United States Department of Justice, https://www
.justice.gov/archive/fbci/progmenu_reentry.html.

9: No Justice, No Peace

62 *the only parent in the household.* Lauren E. Glaze and Laura M. Maruschak, "Parents in Prison and Their Minor Children," Bureau of Justice Statistics Special Report, United States Department of Justice, March 30, 2010.
https://www.bjs.gov/content/pub/pdf/pptmc.pdf.

10: A New Drug

69 *85 percent of people in federal prison for crack offenses are black.* "U.S.
Supreme Court Weighs 100-to-1 Disparity in Crack/Powder Cocaine Sentencing," Press Release, ACLU, October 2, 2007, https://www.aclu.org
/news/us-supreme-court-weighs-100-1-disparity-crackpowder-cocaine
-sentencing.

73 *supplied by the Contras.* Marcus Hoover, "Where All the Madness
Began: A Look at Gang History," *Journals on Poverty and Prejudice: Gangs
of All Colors,* Stanford, May 28, 1999, http://web.stanford.edu/class/e297c
/poverty_prejudice/gangcolor/madness.htm.

73 *was sentenced to life without parole.* Veronica Rocha and Joe Mozingo,
"Former L.A. Cocaine Kingpin 'Freeway' Ricky Ross Arrested in Sonoma
County," *Los Angeles Times,* October 23, 2015, http://www.latimes.com
/local/lanow/la-me-ln-freeway-ricky-ross-arrested-20151023-story.html.

11: Incarceration Nation

75 *one in three black men will see the inside of a jail cell.* T. Bonczar, "Prev-
alence of Imprisonment in the U.S. Population, 1974–2001," Washington,
D.C.: Bureaus of Justice Statistics.

75 *the same as the time whites serve for violent offenses.* "Fair Sentencing
Act," Summary Report, ACLU, https://www.aclu.org/feature/fair-sentencing
-act.

83 *frequent disputes with the phone company.* Vera Bergengruen, "FCC
Gives Inmates Price Break on Prison Phone Calls," *McClatchy DC,* October 22, 2015, http://www.mcclatchydc.com/news/nation-world/national
/article40881675.html.

12: Collateral Damage

85 *the rate is one in nine.* Pew Charitable Trusts, Press Release, "Pew Quan-
tifies the Collateral Costs of Incarceration on the Economic Mobility of
Former Inmates, Their Families, and Their Children," http://famm.org/wp
-content/uploads/2013/09/Pew-Center-on-the-States1.pdf.

85 *shifted from rehabilitation to punishment.* Little Hoover Commission, California State Government, "Solving California's Corrections Crisis," January 25, 2007, http://www.lhc.ca.gov/lhc/185/Report185.pdf.

87 *the state could issue a warrant for your arrest.* Tanzina Vega, "Costly Prison Fees Are Putting Inmates Deep in Debt," *CNN Money,* September 18, 2015, http://money.cnn.com/2015/09/18/news/economy/prison-fees -inmates-debt.

92 *merely sounded good on paper.* Michelle Alexander, "Go to Trial: Crash the Justice System," *New York Times,* March 10, 2012, http://www.nytimes .com/2012/03/11/opinion/sunday/go-to-trial-crash-the-justice-system.html.

92 *"the worst corruption scandal in L.A.P.D. history."* Scott Glover and Matt Lait, "A Tearful Perez Gets 5 Years," *Los Angeles Times,* February 26, 2000, http://articles.latimes.com/2000/feb/26/news/mn-2806.

92 *total settlements estimated around $125 million.* "Rampart Scandal Timeline," *PBS Frontline,* 2001, http://www.pbs.org/wgbh/pages/frontline /shows/lapd/scandal/cron.html.

93 *100 kilos of marijuana (worth a total of around $20,000).* Eric Sterling, "Drug Laws and Snitching: A Primer," *PBS Frontline,* 2001, http://www.pbs .org/wgbh/pages/frontline/shows/snitch/primer. See also Robin Moroney, "Cocaine Keeps Getting Cheaper and Cheaper," *Wall Street Journal,* June 6, 2007, http://blogs.wsj.com/informedreader/2007/06/06/cocaine-keeps -getting-cheaper-and-cheaper; and Lana Harrison, Michael Backenheimer, and James Inciardi, "Cannabis Use in the United States: Implications for Policy," Center for Drug and Alcohol Studies, University of Delaware, June 12, 1995, http://www.cedro-uva.org/lib/harrison.cannabis.pdf.

93 *passed into law without any hearings.* Sterling, "Drug Laws and Snitching." Note: the disparity was revised in the 2010 Fair Sentencing Act to eighteen to one.

13: The Revolving Door

Changed name first appearing in this chapter: Chief

94 *on the taxpayers' dime.* "California Three Strikes Law and Proposition 36 Reforms," Shouse California Law Group, http://www.shouselaw.com /three-strikes.html.

95 *a shocking 80 percent higher.* Adam Liptak, "Justices, 5–4, Tell California to Cut Prisoner Population," *New York Times,* May 23, 2011, http://www .nytimes.com/2011/05/24/us/24scotus.html.

14: The Vicious Cycle

99 *a drug treatment program with a trained professional.* "Drug Addiction Treatment in the Criminal Justice System," National Institute on Drug Abuse, April 2014, https://www.drugabuse.gov/related-topics/criminal-justice/drug-addiction-treatment-in-criminal-justice-system.

103 *you instead had to go cold turkey.* David Cecere, "Inmates Suffer from Chronic Illness, Poor Access to Health Care," *Harvard Gazette*, January 15, 2009, http://news.harvard.edu/gazette/story/2009/01/inmates-suffer-from-chronic-illness-poor-access-to-health-care.

15: Hurt People

107 *victims of physical or sexual abuse.* "Fact Sheet on Domestic Violence and the Criminalization of Survival," Press Release, Prison Rape Elimination Act, ACLU, https://www.aclu.org/other/prison-rape-elimination-act-2003-prea?redirect=prisoners-rights-womens-rights/prison-rape-elimination-act-2003-prea.

109 *"And I want to admit it."* Peter Baker, "Bill Clinton Concedes His Crime Law Jailed Too Many for Too Long," *New York Times*, July 15, 2015, http://www.nytimes.com/2015/07/16/us/politics/bill-clinton-concedes-his-crime-law-jailed-too-many-for-too-long.html.

16: A Tale of Two Systems

Changed name first appearing in this chapter: Ms. B

115 *twice as likely to be incarcerated for drug offenses.* "Women in the Criminal Justice System," Sentencing Project: Research and Advocacy for Reform, May 2007, http://www.sentencingproject.org/wp-content/uploads/2016/01/Women-in-the-Criminal-Justice-System-Briefing-Sheets.pdf.

126 *it was on the brink of being torn down.* Gloria Ohland, "Renaissance in the Barrio," *LA Weekly*, November 18, 2014, http://www.laweekly.com/news/renaissance-in-the-barrio-2139102.

17: A Way Out

127 *increases the likelihood of arrest.* "Child Abuse and Neglect: Consequences," Centers for Disease Control and Prevention, https://www.cdc.gov/violenceprevention/childmaltreatment/consequences.html.

18: Finding Purpose

134 *up to half of those on parole are homeless.* Little Hoover Commission, California State Government, "Solving California's Corrections Crisis," January 25, 2007, http://www.lhc.ca.gov/lhc/185/Report185.pdf.

19: A New Way of Life

Changed names first appearing in this chapter: June, Wanda

143 *released back to their communities at some point.* "Reentry Matters: Strategies and Successes of Second Chance Act Grantees Across the United States," Council of State Governments Justice Center, November 2013, https://csgjusticecenter.org/wp-content/uploads/2013/11/ReentryMatters.pdf.

20: The Wall of No

153 *collateral consequences become a life sentence.* William Hubbard, "1st National Summit on Collateral Consequences," ABA, http://www.americanbar.org/groups/leadership/office_of_the_president/selected-speeches-of-aba-president-william-c--hubbard/1st-national-summit-on-collateral-consequences--february-2015.html.

21: Who's Profiting from Our Pain?

159 *twelve new prisons from 1852 to 1984.* Saki Knafo, "California Prison Guards Union Pushes for Prison Expansion," *Huffington Post*, September 9, 2013, http://www.huffingtonpost.com/2013/09/09/california-prison-guards_n_3894490.html.

164 *misdemeanor drug offenses could lead to deportation.* Grace Meng, "True Drug Reform Includes Immigration Reform," *The Hill*, May 16, 2014, http://thehill.com/blogs/congress-blog/judicial/206284-true-drug-reform-includes-immigration-reform.

168 *"vowed to organize themselves and push to change public policy."* Jocelyn Stewart, "South L.A. Group Aims to Reform Foster Care," *Los Angeles Times*, September 24, 2000, http://articles.latimes.com/2000/sep/24/local/me-26152.

22: Women and Prison

170 *Most women offenders are under thirty years old.* Bloom et al., *Gender-Responsive Strategies*, p. 2.

170 *for black women, it's 1 in 19.* "Women in the Criminal Justice System," Sentencing Project.

171 *jaywalking routinely landed a black man facedown on the street.* Dennis Romero, "The Militarization of Police Started in Los Angeles," *LA Weekly,* August 15, 2014, http://www.laweekly.com/news/the-militarization-of -police-started-in-los-angeles-5010287.

173 *a photo of me, in cap and gown, at my graduation from Southwest College.* Little Hoover Commission, California State Government, Report 177, "Breaking the Barriers for Women on Parole," December 2004, http://www .lhc.ca.gov/studies/177/report177.html.

173 *filled to over 180 percent of its intended capacity.* Paige St. John, "California Adds Another Private Prison," *Los Angeles Times,* April 2, 2014, http:// www.latimes.com/local/political/la-me-ff-california-adds-another-private -prison-20140402-story.html.

174 *bartering sex acts for basic necessities.* "Facts About California Women's Prisons," California Coalition for Women Prisoners, Women for Leadership Development, March 2007, http://www.womenprisoners.org/resources /critical_statistics.html.

175 *forced sterilizations on men and women.* Corey Johnson, "Female Inmates Sterilized in California Prisons Without Approval," *Center for Investigative Reporting,* July 7, 2013, http://cironline.org/reports/female -inmates-sterilized-california-prisons-without-approval-4917.

23: A Kindred Sprit

177 *rate of recidivism drops to a 16 percent chance.* "Literacy Statistics," Begin to Read, WriteExpress Corporation, http://www.begintoread.com /research/literacystatistics.html.

24: Taking Food off the Table

181 *more likely to live in poverty and be hungry.* "Hunger and Mass Incarceration," Bread for the World Institute, http://www.bread.org/sites/default /files/downloads/gar-issues-mass-incarceration.pdf.

181 *3 percent of federal spending goes toward nutrition programs.* "2016 Hunger Report: The Nourishing Effect: Ending Hunger, Improving Health, Reducing Inequality," Bread for the World Institute, http://hungerreport.org /2016/wp-content/uploads/2015/11/HR2016-Full-Report-Web.pdf.

181 *Senator Edward Kennedy called the bill.* Peter Edelman, "The Worst Thing Bill Clinton Had Done," *The Atlantic,* March 1997.

182 *a whopping 40 percent lived in California.* Marc Mauer and Virginia McClamont, "A Lifetime of Punishment: The Impact of the Felony Drug Ban on Welfare Benefits," Sentencing Project, http://sentencingproject.org/wp -content/uploads/2015/12/A-Lifetime-of-Punishment.pdf.

182 *his habit of thwarting his state's legislature and citizens.* Lyndsey Eadler, "Purging the Drug Conviction Ban on Food Stamps in California," *The Scholar*, p. 134, http://lawspace.stmarytx.edu/items/show/1504.

184 *the food stamp ban was, at long last, dead.* Rick Paulas, "California Removes Lifetime Food Stamp Ban for Drug Felons," *KCET*, September 2, 2014, https://www.kcet.org/food/california-removes-lifetime-food-stamp-ban-for-drug-felons.

25: Broke Leg House

185 *with a mother in prison has more than doubled since 1991.* Glaze and Maruschak, "Special Report: Parents in Prison and Their Minor Children."

185 *10 million American children have or have had a parent in prison.* M. Mauer, A. Nellis, and S. Schirmir, "Incarcerated Parents and Their Children: Trends 1991–2007," Sentencing Project, Febuary 2009, http://www.sentencingproject.org.

186 *my personal story and the many barriers to re-entry.* Sandra Murillo, "Helping Women Get a New Start After Prison," *Los Angeles Times*, March 18, 2001, http://articles.latimes.com/2002/mar/18/local/me-sober18.

26: From Trash to Treasure

193 *extremely limited assistance to the poor.* Seymour Martin Lipset, *American Exceptionalism: A Double-Edged Sword* (New York: Norton, 1996). See also Timothy M. Smeeding, "Poverty, Work, and Policy: The United States in Comparative Perspective," in David Grusky (ed.), *Social Stratification: Class, Race, and Gender in Sociological Perspective*, 3rd ed. (Boulder, CO: Westview, 2008), pp. 327–29; and Michael B. Katz, *The Price of Citizenship: Redefining the American Welfare State* (New York: Metropolitan Books, 2001).

196 *"we beat our chest and say we're protecting the public."* James Koren, "State Senate Passes Inmate-Release Plan," *San Bernardino County Sun*, August 20, 2009, http://www.dailybulletin.com/article/ZZ/20090820/NEWS/908209872.

197 *one of the major issues he'd been working to reform when he'd been in office.* Paige St. John, "Early Jail Releases Have Surged Since California's Prison Realignment," *Los Angeles Times*, August 16, 2014.

198 *he went on to serve five consecutive terms. Bridging the Divide: Tom Bradley and the Politics of Race*, dir. Lyn Goldfarb (Los Angeles: PBS, June 2015), http://www.pbs.org/show/bridging-divide-tom-bradley-and-politics-race.

27: All of Us or None

200 *six times more likely than white men to be incarcerated.* "Poverty and Opportunity Profile: Americans with Criminal Records," Half in 10, The Sentencing Project, http://www.sentencingproject.org/wp-content/uploads/2015/11/Americans-with-Criminal-Records-Poverty-and-Opportunity-Profile.pdf.

200 *than adults with no criminal background.* John Schmitt and Kris Warner, "Ex-offenders and the Labor Market," Center for Economic and Policy Research, November 2010, http://cepr.net/documents/publications/ex-offenders-2010-11.pdf.

200 *the 2.2 million Americans currently incarcerated.* "Criminal Justice Facts," Sentencing Project.

201 *giving inmates a voice in civil law issues.* Michael Taylor, "Recalling a Key Figure of Inmate-Rights Movement," *San Francisco Gate*, May 28, 1998.

204 *Ban the Box was further expanded to all public sector job applications.* "AB-218 Employment Applications: Criminal History," California State Legislature, 2013–14, https://leginfo.legislature.ca.gov/faces/billNavClient.xhtml?bill_id=201320140AB218.

28: Treating the Symptoms *and* the Disease

206 *46,600 people are released on parole.* "Reentry Trends in the U.S.," Bureau of Justice Statistics, https://www.bjs.gov/content/reentry/releases.cfm.

206 *would not hire a person with a criminal record.* Harry J. Holzer, Steven Raphael, and Michael A. Stoll, "Employer Demand for Ex-Offenders: Recent Evidence from Los Angeles," March 2003, http://www.urban.org/sites/default/files/alfresco/publication-pdfs/410779-Employer-Demand-for-Ex-Offenders.PDF.

29: The Meaning of *Life*

216 *a man who kills a female partner typically receives two to six years.* "Words from Prison: Women in Prison: An Overview," ACLU, https://www.aclu.org/other/words-prison-did-you-know.

217 *"If I can't have you, no one can!"* Henry Weinstein, "Battered Woman to Be Freed After Killing Man in '86," *Los Angeles Times*, August 4, 2007, http://articles.latimes.com/2007/aug/04/local/me-battered4.

217 *a medical condition and a form of self-defense.* Mary Wimberly, "Defending Victims of Domestic Violence Who Kill Their Batterers: Using the Tri-

al Expert to Change Social Norms," Nashville, TN: Vanderbilt University Law School, 2007, http://www.americanbar.org/content/dam/aba/migrated /domviol/priorwinners/Wimberly2.authcheckdam.pdf.

217 *mistaken for someone else and fatally shot.* "Home for Christmas," December 24, 2007, http://www.sfgate.com/opinion/article/HOME-FOR -CHRISTMAS-3234044.php.

217 *the Board of Prison Terms found her suitable.* National Lawyers Guild, September 2007.

218 *Davis overturned all but six.* National Lawyers Guild.

218 *duct tape covering their mouths.* California Coalition for Women Prisoners.

218 *"she deeply regrets what happened."* Weinstein, "Battered Woman to Be Freed After Killing Man in '86."

30: The Women from Orange County

Changed names first appearing in this chapter: Rachel, Tara, Sonya

222 *Women give significantly more to charity than their male peers.* Debra J. Mesch, "Women Give 2010," https://scholarworks.iupui.edu/bitstream /handle/1805/6337/women_give_2010_report.pdf.

31: Being Beholden

226 *within the first year of release.* "2013 Outcome Evaluation Report," California Department of Corrections and Rehabilitation, http://www.cdcr.ca .gov/Reports_Research/Offender_Information_Services_Branch/Annual /CalPris/CALPRISd2010.pdf.

32: Living an Impossible Life

233 *90 percent of women imprisoned for killing someone close to them.* Rebecca McCray, "When Battered Women Are Punished with Prison." September 24, 2015, http://www.takepart.com/article/2015/09/24/battered-women -prison.

33: The House That Discrimination Built

241 *unable to afford housing after release.* "Who Pays? The True Cost of Incarceration on Families," Ella Baker Center for Human Rights, Forward Together, and Research Action Design, September 2015, http:// whopaysreport.org/key-findings.

241 *deprives people of the right to housing because of their criminal histories.*
"No Second Chance: People with Criminal Records Denied Access to Public Housing," Human Rights Watch, November 17, 2004, https://www.hrw.org/report/2004/11/17/no-second-chance/people-criminal-records-denied-access-public-housing.

34: Women Organizing for Justice and Opportunity

245 *30 percent of all incarcerated women.* "Facts About the Over-Incarceration of Women in the United States," ACLU, https://www.aclu.org/other/facts-about-over-incarceration-women-united-states.

245 *7 percent of the country's population.* United States Census Bureau, https://www.census.gov/quickfacts.

35: What Would Ms. Sybil Brand Think?

255 *a likely preventable death at least every week.* Sara Mayeux, "The Unconstitutional Horrors of Prison Overcrowding," *Newsweek*, March 22, 2015, http://www.newsweek.com/unconstitutional-horrors-prison-overcrowding-315640.

36: Without Representation

260 *Only two states, Maine and Vermont, allow voting from prison.* "State Felon Voting Laws," Procon: Explore Pros and Cons of Controversial Issues, October 5, 2016, http://felonvoting.procon.org/view.resource.php?resourceID=000286.

261 *"save taxpayer dollars by lowering the direct and collateral costs of incarceration."* "Federal Interagency Reentry Council," Justice Center: Council of State Governments, https://csgjusticecenter.org/nrrc/projects/firc.

262 *HUD publicly stated the importance of second chances.* "On Public Housing: Reentry Myth-Buster" and "Federal Interagency Reentry Council," Justice Center: Council of State Governments, https://csgjusticecenter.org/wp-content/uploads/2012/12/Reentry_Council_Mythbuster_Housing.pdf.

37: Prop 47

264 *One in five inmates in California is behind bars.* Paige St. John, "Prop 47 Would Cut Penalties for 1 in 5 Criminals in California," *Los Angeles Times*, October 11, 2014 http://www.latimes.com/local/politics/la-me-ff-pol-proposition47-20141012-story.html.

264 *reduce their sentences, clean up their records, and change their lives.* "My

NOTES   303

Prop 47: Los Angeles," My Prop 47 Organization, http://myprop47.org/la.

265 *ease overcrowding in prisons and jails and save taxpayer money.* Erika Aguilar, "Prop 47 Reduces Drug and Property Crimes to Misdemeanors," Southern California Public Radio, October 9, 2014, http://www.scpr.org/news/2014/10/09/47265/election-2014-prop-47-reduces-drug-and-property-cr.

265 *removing the mandatory twenty-five-years-to-life sentence for a third nonviolent offense.* "California Three Strikes Law and Proposition 36 Reforms," SHouse California Law Group, http://www.shouselaw.com/three-strikes.html.

265 *saving the state an estimated $20 million.* "California Leads on Justice Reform," *New York Times*, October 29, 2014; "Proposition 36 Progress Report," Stanford Law School, Three Strikes Project, https://law.stanford.edu/wp-content/uploads/sites/default/files/child-page/595365/doc/slspublic/ThreeStrikesReport.pdf.

266 *rules about voting rights weren't widely known.* ACLU of Northern California.

267 *impressive 64 percent.* "Statement of Vote: November 14, 2014, General Election," California Secretary of State Office, http://elections.cdn.sos.ca.gov/sov/2014-general/pdf/2014-complete-sov.pdf.

268 *fewer sheriffs than there'd been popes at the Vatican.* Kristin Lapore, "A New Sheriff in Town," Southern California Public Radio, January 16, 2014, http://www.scpr.org/news/2014/01/16/41448/new-sheriff-in-town-a-look-at-8-potential-successo.

268 *rejected the proposed six-month prison sentence as too lenient.* John R. Emshwiller, "Plea Deal Rejected for Former L.A. Sheriff Lee Baca," *Los Angeles Times*, July 18, 2016, http://www.wsj.com/articles/plea-deal-rejected-for-former-l-a-sheriff-lee-baca-1468874393.

268 *Baca got to keep his nearly $330,000 annual pension.* Kim Christensen and Richard Winton, "Why ex-L.A. Sheriff Lee Baca Gets to Keep His Pension Even If He Goes to Jail for Lying," *Los Angeles Times*, February 12, 2016, http://www.latimes.com/local/countygovernment/la-me-baca-pension-20160212-story.html.

270 *Stanford Law School later released a Proposition 47 Progress Report.* "Proposition 47 Progress Report: Year One Implementation," Stanford Justice Advocacy Project, October 2015, https://www-cdn.law.stanford.edu/wp-content/uploads/2015/10/Prop-47-report.pdf.

38: The Movement

273 *police killed at least 102 unarmed black people.* "Unarmed Victims: Key Findings," Mapping Police Violence, http://mappingpoliceviolence.org/unarmed.

274 *months of thwarted voter registration efforts.* Christopher Klein, "Remember Selma's 'Bloody Sunday,'" History Channel, March 6, 2015, http:// www.history.com/news/selmas-bloody-sunday-50-years-ago.

274 *a third of the population living below the poverty line.* "Selma Updates: Recalling 'Bloody Sunday,' Crowds Cross Edmund Pettus Bridge," *Los Angeles Times,* March 8, 2015, http://www.latimes.com/nation/la-na-selma-live -updates-20150308-htmlstory.html.

39: The Arc Bends Toward Justice

276 *that's one in three Americans.* "Poverty and Opportunity Profile: Americans with Criminal Records," Sentencing Project, http://www .sentencingproject.org/wp-content/uploads/2015/11/Americans-with -Criminal-Records-Poverty-and-Opportunity-Profile.pdf.

278 *Obama believed the gap should have been closed entirely.* Zachary Norris, "SB 1010: Fixing California's Racist Drug Laws," *Huffington Post,* October 12, 2014, http://www.huffingtonpost.com/zachary-norris/sb-1010-fixing -california_b_5670206.html.

279 *four to five dollars would be saved on re-incarceration costs.* Lois M. Davis et al., "Evaluating the Effectiveness of Correctional Education," RAND Corporation, 2013, http://www.rand.org/pubs/research_reports/RR266.html.

279 *offer Pell Grants and education for inmates.* "12,000 Incarcerated Students to Enroll in Postsecondary Educational and Training Programs Through Education Department's New Second Chance Pell Pilot Program," U.S. Department of Education, June 24, 2016, http://www.ed.gov/news/press -releases/12000-incarcerated-students-enroll-postsecondary-educational -and-training-programs-through-education-departments-new-second -chance-pell-pilot-program.

279 *affected a mere 11 percent of federal inmates.* Matt Zapotosky and Chico Harlan, "Justice Department Says It Will End Use of Private Prisons," *Washington Post,* August 18, 2016, https://www.washingtonpost.com/news/post -nation/wp/2016/08/18/justice-department-says-it-will-end-use-of-private -prisons/?utm_term=.2df602ce04d7; and Juleyka Lantigua-Williams, "Feds End Use of Private Prisons, but Questions Remain," *The Atlantic,* August 18, 2016, http://www.theatlantic.com/politics/archive/2016/08/end-of-private -prison-contracts-with-federal-government/496469.

ABOUT THE AUTHORS

Susan Burton is the founder and executive director of A New Way of Life, a nonprofit that provides sober housing and other support to formerly incarcerated women. She is nationally known as an advocate for restoring basic civil and human rights to those who have served time. She has been a Starbucks® "Upstander," a CNN Top 10 Hero, a Soros Justice Fellow, and a Women's Policy Institute Fellow at the California Wellness Foundation. She lives in Los Angeles.

Cari Lynn is a journalist and the author of a historical novel and several books of nonfiction, including *The Whistleblower: Sex Trafficking, Military Contractors, and One Woman's Fight for Justice*, with Kathryn Bolkovac, and *Leg the Spread: A Woman's Adventures Inside the Trillion-Dollar Boys' Club of Commodities Trading*. She lives in Los Angeles.

A NEW WAY OF LIFE

Please consider supporting the creation of more safe houses and rehabilitation services for formerly incarcerated women and their children with a tax-deductible donation to A New Way of Life.

http://www.anewwayoflife.org
P.O. Box 875288
Los Angeles, CA 90087

READING GROUP GUIDE

Family and Early Life

1. What was Susan Burton's early childhood like? Who were her parents, where did they come from, and why did they move to Los Angeles? Why did Susan's father move to Syracuse? How did this affect Susan and the rest of her family?

2. "Sue" loved going to school as a child—she called it her "safe place"—but then she got pushed out. What happened? Why did her relationship to school change? Could anything have been done to prevent her from dropping out?

3. Susan experienced sexual abuse throughout her childhood, often at the hands of those close to her. How did the trauma Susan experienced alter her perception of herself and her life? How did it change her relationships with her mother, siblings, friends, school, and community? What might have prevented the type of violence Susan experienced in her youth?

4. How are larger forces in society connected to violence and trauma? What role does community violence play? How do racism and gender come into play? How do low wages or poverty, poor schools, and substandard housing threaten families? Have you experienced any of these problems in your life?

5. People who work in trauma services sometimes use the phrase "hurt people hurt people." What does this mean?

6. At Booth Memorial Maternity Home, Susan felt different from the other girls. How was she different from them? And how was she treated differently?

7. Susan had her daughter, Toni, on the day before her fifteenth birthday. What was their relationship like in Toni's early years? Growing up, what did Toni think of her mother, and why? Susan's brothers were important figures in her life but they too had many struggles. How might their lives have been different if there had been good schools and decent jobs available to them?

8. After she ran away from home as a teenager, Susan lived with various men to survive and make a living. What was her life like during this time? How did it affect her relationships with her family?

9. Susan's son, Marque ("K.K."), was five years old when he was run over and killed by an unmarked police department van outside their house. How did this tragedy fundamentally change her life? What kinds of community resources did Susan need in the wake of the accident? How did this tragedy affect her daughter, Toni? Might some of the circumstances— and Susan's experience—have been different if the accident hadn't occurred in a poor neighborhood?

Mass Incarceration

10. In the prologue, Susan tells the story of Ingrid, who was re-incarcerated after leaving her baby in the car for ten minutes while she was in the Dollar General Store. Susan writes, "Had Ingrid been a person of means . . . had she not been black, would she have been sentenced to years in prison?" Looking at Susan, Ingrid, and other women featured in the book, in what ways do you think race and class help determine who ends up being incarcerated? How do race and class affect your own life?

11. While the number of men incarcerated is higher than the number of women, the rate of incarceration for women has risen more than 700 percent since 1980. How is the experience of incarceration different or similar for men and women? What challenges are faced by people who identify as queer or gender nonconforming when they go to jail and prison?

12. With a population of 2.2 million behind bars, the United States incarcerates more people than any other country in the world, and black Americans are incarcerated at nearly six times the rate of whites. Why is the prison population so high and disproportionately made up of people of color, according to the research doumented by scholars?

13. How are families—spouses, children, and other loved ones— affected when their relatives go to prison? How are communities impacted when many people from a neighborhood are incarcerated or returning home from prison?

14. Susan cycled in and out of prison for six sentences over more than fifteen years (recall the prison guard who predicted she'd return, saying they would keep a bed waiting for her). Why did Susan keep ending up back in prison? Why is it so easy for formerly incarcerated people to become incarcerated again? What can be done to reduce recidivism?

15. Susan lived in South Los Angeles in the 1980s, at the height of the War on Drugs. How were she and her family affected? What did the War on Drugs look like in her community and across the United States?

16. What jobs and educational opportunities were available to Susan in prison? How does she respond to her assignments?

17. How does Susan navigate life in prison? What does she try to avoid, and what does she—and other female inmates she encounters both during her incarceration and after—have to look forward to or enjoy?

18. Susan describes various experiences with parole officers. How did these experiences differ and what role did parole officers play in Susan's life?

Recovery, Re-entry, and A New Way of Life

19. One of the highlights of Susan's book is the description of Susan making it to a recovery center and finally getting the treatment she needed to begin to heal and make a new start in life. How did she finally get help? Who were the various people who helped her? What did they offer that transformed Susan's life? Why did it take so long for her to get the support she needed?

20. At the CLARE center in Santa Monica, Susan learns concepts and receives support that allows her to reckon with her past, as well as with her trauma and addictions. What are some of the lessons and techniques for recovery she learns in the 12-Step Program? How does recovery begin to transform her sense of purpose in life?

21. Throughout her life, Susan is made to feel singularly responsible for her problems. Her aunt calls her a "dirty little girl" when she discovers that her boyfriend is abusing Susan; her mother calls her a "bad seed" and says she is "rotten to the core." What other messages of blame do Susan and others who become caught up in the criminal justice system hear from family, friends, community, and society as a whole? Have you ever been affected by negative messages about you or your life?

22. Thinking of examples from the book, how do these messages, which blame the victim, affect the people receiving them? How does victim-blaming prevent healing and the possibility of rebuilding one's life? Are there ways to address or challenge someone who is victim-blaming?

23. What are the challenges facing women of color upon re-entering society? What are some of the ways that Susan and A New Way of Life tackle these challenges?

24. The annual cost per woman at A New Way of Life is $16,000, while the annual cost of imprisoning a woman in California is $60,000. Why does this country spend so much money keep-

ing people behind bars? Does incarceration reduce crime and keep people safe? What would it take to change the current thinking and approach to crime and incarceration? What is needed to make communities truly safe?

25. Not long after founding A New Way of Life, Susan became an activist and began to work to change the system more broadly. What is All of Us or None? Who does Susan work with on the state and national levels? What are some of the policy measures and structural changes she thinks would dramatically change the lives of people who have been incarcerated?

26. After reading *The New Jim Crow* and other books and talking to her new friends in the criminal justice reform movement, Susan came to understand the larger political and societal forces that affected her and her family. She began to believe that the criminal justice system, as well as other social systems and power structures, is designed to disadvantage and oppress poor people of color. What does she mean by that? How did the criminal justice system become this way? Do you agree or disagree with her beliefs about how these systems can harm people rather than help people? Have you been part of social systems that diminished you as an individual?

27. When formerly incarcerated people try to re-enter society, they encounter what Susan calls a "Wall of No." What is that wall, and how can it be torn down?

28. What is Ban the Box? How did "the box" eventually become banned from state and federal agencies, and why was it so important to All of Us or None?

29. What is California's Proposition 47? What lessons for organizers might we draw from its successful passage?

30. Susan offers portraits of people—including Saúl Sarabia, Dorsey Nunn, Senator Rod Wright, the women of Orange County, Joshua Kim—who volunteer, donate, and assist her in running and expanding A New Way of Life. What do these

310 READING GROUP GUIDE

people have in common and what inspires them to work with
A New Way of Life?

31. What role has advocacy work played in Susan's recovery? Why does Susan think this type of advocacy and leadership development is so important?

32. Are you or do you have friends, family members, or community members who have been or are currently incarcerated? In what ways is your path, or the paths of people you know, similar to Susan's? In what ways is it different? What can we do to help more people?

33. Has Susan's story changed the way you view criminality, punishment, and mass incarceration in America? How?

34. At some point, Susan was able to forgive herself for some of the poor choices she made and she is open in the book about some of things she did that she now regrets. She was eventually able to reconnect with her daughter and other members of her family. What role do social policies play? And what role do professional support, forgiveness of others and of yourself, and taking responsibility for yourself and your actions play in helping someone like Susan get to this new place in their understanding of their lives?

35. Susan Burton believes that there are "no throwaway lives." Do you? What will it take for formerly and currently incarcerated people to be treated humanely and with dignity in America? Is it possible to achieve the full restoration of the civil and human rights of all formerly incarcerated people?